The COMPASSIONATE EDUCATOR

The COMPASSIONATE EDUCATOR

Understanding Social Issues and the Ethics of Care in Canadian Schools

Edited by Allyson Jule

CANADIAN
SCHOLARS

Toronto | Vancouver

The Compassionate Educator: Understanding Social Issues and the Ethics of Care in Canadian Schools
Edited by Allyson Jule

First published in 2019 by
Canadian Scholars, an imprint of CSP Books Inc.
425 Adelaide Street West, Suite 200
Toronto, Ontario
M5V 3C1

www.canadianscholars.ca

Library and Archives Canada Cataloguing in Publication

Title: The compassionate educator : understanding social issues and the ethics of care in Canadian schools / edited by Allyson Jule.
Names: Julé, Allyson, 1965- editor.
Description: Includes bibliographical references and index.
Identifiers: Canadiana (print) 2019017062X | Canadiana (ebook) 20190170638 |
    ISBN 9781773381336 (softcover) | ISBN 9781773381343 (PDF) |
    ISBN 9781773381350 (EPUB)
Subjects: LCSH: Culturally relevant pedagogy—Canada. | LCSH: Teaching—Social aspects—Canada. | LCSH: Teacher-student relationships—Canada. | LCSH: Compassion—Canada. | LCSH: Caring—Canada.
Classification: LCC LC1099.5.C3 C63 2019 | DDC 370.1170971—dc23

Page layout by S4Carlisle Publishing Services
Cover design by Liz Harasymczuk

19   20   21   22   23   5   4   3   2   1

Printed and bound in Ontario, Canada

Canadä

*"Compassion is a way of being in relationship
—a way of acting and interacting."*
(Hart & Hodson, 2004)

TABLE OF CONTENTS

ACKNOWLEDGEMENTS

There are countless people to thank for their roles in producing this edited collection. Certainly, the authors themselves are to be thanked for their hard work in creating such informative and meaningful chapters on various social issues in Canadian schools today. Their terrific ability to keep to deadlines and to respond quickly to my many questions made all the difference.

My personal thanks goes to Cheryl Wall for all her continued support and to Julie Sutherland for her keen eye for detail.

The wonderful people at Canadian Scholars sought out this book, provided key support in the assembling of various scholars in the field, and remained encouraging and supportive throughout the entire process of publishing this important book. Thank you.

And to all the people who support our scholarship behind the scenes—our family, friends, and colleagues; our many thanks.

INTRODUCTION

Allyson Jule

Schools in Canada today are complex places, and the teachers therein must be prepared to respond to an increasing variety of students from a wide range of backgrounds and experiences. Fifty years ago, the Canadian population was just over 18 million, with people of English ancestry making up about 44 percent. Today, with a population just over 37 million, only 20 percent of Canadians are of English descent; 80 percent are not (World Population Review, 2018). This shift alone has had an impact on neighbourhoods and schools. What was largely a country of former Europeans is now considered to be the most diverse of all the G8 countries. Differences in student populations tend to be both visible (e.g., race, ethnicity, culture, some religious affiliations, and visible (dis)abilities) and non-visible (e.g., class, invisible (dis)abilities, and sexual orientation) (Harvey & Houle, 2006; Ryan, Pollack, & Antonelli, 2006).

During the 50-year period from 1961 to 2011, considerable social and economic changes occurred in Canada. The early 1960s marked the end of the baby boom period (1946 to 1965), when many people married at a fairly young age and had relatively large families. At that time, the majority of Canadians were of European origin. There were incredible social changes during that period, such as the legalization of the birth control pill, the introduction of "no fault" divorce, the growing participation of women in higher education, and, importantly, immigration, which is a central fact of Canadian life and has become more diverse since the mid-1960s. Such shifts have heavily influenced the makeup of Canadian classrooms. Developing out of a largely homogenous population 50 years ago, the Canadian school population today is considerably more varied. More than 200 ethnic origins were reported across Canada in the 2011 National Household Survey (NHS). In 2011, 13 different ethnic origins had surpassed the 1-million mark. Of the immigrants who had a single language, less than one quarter (23.8 percent) reported English as their mother tongue. Chinese languages are the most common, followed by Tagalog (a language of the Philippines), Spanish, and Punjabi (Statistics Canada, 2011).

Too often, Canadian teachers are not prepared for the incredible diversity of their students. As a result, their compassion may fall short of the mark.

Many emerging (as well as many experienced) teachers are frequently unaware of the complexities and opportunities that surround their students' lived realities. This edited collection presents the research of educational scholars from across Canada regarding a variety of social situations that impact Canadian K-12 education. This scholarship is centred on the need—and the wisdom required—for exercising compassion in Canadian classrooms. Each chapter focuses on a specific social issue and applies the notion of compassion and the ethics of care to improving relationships between teachers and their students in a variety of ways. Teachers in Canadian schools encounter various situations in need of a deep understanding of diversity and the significance of compassion as a necessary place of response.

In most Canadian provincial school systems, full inclusion is the philosophy. It is also the basis of Canadian values and the human rights encoded in the *Canadian Charter of Rights and Freedoms* of 1981. Certainly, official school policies promote respect and care for all students, by all teachers. But lived realities do not necessarily reflect this. Teachers are taught how to teach, how to create and manage learning experiences, and how to assess and plan units, but are not necessarily taught to be compassionate educators. Where and how does compassion fit into Canadian curricula? Compassion requires well-prepared classroom teachers who understand the complexities of Canadian society and the inclusive values that characterize it. Focusing on Canadian schools, this book is for seasoned teachers, in-service teachers, pre-service teachers, school administrators, and educational researchers who desire to better understand the role of compassion in the classroom. Our overarching objective is to demonstrate that teachers who practice compassion can help students move from merely surviving public education to thriving in it—that is, the compassionate educator cares for the full flourishing of all students and acts in particular ways because of this.

From a global perspective, Canadian education is uniquely diverse. Notably, it is located in a (largely) peaceful, multicultural, and open society. It functions as a "lumper" system—a "fully inclusive" set of provincial systems providing regulated mainstream classrooms that incorporate all students regardless of their abilities, learning styles, special educational needs, social class, immigrant status, race, gender, or sexuality. All successful students receive a standardized high school diploma upon graduation, and career choices are made after high school. Most Canadian students (97 percent) attend publicly funded schools that are consistently governed by inclusive pedagogy.

A central theme in this book is the "ethic of care." Caring in Canadian schools is central to the pluralistic values and ideals embedded in the Canadian psyche. The drastic changes in the geopolitics of the 21st century have highlighted the urgent need for compassion. The rise of nationalism in some Western nations (in particular, the United States) concerns Canadian educators who see education as a powerful component in the creation and maintenance of a caring society. The writings of scholars exploring the "ethic of care" since the 1990s (e.g., Noddings, 1992; Thompson, 1998) have emphasized the importance of caring teachers in all teaching, all learning, and all student-teacher relationships. Nel Noddings, one of the most recognized and well-cited scholars of caring in education (including in this collection), says caring "is the very bedrock of all successful education" (1992, p. 27). When it becomes an integral part of teaching and learning, caring transforms education at all levels. Part of achieving this level of care is the obligation for teachers to encourage students to articulate how they are feeling. Teachers need to actively listen to their students' self-evaluations, evaluate their purposes, and help them grow as participants in caring relationships. This orientation suggests that caring teachers exhibit an array of practices and behaviours underpinned by a relational approach to pedagogy that puts pedagogic bonds at the centre of teaching. This relational approach is translated into specific pedagogic actions such as good context-based planning, rich questioning and dialogue techniques, high levels of aspiration, and the expectation of meaningful classroom experiences for all students (Walker & Gleaves, 2016).

Compassionate teachers and caring classroom environments are vital components of student learning, and they can be central in positive learning outcomes. In many ways, *compassionate* and *caring* are used interchangeably throughout the book. McKamey (2004) outlines three theories of caring teachers:

1. the caring teacher behaviour theory;
2. the caring capacity theory; and
3. the caring difference theory.

The caring teacher behaviour theory locates caring in teacher behaviours. It sees a causal relationship between teachers' compassionate actions and student success. From this perspective, there are specific actions a teacher can make to enhance student-teacher interactions, including active listening and asking meaningful questions. Students' responses to such teacher behaviours could include an increase in student motivation and engagement.

The caring capacity theory locates caring within the capacities of all participants in a given classroom community. This theory assumes that educational settings have the capacity to provide caring contexts for students who are not recipients of a caring experience outside of the classroom. This view is at odds with some educational ideas that focus only on teaching methods and teacher competence and give little, if any, importance to teachers' own capacity of compassion.

The caring difference theory locates caring within a variety of social groups. It explores the differences in the ways that social, ethnic, class, and gender groups express caring. The underlying assumption is that a caring orientation is informed by social, ethnic, class, and gender practices. In such a model, denying someone's "orientation" is renouncing someone's identity (McKamey, 2004, p. 9). This theory addresses "the issues of power relations and seeks to empower students by attending to their personal lives and their cultural traditions" (Zembylas, 2017, p. 5).

Michalinos Zembylas (2017) outlines some important limitations of these theories. *The caring teacher behaviour theory* is deterministic, insofar as it assumes all students will benefit from an agreed upon style of caring. *The caring capacity theory*, says Zembylas, relies on a deficiency model where society considers some people and certain communities to be deficient in compassion and in need of certain competencies in order to rectify their shortcomings. This is significant in the context of this book, because such theories "pathologize" students who may not fit the expectations of educational institutions and seek to change the students into a narrow set of idealized norms.

The caring difference theory falls into the same challenges to theories of multiculturalism, because it focuses on differences between "us" and "them." While the theory celebrates differences, it also re-establishes cultural and social divisions (McKamey, 2004; Zembylas, Bozalek, & Shefer, 2014). Despite considerable contributions from relation-based theorists (such as Noddings and Carol Gilligan) to educational theory, there remains a problem in assuming teachers naturally have compassionate values and ways of thinking. In response to the criticisms of these theories, McKamey suggests a fourth way: *process theory*, or a theory of *critical care*. This theory engages in a deeper exploration of the complexities of meanings and enactments of compassion in various educational communities.

This book uses the word *compassion* to mean *caring*, in particular what I call *critical caring*—a deep connection and commitment to compassion as the centre of school life. In this sense, teacher enactments may be incredibly caring and enacted in various ways in a variety of circumstances. My motivation as the editor of this collection is to highlight the theme of critical caring by drawing on the experiences of a number of experts in a range of educational settings and with diverse educational experiences. The contributors have brought their collective years as educational researchers to the task of articulating how the exercising of compassion by teachers can help to create better experiences for all students. Thus, the writing of *The Compassionate Educator* has been a fully collaborative process.

Every young person benefits from a compassionate educator because each young person can observe how powerful compassion is in helping to resolve tensions—a helpful and constructive posture of dealing with the world experienced inside and outside of school life. A teacher must be both intellectual and kind in order to connect deeply using empathetic gestures. It follows, then, that Canadian teachers need to embody compassion so as to model how a diverse society can transcend its differences and genuinely honour, protect, and promote diversity. Creating and sustaining a peaceful country entails an appreciation of the range of values, dreams, desires, and needs that exist in everyone.

With its overarching objective—compassion in education—always in mind, this book seeks to outline some situations where a teacher's compassion is central to meaningful learning experiences and to tensions. The first two chapters discuss the urgent need for compassion in today's educational context. Both draw heavily on Nel Noddings's (1992) "ethic of care"—the philosophical foundation Noddings articulates in regards to establishing life-affirming teacher-student relationships. The contributors of this collection seek to address a range of situations, including how teachers can act on truth and reconciliation commitments to Indigenous students and engage with similar commitments to queer-identified students, students who live with mental health problems, English-language learners, refugee students, those with (dis)abilities, students living in poverty, and students who come from various religious homes. Not all topics related to social issues could be included. Some notable exceptions include gender in education, sexuality in the classroom, children and youth in foster care, and the geopolitical pressures on GSAs (Gay Straight Alliances) across the country—as well as many other intersections where compassion would be critically important.

The fourteen chapters in this collection begin with two foundational chapters, while the following chapters focus on more particular issues. Verna McDonald and Ed Harrison, in Chapter 1, explore "layers of complex and urgent sociocultural issues." Kumari Beck and Wanda Cassidy, in Chapter 2, discuss the "promise of care ethics" for educators in today's complex environments, with their contribution entitled "Teaching in Difficult Times." These first two chapters discuss the notion of compassion and set the stage for the subsequent chapters.

In Chapter 3, Joanna Black connects Indigenous history and culture with the "educators' journey" in the current reconciliation process through art. With Canada at a crossroads with Indigenous Peoples, her chapter is critical reading for all teachers. Leigh Potvin, in Chapter 4, writes an absorbing and powerful chapter on the need for compassion by straight teachers in relation to their queer students. Here, the notion of "allies" is particularly compelling.

In Chapter 5, Christina Luzius-Vanin and Alana Butler discuss the role compassion can play in dealing with mental health issues in Canadian schools. In Chapter 6, five educational researchers—Francis Bangou, Stephanie Arnott, Carole Fleuret, Douglas Fleming, and Marie-Josée Vignola—join together to offer their insights into compassion and language education and into the social issues that are central to language teaching in Canada. Aiming their attention at the current global refugee crisis, Doug Checkley and Sharon Pelech in Chapter 7 focus on compassion in response to high school students who come to Canada as refugees. It is central to their discussion that teachers' caring for refugee students must and can only come from a place of deep compassion. In Chapter 8, Jeff Brown and Brett Reynolds discuss English-language learners in Canadian classrooms and the praxis of respect needed for these students.

The next two chapters focus on relationships with parents or guardians. A significant part of a teacher's life is dealing with parents or guardians, especially in the face of increasingly varied issues experienced by children in many Canadian schools. In Chapter 9, Dawn McBride and Alyson Worrall write about teachers' helpful responses to parents who may be in crisis with regards to their children and who, consequently, may lash out at their child's teacher. In Chapter 10, Kyle Robinson and Nancy Hutchinson focus their discussion of teacher-parent communications on students with (dis)abilities. In these circumstances, the role of compassion is powerful, to be sure; they require teachers who can initiate and respond to relationships compassionately and insightfully.

The next chapters present some important aspects of religious diversity in Canadian schools, especially in light of the growing concern in schools about very religious communities. For example, in Chapter 11, David Young and Kendra Gottschall tackle the complexity of balancing religious with non-religious views of students within classrooms. Chapter 12, by Dilmurat Mahmut, Helal Hossain Dhali, and Ratna Ghosh, explores the radicalization of young people in the West and considers how Canadian teachers can effectively approach this sensitive issue.

In Chapter 13, Pam Bishop provides readers with a frank and honest look at the role poverty plays in Canadian education and explores how compassionate educators can play an important role in creating classrooms of safety and acceptance. The final contribution, Chapter 14, concludes the collection with a discussion of the critical need for anti-racist pedagogy, with a focus on the pedagogy of power and systemic privilege. George Sefa Dei and Rowena Linton issue a rallying cry for some serious rejigging of a system too long situated in unaccount-able privilege. Theirs seems an apt chapter on which to conclude this book. There are countless social issues not discussed in this collection but which nevertheless rest on an understanding of the role of compassion in the lives of educators who seek to respond to a variety of challenging issues and see them as opportunities for fostering community, inclusion, and care.

All of the contributors agree that schools must be places where students feel safe, accepted, and respected. Compassion may sound sweet, but it is so much grittier than the word often connotes. Compassion involves strength and per-sistence. It is the hard, everyday discipline of finding ever-new ways to engage all children in the learning experience. This reality is what teachers must reckon with. Teachers are not so much founts of content information and technicians of methodology or classroom management (though these are very important as well); rather, teachers are the hope-holders and moulders of the next generation. They have incredible influence on how Canadian children come to see the world and how Canadians can contribute to the continuing enterprise of protecting a civil society for all. It is my wish that the learning objectives, questions for critical thought, and glossary in each chapter provide helpful learning aids to all readers. May all readers find this collection of chapters of great help in under-standing and interacting with Canadian classrooms today and be inspired by the ethics of care at the soul of the teacher-student relationship wherever they find it.

REFERENCES

Hart, S., & Hodson, V. K. (2004). *The compassionate classroom: Relationship-based teaching and learning*. Encinitas, GA: Puddle Dancer Press.

Harvey, E., & Houle, R. (2006). *Demographic changes in Canada and their impact on public education*. Toronto: The Learning Partnership.

McKamey, C. (2004). *Competing theories of care in education: A critical review and analysis of the literature*. Paper presented at the annual meeting of the American Educational Research Association (AERA), San Diego, CA.

Noddings, N. (1992). *Caring: A feminine approach to ethics and moral education*. Berkeley, CA: University of California Press.

Ryan, J., Pollack, K., & Antonelli, F. (2006). Teacher diversity in Canada: Leaky pipelines, bottlenecks, and glass ceilings. *Canadian Journal of Education*, 32(3), 591–617.

Statistics Canada. (2011). *Immigration and ethno-cultural diversity in Canada*. Retrieved from https://www12.statcan.gc.ca/nhs-enm/2011/as-sa/99-010-x/99-010-x2011001-eng.cfm.

Thompson, A. (1998). Not the colour purple: Black feminist lessons for educational caring. *Communication Education, 50*(3), 159–169.

Walker, C., & Gleaves, A. (2016). Constructing the caring higher education teacher: A theoretical framework. *Teaching and Education, 54,* 65–76.

World Population Review. (2018). *Canada population 2018*. Retrieved from http://worldpopulationreview.com/countries/canada-population.

Zembylas, M. (2017). Practicing an ethic of discomfort as an ethic of care in higher education. *Cristal: Critical Studies in Teaching and Learning, 5*(1), 1–17.

Zembylas, M., Bozalek, V., & Shefer, T. (2014). Tronto's notion of privileged irresponsibility and the reconceptualization of care: Implications for critical pedagogies of emotion. *Gender and Education, 26*(3), 200–214.

CHAPTER 1

The Compassionate Educator: Uncovering and Addressing Layers of Complex and Urgent Sociocultural Realities

Verna L. McDonald and Ed Harrison

LEARNING OBJECTIVES

1. To develop definitions and examples of compassionate cross-cultural teacher action in classrooms and in communities.
2. To consider compassionate teacher action, including in local classrooms and in local communities.
3. To reflect on observations and choices about compassionate action in classroom situations teachers have been involved in.

INTRODUCTION

The word *compassion* originates in the Greek *sympatheia*, an affinity of parts to the organic whole and mutual interdependence (Holiday & Hanselman, 2016). To have affinity for the parts suggests both an understanding of the whole and an understanding of the individual parts—as well as perceiving how they are related. Merriam-Webster (2004, p. 1266) defines *compassion* from a Latin perspective as "to sympathize"; "to bear, suffer"; and "sympathetic consciousness of others' distress together with a desire to alleviate it". Teacher action is implied *in loco parentis* towards the alleviation of the distress in the absence of family. Teacher action follows if the experience of sympathy, "having common feelings," and "unity or harmony in action or affect" is present (p. 1267). Sometimes these feelings may not be acted upon or even be opposite reactions such as the antonyms "indifference, cold-bloodedness, disregard" instead of the synonyms "sympathy, empathy, feeling, heart, pity, mercy, love, charity, grace, commiseration, concern, kindness" (McCutcheon, 2003, p. 120). Compassion is thus experienced in emotional energy that emanates from, and oscillates between, each person involved. Compassion in classrooms is an emotional oscillation between acting or not acting, in response to the person needing compassionate action.

This chapter defines and discusses compassion before giving examples of and offering challenges to some of the many cultures in Canadian classrooms.

COMPASSION IN CLASSROOMS

What assumptions are made about teaching and compassion in the classroom? If you were to ask teachers if they thought about "compassion" in their daily work with children, they might respond, "It's something I do. I don't really think about it, I just do it." Teacher education courses rarely include instruction on acting with compassion, but it appears that compassion in teaching is considered by instructors to be an important part of a learning program. Teacher candidates may be encouraged to have empathy, care, and connection with their students. Perhaps a program assumption would be that teachers should try to understand the sociocultural environment that their students come from, as well as their ethnic background, socioeconomic status, or living conditions. In order to do this, teacher candidates may be encouraged to observe how their students arrive at school: Did they walk or bike alone or in groups? Did their parents drive them? Are they living with grandparents, in a single-parent home, or with same-gender partners? Are they themselves new immigrants, speaking English as a first or second language? Where do they live? Are they in housing developments, single detached houses, farms, couch surfing situations, or apartments?

The question that really needs to be asked is: How do you, as a teacher candidate, observe, feel, and respond to student information? Will the way you feel about what you observe influence the way you teach your students? How you *feel* is a very vague and imprecise term. Yet it is assumed that student teachers are able to act in a compassionate manner when working with children. While student teachers may know a general definition of the word *compassion*, or experience compassion as positive, they may or may not unpack the deeper meanings of compassion in their own lived experiences in classrooms. Can new teachers from any experiential background act compassionately towards all students who may be of different or similar backgrounds?

COMPASSION: DEFINITIONS AND PERSPECTIVES

European settlements generally evolved as mimics of their homelands (governance structures, school systems, economic emphases, policing, courts, and so on). Indigenous Peoples had a difficult time counteracting the impacts of settlement, including wars, cultural genocide, the spread of new diseases, and treaties written in English. Colonial economics, as well as gendered and social class exploitations, are still being reconstructed by all raised and living in a colonially founded context—if they are not actively deconstructing that colonial foundation. Once the process of deculturalization was complete, Indigenous lands became fertile ground for ever subtler recolonization. Indigenous stories, as very different perspectives on human development, must be part of education in Canada today in order for students to see continual iterations of settler dominance and to learn to act differently. New teachers can work towards becoming allies rather than subtly perpetuating colonial structures that benefit settlers over First Peoples (Manuel & Derrikson, 2017).

The *Merriam-Webster* dictionary definition from the opening paragraph captures the basics of the term *compassion*. It is important to recognize that this definition is geographically based: it has a European origin. The core meaning of the word in European languages is similar: In Spanish, *compasión* means sympathy, or pity. In German the meaning of compassion, *mitleid*, can be varied, meaning pity, sympathy, or mercy.

As European nations expanded and established colonies, the languages of the colonizers came with them. Therefore, when *compassion* is discussed in relation to a teacher education program, there are different understandings of the word. For example, teachers may have sympathy for the child who has skinned a knee. They may work to help the student who has a learning disability. New teachers may design curriculum and visual learning activities for new immigrants learning English.

The word *compassion*, however, has many dimensions. At its core is an action, whether it is cognitive or physical or both; it is not a passive word. But at the same time, it is not apolitical—it cannot be neutral. For teachers, there is a demand from parents, the school, and/or the community that something be done about a situation. The action that occurs is dependent upon a reflective capacity to see what needs to be done. In the case of the student with the skinned knee, it is important to locate a bandage and provide comfort. But what of poverty in a nearby community? How is that addressed? What about the plight of school girls kidnapped by Boko Haram in 2014 and 2018? The plight of the working poor in the southern United States? The Muslim people of Europe who are viewed as second-class citizens? These all test our active understanding of compassion as it is applied in the classroom or teacher education programs. Do we take personal action or not? Are we keeping in mind that remaining silent or passive is an action as well?

Some dimensions of compassion and aspects of compassionate action are summarized at the end of the chapter. You are invited to build your own diagram for your schools and community context.

Western schools of education are often created with an understanding that acts of compassion are important as they pertain to children and their future successes. Central to this vision is establishing a social-emotional connection with the children that teacher candidates teach. But within this context, it is significant that compassion is often defined and understood through the world view of settlers acculturated in colonial ways—that is, via a Western European structuring of colonial empire (the Commonwealth). When the word is used in an education setting, it is employed in ways that strictly pertain to its English definition. Indeed, teachers often fail to question how the word should perhaps be applied differently when they are in cross-cultural settings. However, the demographics of Canada are rapidly changing, and new teachers should also embrace the examination of social change in their classrooms. As an action word, *compassion* comes with the assumption that its components will be universally understood and applied. If the people taking action are Western European or Euro-Canadian, they may assume that the person(s) receiving the compassion will understand it in the same manner (Hao, 2011, p. 93). Often the recipients' understanding and expectations are quite different.

A child or family member may interpret an act of compassion by a teacher in a completely different manner than intended—for example, a child from the Punjab that the student teacher wants to help be successful academically. The new teacher may perceive their actions as compassionate and understanding. But how is the child or family viewing it? Perhaps since the extended family is not involved—as they would be in their culture—a different act and a developmental focus is expected from what the teacher's **acculturation** would call for. A common example is the including of family (and community) in academic decision-making and in discipline. Many Canadian student teachers are likely to experience home and classroom norms that focus on the individual; however, children may have a family and community focus. Another example is heritage Hawai'ian or Chinese students coming from a home language with no individual pronouns (I, me, mine). A family and community focus are expected.

DEFINITIONS FROM OUR LOCAL CULTURES: GITXSAN, PILIPINO, AND NISGA'A

Local **cross-cultural** definitions of the term *compassion* are important, rather than assuming one universal meaning (usually the European/English version). Recognizing that there are other possible cultural definitions for a term is related to the very essence of compassionate teaching as being more deeply human than simply responding to our own acculturation. For those of us in Northwest British Columbia, the importance of Indigenous understandings is central. For example, when we consider a Gitxsan knowledge-holder's definition of the term *hlo'omsxw*, their understanding centres upon the concept of respect or honour as shown by action. It is close to the heart of what it means to be Gitxsan. In Gitxsan communities, it is actively interfering with a cultural norm to discourage the extended family to show honour or respect of the kinship connection web by supporting a family member who is ill in the hospital. If the Gitxsan people visiting the patient are asked to leave the hospital, the culture has been asked to leave as well, in the Gitxsan visitor's perception, and the patient is left with the possibility of dying alone. "By removing the Gitxsan people, their Gitxsan-ness is no longer involved in the healing: they belong to someone else but not Gitxsan, since they do not know their ways of being" (A. Woods, personal conversation, April 18, 2018).

The Gitxsan definition of *compassion* emerges when the dissonance of the English meaning appears. The English meaning is closely defined in terms of the individual patient in a hospital setting. Cultural dominance appears in this disjuncture of Western medical practice and Gitxsan healing beliefs, by demanding that there is another way of being that is not Gitxsan, and that other cultural meanings will supersede Gitxsan healing practices. It is the dominant culture/hospital beliefs centred on the European definition of *compassion* that is expected, with a few nuclear family visitors in designated time slots.

Santos (2014, p. 138) suggests that there are three principles related to Western beliefs: "[1] Regulation … constituted by the principle of the state, formulated most prominently by Hobbes, [2] the principle of the market, developed by Locke and Adam Smith in particular, and [3] the principle of the community, which presides over Rousseau's political theory." There is a tension between regulation and emancipation: regulation constantly seeks to make order from the predominant social structures while emancipation seeks those forces that probe and reveal the over-regulation of the state. Santos (2014, p. 139) indicates that knowledge generated in power relations has overpowered knowledge-as-emancipation, each one feeding back on the other. In the example of the Gitxsan, the understanding of compassion is in danger of being overwhelmed by the prevailing colonizers' definition of *compassion*.

Other cultures also describe compassion differently. Pilipino people have two words that relate to compassion: *habag* and *awa*. *Habag* means "I sincerely feel your pain" or "I'm deeply sorry." *Awa* means "I feel for you." These words, however, place different emphasis on the relationship between the speaker and the event. *Habag* is a broad feeling: "I will take on your pain." It is often preceded by the term *nakaka*, meaning "I feel for you," but not at the intensely personal level. *Awa*, on the other hand, means "I am so sorry for you having experienced that, because I …" Another way of understanding it is as follows: "I am almost in tears because of what you have gone through." Pilipino compassion is intensely personal (A. Avila, personal communication, June 28, 2018). There is recognition that the other person is human, and there is a very close relationship established between the two. This is very different from the commonly required rote, or even mandated, apology frequent in a Canadian context.

The Nisga'a (Sim'algax) language of Northern British Columbia bases the word *compassion* on "feeling" and "heart." The word they use is *k'e'em goot*. *Goot* means heart. Peter McKay describes the use of the word this way: "When one shows or demonstrates *k'e'em goot*, they are doing this with their entire being and not for self-gratification" (personal communication, June 8, 2018). This definition reflects an intense personal relationship that is centred on valuing and building a relationship with the other person. It moves well beyond the terms *sympathy* and *pity*. We are reminded of seeing staff talking with children fighting on the playground. Is an apology helpful? Spontaneous? Mandated? Authentic?

HOW CULTURAL DEFINITIONS OF COMPASSION DIFFER FROM EACH OTHER: WHY DOES IT MATTER?

The definitions of the term *compassion* describe the sociocultural practices around which the actions or non-actions with respect to the word occur. The descriptions are not neutral or inert. Compassion lies at the heart of educators' understanding in their work. It may not be overtly expressed as such, but it reveals itself in each action; it is almost like a silent partner. For example, Mary was sheltering her feelings—hiding, by herself, in the corner of the room; or Bill was consistently standing by himself on the playground. A struggle is initiated within the teacher: how should I approach this student? This question suggests that the teacher is observing, thinking about the situation, and perhaps acting. The teacher is drawing upon past experience with children and relating it to the current event. Cummings and Bennett (2012) describe this as "intelligent kindness." Olshansky (2007, p. 247), when discussing nursing practice, suggests "there [are] multiple interpretations of compassion, and how it relates to practice can be unclear."

The experienced teacher may assess the situation quickly and act upon it. The newer teacher may act with less assuredness. Effective teaching practice requires both a thoughtful approach and a different set of cultural skills. Take, for instance, the following: Carol cannot read at a Grade 3 level even though she is in Grade 5. This situation not only requires an understanding of knowledge and classroom practice, but it also places the teacher in a quandary: should the teacher act or not act in this situation? Success for the student requires that the teacher become involved in the politics of the situation. In British Columbia between 2002 and 2017, the underfunding of education, particularly special education, meant that Carol may not have had the help that she required. In order to obtain the help, the teacher would have needed to become politically active, balancing activism with social regulation. No action in such a situation could be perceived as neutral by the teacher. Neutral is not an option.

There is a poem addressing the complexity of new teacher decision-making. Decisions may be made up in the moment, without yet having learned a set of effective actions, or having an experience bank of teaching or learning:

> How am I supposed to feel [act?]
> With all my learning and concentration, I should be able to help you, but
>   this isn't how it sounded in the book
>
> (Jack & Tetley, 2016, p. 4)

Who will lose in the struggle to compassionately provide Carol with the skills she requires? A neoliberal position may scale compassion to the level of funding available, while an emancipation position would argue that Carol's quality of life is most important. But at the same time, questions of relevance apply along with their variations. Britzman (2003, p. 4) describes a student teacher's dilemma as follows: "And while, of course, familiarity with the teacher's work does matter it is not a direct line to insight. For the newcomer, more is at stake because he or she already feels the teacher's work as uncannily familiar and utterly strange." Familiar because they have attended schools and therefore know the routines and beliefs of school. The well-known beliefs and routines of schools are comfortable, since the student teachers have attended schools as students. In their new role as teachers, they may feel utterly strange when in charge and planning action. Teachers in situations like Carol's often feel new and lost.

HOW DO DEFINITIONS OSCILLATE, IN SYNC AND OUT OF SYNC, IN THE GLOBAL CULTURE?

Carson and Johnston (2000, pp. 3–4) remind us teaching is a "psychic event ... that involves something other than consciousness." The belief that one must act in Carol's situation raises the question: Act for what and against what? The line of sight for some would be to use whatever skills and strategies are available to work with Carol. On the other hand, the budget may only afford or allow so much time for the work to achieve the best results. In more serious situations, such as the death of a child or parent, Hamilton (2008) describes her reaction as follows: "Involvement with such incidents requires a certain emotional detachment, in order to support those in crisis, counselors find a way to put their own feelings aside. While emotionally detaching may be possible and even automatic for some ..." (p. 9). Teachers are drawn into the situation and at the same time hold themselves detached from it, as their role is institutional rather than personal. The detachment becomes part of an induced filter at least for a short period of time before the person begins to reconsider it upon reflection. Other times, the new teacher may become immersed in emotional turmoil themselves and be unable to reflect or make thoughtful decisions until the emotional reaction subsides. In such situations, emotional regulation strategies may assist the teacher in a wider range of options to fit different contexts and cultures.

Compassion is, however, a multifaceted concept, and, because of that, compassion actively travels between the person/situation that requires compassion and the individual(s) who may or may not act to assist compassionately. As a concept conveyed by an act, compassion is first grasped only in parts that are integrated as a whole, but that whole, as we have seen, is bound to culture. The compassionate action of teachers, in whatever form, has different meanings depending upon the cultural backgrounds that are applied in the moment. Neumann and Nunning (2012, p. 3) suggest that "concepts are thus not to be understood as static abstractions, but also as dynamic re-arrangements of symbolic forms—a dynamic that travels in the space between cultural practices and academic theory." In that oscillating space of concepts, emotions, acculturation, and possible actions, it is possible that new forms of action and definition begin to emerge as hybrid cultural responses.

These emergent responses are open to changes in ways that are both positive and negative—that is, the redefinition of the term may be found to be disagreeable. There may be no further action for a problem; the helper has reached their limit. In another culture, the problem itself may not even be recognized as a problem, even if the question is raised. For example, take the statement "80 percent of our children are not able to attend school." This could be an accurate statement that the educator has no knowledge of and is not acting on. There is, then, a tension between what is known and not acted upon. Where does our compassion lie, and how will we act for the 80 percent of children not in school? But perhaps from the other culture's perspective, the question cannot be addressed in their current circumstance. Is compassion felt by the educator? Sufficient compassion to motivate research? To motivate an action plan? To carry through with intervention on this major community need? To see it through to change?

Perhaps what is more important to the family in the example above is that the 80 percent of children help to contribute to the family's resources so that the needed farm fertilizer may be purchased for the coming year. In this case, the term *compassionate* becomes culturally relative.

These constantly shifting meanings make it difficult to specify and create a definitive understanding of the term. Is it possible to define a term that is different in every context? The metaphor for sound vibration helps define aspects of compassionate experiences—they "oscillate" into action, or not. The definition shifts from culture to culture and perhaps even from place to place within a culture. The facility with which individuals or groups notice, respond to, and are open to acting compassionately for the good of the whole (not just their own individual needs as they perceive them at the moment) will impact every aspect of a situation. Consider, for example, the Nisga'a description of the term *compassion*. When a person or family demonstrates *k'e'em goot*, is it understood commonly, or does the interpretation of the term vary given the situation and the individual? In the aftermath of a colonial deconstruction of a culture, it is likely to be a tense mixture. What does this tell us about the experience of compassion for Nisga'a families and for teachers?

RELEVANCE TO EDUCATION

To meet children's needs in complex cross-cultural public schools today, teacher education programs need to articulate difficult emotional and conceptual responses into action-based experiences; one example is sharing materials in groups. Cultural and other developmental dynamics, which are all impacting the whole group as their interactions oscillate faster and faster, become visible from compassion. This is essential when the children's interactions begin to escalate into conflict. Once this cultural and dynamic perspective is clear, more positive outcomes can occur from compassionate action. The continuum that runs from individual to global becomes increasingly visible as children progress through schooling. Central questions present in all schooling include: Can compassionate "understanding in action" from teachers and students transform socially constructed inequities? Will teachers choose to bridge economic, racial, gender, and other socially constructed points of hierarchical privilege by changing their focus to deeper contextually responsive expressions of compassion-in-action, such as sharing in groups?

Perhaps the greatest compassion question facing the human collective is: Can enough human beings mature to act compassionately in all areas of development in order to focus our individual and collective resources on cooperative sustainability? This level of human development will require rapid cognitive, cultural, emotional, linguistic, physical, and social maturity to make the compassionate and interdependent well-being of the whole planet a consistent priority.

Example of an Action-Based, Compassion-Focused Educator Response

A common social development example from the complexities of bullying in the age of accelerating screen time involves families and school staff noticing, documenting, reporting, and intervening in what is now a widespread behaviour—cyberbullying. A recent CBC news article (Skinner, 2017) stated that a million Canadian children have been cyberbullied, with that number continually increasing, particularly in Grades 3 and 4. Bullying has become a serious high-risk situation. Many children do not have intergenerational and interwoven community support networks they trust and confide in. For children who are constantly getting the "thumbs down" social media response, a compassionate peer, coach, neighbour, mentor, or teacher may be the link to uncovering the deeper issues and getting out of the cycle of bullying or being bullied (Twenge, 2017). Compassion at every stage of the process, from all the peers and adults involved, may go a long way towards reducing and ameliorating incidents of bullying.

UNDERSTANDING THE CHANGING NATURE OF COMPASSION IN THE WORLD TODAY

Developmental research by Albert Bandura in the 1960s taught psychologists that children's aggressive or compassionate responses are highly influenced by the modelling of adults. He used a one-way glass observation room to record the behaviour of children after an adult modelled either violently knocking down the "bobo doll" in the room or coming in to help the children share a snack. The responses to sharing the snack varied depending on the behaviour of the adult (either aggressive or compassionate). This research has been replicated many times and used in many applications of the power of social modelling (Bandura, 1965).

Important research that followed in succeeding decades attempted to understand bystanders who do not act compassionately. "The bystander effect occurs when the presence of others discourages an individual from intervening in an emergency situation" (*Psychology Today*, n.d.). After the stabbing murder of a woman in New York City, "while bystanders who observed the crime did not step in to assist or call the police," researchers "attributed the bystander effect to the perceived diffusion of responsibility (onlookers are less likely to intervene if there are other witnesses who are perceived as likely to do so)." Another aspect of inaction was "social influence (individuals in a group monitor the behavior of those around them to determine how to act)." Researchers determined that "each onlooker concluded from their neighbors' inaction that their own personal help was not needed" (*Psychology Today*, n.d.).

In each of these examples, social modelling strongly influences behaviour. Teachers will find many examples of modelling impacting student behaviour—from compassionate responses on the playground, to compliance with social modelling in groups, to uses and abuses of social power in aggressive "leadership," to being "cool." Children and adults on school campuses often feel overwhelmed at the choices involved in intervention.

By the time the marketing of internet-capable devices to children peaked in 2007, wired and wireless devices were increasingly common in many homes. Blue screen time for children (and adults) more rapidly replaced activities with family and friends, social interaction time, and playtime, as well as supplanting other developmental activities (Twenge, 2017). The emotional and relational capacity for compassion may become overshadowed in the escalating states of clinical anxiety and depression occurring when screen time is substituted for people time (Twenge, 2017, pp. 300–302).

Teen research has shown young people expecting themselves to respond to every tweet, text, Instagram photo share, Facebook post, and so on. In their peer groups, this is their version of a "timely" response. In Twenge's (2017) research, teens were willing to stay up all or most of the night to catch up on screen, then fall asleep at school. Face-to-face time often becomes frustrating for both adolescents and adults as peers continue interacting on-screen, and those wanting actual social interaction are made to feel old-fashioned and uncool. The experience of frustration with friends face-to-face, when their peer continues with interaction online, can replace the connectiveness with people and relationships that builds compassion.

Additionally, it is a common belief that our brains can fluidly multitask, but this is untrue. The brain actually prioritizes focus, then moves from one activity to another, often making many micro-decisions and responding to snippets of information superficially processed in rapid sequence. The anxiety of the attempt to keep all the input prioritized and acted upon increases as the perceived or actual priority goes up. One common example is kids pressuring peers for immediate responses in a dramatic dating "crisis." The person in the dating situation looking for assistance then drops the first peer who could not respond. They call someone who is more immediately responsive to the young person's phone missives (Twenge, 2017).

In 2011, the aggressive marketing campaign to younger students using the term *smartphone* stirred a competitive spirit that tapped into aggressive consumerism in a new way, and "2011-12 was exactly when the majority of Americans started to own cell phones that could access the Internet" (Twenge, 2017, p. 4). Since then, newer versions of phones have become markers of social value and "withitness." A spiky but steadily increasing pattern at the turn of the 21st century was replaced by a steep and rapid rise in screen time, anxiety, and reduced face-to-face time with family and friends. Cyberbullying, suicides, and other behaviours increased rapidly (Twenge, 2017; Turkle, 2011). Even as families and educators continue attempting to teach compassion, they are faced with an increasingly compassionless social media environment.

The steady escalation in children's exposure to violence, and the general population's increasing anxiety experiences, affect teachers' ability to calm student emotions and create an academic focus. Teachers who work with mindfulness as a precursor skill are often able to teach social skills like noticing, discussing, and brainstorming conflict interventions. Children can gain self-management skills along the continuum of feeling anxiety, making snarky comments, and using coercion in early bullying, all the way to classroom violence, domestic violence, and campus violence. These many influences against a thoughtful, kind, and compassionate model have increased children's mental health issues rapidly. From anxiety to suicide, schools are attempting to influence this trajectory with compassionate professionals, academics, families, collaborative data gathering, and coming up with combined interventions.

COMPASSION UNDER STRESS

In the face of these 21st century realities, now present on a scale and in a variety of forms previously unknown, new teachers are faced with many experiences, decisions, and interactions that are stressful in new ways. Schools with the highest turnover of staff, often those with students needing support at all levels of development, are the most likely to hire new teachers. Sometimes they are hired even before completing teacher education programs for certification. The teachers may have had very different experiences in their own K-12 school years than the students they are now teaching. For example, "In 2015, 50,280 or 18.5% of BC's youngest children were still living in poverty. The only positive note is the movement of the under-6 poverty rate down from 20.1% in 2014, closer to the overall child poverty rate of 18.3% in 2015. BC children are poor—higher than the national average" (First Call, 2017, p. 11). As Kreassig notes, "teachers must be more expert at diagnosing student learning, and psychological needs, in addition to sometimes complex academic needs" (Kreassig, 2018, p. 8). They must also be "effective teachers, using sound instructional practices, and providing additional student support services" (2018, p. 8).

For the teacher, the question "Is **teacher compassion** cultural or cognitive, conceptual or evident as action?" is a constant as each day unfolds. **Compassion fatigue**, a term common in medical and social/psychological work settings, may be increasingly relevant in schools. New teachers are making an effort to address learning in many dimensions new to them, and often new to their school sites. For example, literacy online brings a vast range of content with an equally wide range of quality. A continuum from material developed from a single cultural perspective with resultant biases, to high quality cross-cultural materials for building impactful learning for all children.

Merriman (2015) explores the professional concept of compassion fatigue. A description of compassion fatigue related to educators could include: "a state of tension and preoccupation" with traumatized students; "a deep physical, emotional and spiritual exhaustion accompanied by acute emotional pain"; "a condition that is a consequence of a depletion of internal emotional resources"; and "perceived demands outweighing perceived resources" (Merriman, 2015, p. 371). These consequences of increasing societal, economic, cultural, and environmental factors impacting children, families, and their schools may be applicable in many ways for teachers.

COMPASSIONATE INTERVENTIONS INTERFERING WITH GROWTH

A very different perspective on responding to current pressures on children, families, and schools is presented in a dissertation by Mintz, in which the argument is made that "compassion leads many teachers to unreflectively alleviate student struggles" (in Jonas, 2010, p. 2). The intervention may be interfering with the development of "self-mastery in human beings" (Jonas, 2010, p. 1) acquired through dealing with adversity successfully, and then having the confidence and skills to take on further growth and education. In this view, interventions in social or learning issues—different from interventions in high-risk behaviours—may reduce students' social and emotional growth. Examples of areas that may be affected are self-efficacy, confidence, internal locus of control, degree of effort invested, academic growth through failure, accurate self-image as a learner, student teachers resisting the push for grade inflation, and setting realistic improvement goals for children or new teachers.

These very different lenses—of compassion fatigue and growth through suffering—allow reflective teachers to look at possible teacher responses to difficult situations as points of choice that can help them to articulate and shape learning with children. Self-mastery learning for both student and teacher can assist them in building strengths that will serve them in the long term; indeed, this mode of learning will help them enhance ways in which they deal with escalating and difficult social changes.

AN INCREASINGLY ABSENT SKILL IN THE PRESENCE OF STRESS

Costa and Costa (2016) look at another aspect of compassion, from the perspective of medical professionals. They ask the reader if credibility for greater compassion in patient care could be based on looking at compassion through the lens of neuroscience. Costa and Costa (2016, p. 281) explore building empathy by understanding "a specific brain core neural network that is responsive to emotions designated as belonging to the 'pain-empathy network' … activated in response to one's own personal experiences or to observations of others." This documentable brain activity is used to suggest brain modulation imaging studies or biofeedback sessions could be used for educational interventions intended to increase physician compassion. In the context of teacher education, one of the questions Twenge (2017) raises is whether similar disregard for affective components of professional decision-making and interaction can be remedied. Intervention is needed before task- or goal-oriented teachers are solely responsible for the development of children needing stronger affective skills in complex and technology-based social situations. Thus, relationship building could be helpful for both students and teachers. Otherwise, what happens if both teacher and student lack the developmental depth for understanding, coaching, and using such relationship and conflict skills—especially when these skills are increasingly vital for campus success?

INTEGRATION OF NEW IMMIGRANTS OR DISENFRANCHISED STUDENTS REQUIRES COMPASSIONATE EDUCATORS

Boyden (2009) discusses the concepts of educational compassion for refugee children in the UK, with a powerful parallel for Canadian Indigenous children: "A version of compassion founded on social justice would seem to be very different from one based in the notion of care, since this approach gives prominence to the political economy of forced migration and calls up notions of power, equity and rights" (p. 273). For Canadian Indigenous children, there may be some difference between their experience and that of refugee children in the UK, given their social justice issues stem from forced subjugation onto federally designated reserves, into residential schools, and out of their home communities to families far from their home territory. However, both are examples of the backgrounds children bring to school. For Canadian teachers, compassion and accurate knowledge bases are required to address the next generation of social justice issues, and it is important that they have an understanding of colonial history and its resulting practices. This learning can then become part of compassionate cultural regeneration. A larger sociocultural context influences every aspect of classrooms and instruction, whether consciously or **dysconsciously.**

DISCUSSION AND SUGGESTIONS

The definition of *compassion* is varied, and expanded meanings are often ignored in favour of the Western European definition that dominates in our schools. With the increasing global migration/immigration of peoples, it is important to recognize that the definition of the term *compassion* in North America is changing. It must also be understood that the increasing recognition of Indigenous peoples in Canada means that their ways of defining the term are contributing to this change. When there is no longer one assured Western definition, families of many cultures can develop a culturally congruent place with the teacher. The example of relatives being part of the healing in hospitals is an illustration of a cultural intersection for positive change. In classrooms, connections with extended family are critical components of children's balanced development. When peers and pop culture influences replace time with grandparents, uncles, aunts, siblings, and cousins, we all lose in a thinner social fabric supporting children.

As with other concepts, the meanings of *compassion* change as they come in contact with other culturally similar terms—for example, the Pilipino interpretation of compassion as "I am almost in tears ..." and the Nisga'a basis for compassion "from feeling and heart," described earlier. Consider for a moment a young Indigenous student who has been the recipient of racial comments on school grounds. Their white teacher acts quickly to deal with the situation, sending the children responsible to the principal's office. The parents of the boys come to the school, as do members of the Indigenous student's extended family. Why are they involved? They have compassion for their family member, the child.

Schools are perhaps the best examples of places where various cultures of a community mix and mingle. Have you considered that in the case above, the meaning of compassion that is perceived by each family is not two separate definitions but rather one? With thoughtful communication, one new, combined definition emerges—one that has adopted the characteristics of the two definitions. The families are partners in supervising the children's restorative action plan.

Restorative thinking places the compassionate teacher in a new role—one that involves a sensitive, reflective capacity for understanding the role of culture on the playground, as well as in the classroom, school, and community. The teacher must learn to step back after an event and understand how each person can be involved from compassion to co-create the outcome. The teacher in such a process is also a learner. They become learners who more deeply know their students and are able to help them in a constructive manner. As the teacher comes to comprehend the oscillations among different people, they become sensitive to the cultural complexities of the event. The next time a situation arises, the teacher may thoughtfully scaffold the support necessary for their student. Increasing cultural congruence will reduce frictions among students and infuse a new version of compassion that benefits everyone.

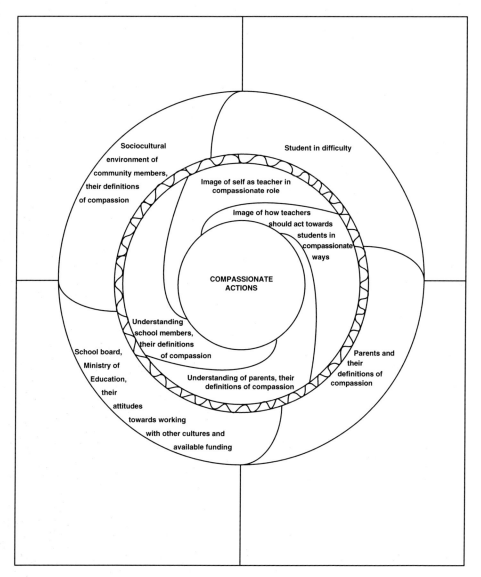

Figure 1.1: Compassion in Motion: Oscillations into Action

Source: Authors, using concepts from Mignolo (2000).

CONCLUSION

Compassionate thinking, in action with families, places the teacher in a new role. It is a role that requires an understanding of the interplay of cultures on the playground, in the classroom, in the school, and in the community. Increasing cultural congruence will reduce frictions among students and infuse a new version of compassion that benefits everyone, even as global change magnifies both tensions and possible connections. The new congruence could provide teachers with a basis from which to integrate their own cultural growth and create a cross-cultural teaching framework that continues to evolve throughout their career.

THREE CASES TO DISCUSS

Case #1

A kindergarten teacher is upset that the mother of a student, James, does not agree that her child needs additional learning support. James still cannot really speak more than a few words, but the parent is adamant that he does not need help: "He is learning." The teacher has tried and tried to create an agreement with the parent for specific speech and language testing and support, at parent night, at personal meetings, with a school-based team, and at a meeting including the principal. None of these interventions have resulted in a successful partnership providing more specific language learning support. Apart from making more sounds, and sometimes using words, James has not progressed to phrases, sentences, or conversation.

Put yourself in this teacher's shoes. *Tasks:* What would you have documented so far? What would you have researched? What would the best outcome for all be in your opinion and why? *Action steps:* What compassionate action steps could you propose next, for the short term and for the long term?

Case #2

A non-Indigenous teacher has two Indigenous students who are not passing her course. There are, however, extenuating circumstances. One has recently been in the hospital, and the other has a recently identified learning disability. The rules of the school are very clear on the point: all students must complete all assignments and tests on time or suffer the consequences, such as failing grades.

Put yourself in this teacher's shoes. *Tasks:* What would you have documented so far? What would you have researched? What would the best outcome for all be in your opinion and why? *Action steps:* What compassionate steps could you propose next, for the short term and for the long term?

Case #3

A middle school student is suspended from a teacher's class by the office for being on campus intoxicated and with liquor in her possession. When she returns in three days, most of her classmates are focused on her and the story of what was going on a few nights before. She's been away for three days, after all. They discuss the morning of the suspension, including "hook-up" rumours with a member of the soccer team who is also in the class. The social dynamics are so intense the teacher cannot refocus the class, except for a few students who valiantly try to continue with class in the face of so much distraction.

Put yourself in this teacher's shoes. *Tasks:* What would you have documented so far? What would you have researched? What would the best outcome for all be in your opinion and why? *Action steps:* What compassionate steps could you propose next, for the short term and for the long term?

QUESTIONS FOR CRITICAL THOUGHT

1. Think of a situation where a teacher acted compassionately. Your example could be from your own school years, or at any time in your experience of classrooms. Describe the context, action or inaction, and the impact on learning.
2. What is an example from your community of a cross-cultural dynamic that often affects children in classrooms and needs a compassionate teacher response?
3. What are some of the factors involved in learning, valuing, and choosing to act upon compassionate feelings, while using complex teacher skill sets to resolve student issues? What are some of the situations requiring intervention that may become challenges to new teachers and require support and mentoring?

GLOSSARY

Acculturation: The process by which culture is passed on to the next generation, often not consciously transmitted or received. Culture is more often in conscious awareness when two or more cultures begin to mix together or when one culture, typically the dominant one, mandates "normal cultural practice."

Compassion fatigue: Broadly defined as a reduced capacity for empathy, as manifested through emotional, behavioural, physical, spiritual, inter-personal, and cognitive reactions experienced by any individual helping a traumatized person.

Cross-cultural: Elements, including ideas, customs, and social behaviour, from different ethnic backgrounds, as well as languages and other differences in-volving students who have lived varying lengths of time in the host country. Differences constantly navigated by Indigenous and settler peoples. For exam-ple, patterns of self- and individual focus, or of family and community focus.

Dysconsciousness: "Refers to an uncritical habit of mind (including perceptions, attitudes, assumptions, and beliefs) that justifies inequity and exploitation by accepting the existing order of things as a given" (Joyce E. King, in Banks, 2012, p. 1).

Teacher compassion: When the teacher understands more intervention is required and becomes involved in supporting the student in new ways by drawing on feelings of empathy and kindness.

REFERENCES

Bandura, A. (1965). Influence of models' reinforcement contingencies on the acquisition of imitative responses. *Journal of Personality and Social Psychology,* 1(6), 589–595.

Banks, J. A. (2012). *Encyclopedia of diversity in education.* Thousand Oaks, CA: Sage Publications.

Boyden, J. (2009). What place the politics of compassion in education surrounding non-citizen children? *Educational Review,* 61(3), 265–276.

Britzman, D. (2003). *Practice makes practice: A critical study of learning to teach.* New York: SUNY Press.

Carson, T., & Johnston, I. (2000). The difficulty with difference in teacher education: Toward a pedagogy of compassion. *Alberta Journal of Educational Research,* 46(1), 75–83.

compasión. (n.d.). In *Collins Spanish Dictionary.* Retrieved from https://www. collinsdictionary.com/dictionary/spanish-english/compasion%C3%B3.

compassion. (2018). In *Merriam-Webster.com.* Retrieved from https://www.merriam -webster.com/dictionary/compassion.

compassion. (2004). In *Merriam-Webster's Collegiate Dictionary* (11th ed.). Springfield, MA: Merriam-Webster, Incorporated.

Costa, M., & Costa, P. (2016). Nurturing empathy and compassion: What might the neurosciences have to offer? *Medical Education, 50*, 271–281.

Cummings, J., & Bennett, V. (2012). *Compassion in practice: Nursing, midwifery and care.* Retrieved from https://www.england.nhs.uk/wp-content/uploads/2012/12/compassion-in-practice.

First Call: BC Child and Youth Advocacy Coalition. (2017). 2017 BC child poverty report card. Retrieved from https://www.sparc.bc.ca/wp-content/uploads/2017/12/2017-BC-Child-Poverty-Report-Card.pdf.

Hamilton, M. (2008). Compassion fatigue: What school counsellors should know about secondary traumatic stress. *Alberta Counselor, 30*(1), 9–21.

Hao, R. H. (2011). Critical compassionate pedagogy and the teacher's role in first-generation student success. *New Directions for Teaching and Learning, 127*(Fall), 91–98. https://doi.org/10.1002/tl.460.

Holiday, R., & Hanselman, H. (2016). Glossary. *Daily Stoic.* Retrieved from https://dailystoic.com/glossary.

Jack, K., & Tetley, J. (2016). Using poems to explore the meaning of compassion to undergraduate nursing students. *International Practice Development Journal, 6*(1). https://doi.org/10.19043/ipdj.61.004.

Jonas, M. (2010). When teachers must let education hurt: Rousseau and Nietzsche on compassion and the educational value of suffering. *Journal of Philosophy of Education, 44*(1), 45–60.

Kreassig, K. (2018). Challenges of student teachers placed in poverty schools. *Journal of Education & Social Policy, 5*(1), 6–16.

Manuel, A., & Derrikson, R. (2017). *The reconciliation manifesto: Recovering the land, rebuilding the economy.* Toronto: James Lorimer.

McCutcheon, M. (2003). *Roget's Super Thesaurus* (3rd ed.). Cincinnati, OH: Writer's Digest Books.

Merriman, J. (2015). Enhancing counselor supervision through compassion fatigue education. *Journal of Counseling and Development, 93*, 370–378.

Mignolo, W. D. (2000). *Local histories/global designs: Coloniality, subaltern knowledges and border thinking.* Princeton, NJ: Princeton University Press.

Mitleid. (n.d.). In *dict.cc.* Retrieved from https://www.dict.cc/german-english/Mitleid.html.

Neumann, B., & Nunning, A. (Eds.). (2012). *Travelling for the study of culture.* Boston: Walter de Gruyer GmbH & Co.

Olshansky, E. (2007). What do we mean by compassion and caring in nursing and what does it matter anyway? *Journal of Professional Nursing, 23*(5), 247–248.

Psychology Today. (n.d.). *Bystander Effect.* Retrieved from https://www.psychologytoday. com/us/basics/bystander-effect.

Santos, B. de S. (2014). *Epistemologies of the south: Justice against epistemcide.* Boulder, CO: Paradigm Publishers.

Skinner, R. J. (2017, October 10). Your kids' smartphones may be putting them at a higher risk for cyberbullying. *CBC Life.* Retrieved from https://www.cbc.ca/life/wellness/ your-kids-smartphones-may-be-putting-them-at-a-higher-risk-for -cyberbullying-1.4348254.

sympatheia. (2016). In *Daily Stoic.* Retrieved from https://dailystoic.com/glossary.

Turkle, S. (2011). *Alone together: Why we expect more from technology and less from each other* (3rd ed.). New York: Basic Books.

Twenge, J. (2017). *iGen: Why today's super-connected kids are growing up less rebellious, more tolerant, less happy—and completely unprepared for adulthood.* New York: Simon and Schuster.

CHAPTER 2

Teaching in Difficult Times: The Promise of Care Ethics

Kumari Beck and Wanda Cassidy

LEARNING OBJECTIVES

1. To introduce readers to the ethic of care.
2. To understand how ethical care focuses on relationships, other-directedness, dialogue, and reciprocity.
3. To engage with stories from educators who have enacted ethical caring in their schools.
4. To consider how to enhance practice through strategies reflecting an ethic of care.

INTRODUCTION

We live in difficult times: social, cultural, economic, environmental, and political conditions are making our daily lives unpredictable, uncertain, and for too many, life threatening and unsafe. These conditions contribute to what we believe is a critical moment in education generally, and for teacher education more specifically.

Today's classrooms, particularly in urban and suburban contexts, include students from diverse backgrounds from all parts of the world; some are refugees displaced by war, terror, or genocide, and many are learning English as their second or third language. We see a growing number of Indigenous children and youth who are trying to recover from the legacy of colonization. Too many of our young people struggle with mental health issues, have learning challenges, and/or live in poverty. Yet all students, no matter their background, come to school wanting to succeed academically (Cassidy & Bates, 2005; Hayes, Ryan, & Zseller, 1994) and to fit in socially (van der Putten, 2017). Each child wants to belong and to have hope. Hoot (2011) confirms the essential role that education plays in creating a sense of belonging and preserving hope among students in school.

We see "difficult times" as opportunities for teachers to "do school differently" (Beck & Cassidy, 2009, p. 55), to bring a relational caring ethic to a school system still rooted in an industrial model, and to provide success for students often relegated to the margins because they are labelled as "challenging." We find it distressing that 15 percent of children who started kindergarten with joy and hope fail to graduate in our public education system, with even higher percentages for Indigenous youth (30 percent) and students with special needs (29 percent) (British Columbia Teachers' Federation, 2019a, 2019b). These youth are the "push-outs" in a system that espouses diversity but does not embrace students' differences. We take a social justice perspective rather than an individual deficit approach (Cassidy & Bates, 2005; McDowell, 2011; Wotherspoon & Schissel, 2001) to the issue of "teaching in difficult times"; that is, we see the challenge residing in a school system that needs changing rather than in students that need to adapt to fit the norm. In other words, to use a horticultural analogy, if a plant is failing to thrive, we see the problem residing with the soil and the environment (light, heat, moisture) rather than with the plant needing to be pruned or discarded.

In this chapter, we discuss the **ethic of care** and how enacting this ethic in our teaching and in school policies and practices creates "wiggle room" (Parker, 2011) in a school system that currently fails to provide success for all students, and creates a vision of healing and ethical power to act for the betterment of all (Greene, 1991). Nel Noddings, Professor Emerita from Stanford and a prominent scholar for the caring ethic, described a school system that tends to work against care, while "the need for care may be greater than ever" (1992, p. 20). Noddings's words continue to ring true 27 years later.

We begin by discussing what is meant by the ethic of care, as opposed to natural caring or virtue caring. We then present stories from our research with Canadian teachers and school administrators who embraced this ethic, modelling and practicing its principles in their respective schools, and reflect upon the impact this enactment had on their practice as educators, on their students, and on their **school cultures** as a whole.[1] We conclude with a brief discussion of the implications for classroom practice.

WHAT IS THE ETHIC OF CARE?

> Caring—far more than a fuzzy feeling—is a moral way of life. (Noddings, 2012, p. 56)

A common response when teachers are asked why they chose teaching as a career is that they care about children and want to make a difference in their lives. We would be hard-pressed to find teachers who did not describe themselves as caring individuals. Yet too many studies show that when students are asked if their teachers are caring, students reply in the negative (McDowell, 2011). There is a disconnect between what teachers perceive their actions to be and what students are experiencing.

One reason for this is that caring typically is seen as residing in the carer, as an expression of a virtue that the carer possesses. So a teacher self-identifies as a kind, nice, or pleasant person—someone who has a set of positive attributes. This is not the ethical caring that Noddings (1984, 2012) and others (Bergman, 2007) talk about, nor is it the "natural caring" that a person feels when interacting with a loved one—a good example being the relationship between mother and infant where the motivation to care arises on its own (Noddings, 1984).

Ethical caring is a relational ethic that is based on the carer responding to the expressed needs of the other. This ethic requires that a connection be established between the carer and the receiver of the caring act. The carer perceives that there is a need for care, or that need for care is communicated by the one about to receive the care, and then the care is offered in response to those needs. Ethical caring involves **reciprocity** and **mutuality**: the one receiving the care responds to the act of care, thus building a sense of mutuality in the circle of care. In fact, if the care is not received, it is not considered ethical caring; the actions have gone awry—what the carer thought was a caring action was not what was needed and was, therefore, rejected. The circle was not completed. So, unlike virtue caring, ethical caring is not an attribute or a particular behaviour, nor is it a one-way process. Rather, it is constituted in the relationship between the carer and the cared-for, with the cared-for actively participating in the process.

So how can this caring relationship be established in schools? There is no set of rules, specific behaviours, or a template that can be followed, nor a program that can be purchased and implemented. Rather, ethical caring requires the teacher to see ethical possibilities in everyday interactions with students, opportunities to build relationships, to listen attentively to the other, and to offer unique responses to expressed needs. As Montabello notes, "a caring response cannot be achieved by formula" (2008, p. 36).

In what follows, we identify four broad working principles that may guide teachers to a better understanding of ethical caring.

Determining the Needs of the Other

Because ethical caring involves responding to the expressed needs of the other, it is important that teachers take time to attentively listen to students' needs, to discern what those needs might be even if not directly and overtly expressed. This requires opportunities to have one-on-one conversations and interactions with students, to get to know each as individuals with unique needs and aspirations. At the secondary school level, in particular, this is more challenging with teachers teaching multiple classes. Gillespie (2015) offers some suggestions: greeting students by name; spending the beginning of every class making connections with students rather than delving right into the formal lesson; taking time to chat with students in the hallways, at lunch, and at clubs, sports, and arts events; and acknowledging students' accomplishments.

Noddings talks about the need for teachers to "apprehend the other's reality" (1984, p. 16), while Rauner (2000) discusses the importance of "attentive listening," rather than projecting one's own agenda on the other or assuming needs that are not there. Bergman (2007) discusses Noddings's concept of "engrossment" to describe the act of being fully present.

Wise Actions in the Other's Best Interests

Ethical caring is more than a feeling or an intention; it involves action in response to the expressed or perceived needs of the other. Determining how best to respond comes from an empathetic "reading of the other that engenders both feeling and understanding" (Noddings, 2012, p. 54). The process involves self-reflectivity and the setting aside of one's ego and preconceived solutions. Mayeroff (1971) calls for a responsiveness to needs and action that is wise and personalized. In the school system, this means refraining from one-size-fits-all solutions to what the teacher perceives as the problems that need fixing.

Making Relationships a Priority

Often teachers get caught up in the expectations of the required
the pressures to increase students' achievement on standardized te
aminations, the demands of creating daily lesson plans, and the ma
of classroom behaviour. But schooling, as far back as Dewey (1916), stresses
the importance of students building connections inside the classroom as well as
with the wider community, cultivating the values that undergird democracy, and
learning social skills and attributes. Education should be viewed as engaging the
whole person, not just the mind. This focus on the informal curriculum of relationship building can take place simultaneously with implementing the formal
curriculum, if teachers consciously attend to this broader purpose of education.

Modelling, Practice, Dialogue, and Confirmation

Noddings (1992, 2012) suggests that the caring ethic may be attended to
through modelling, practice, dialogue, and confirmation. The most powerful
teacher is often what is being modelled and practiced through daily interactions
(Jackson, Boostrom, & Hansen, 1993). Certainly, we know that children learn
more from growing up in families and what they observe there, than from the
oral lessons they are taught by their parents. By modelling and practicing care,
students know that they matter, and it grows their own capacity to care (Beck
& Cassidy, 2009). Noddings draws on Freire's (1970) concept of dialogue, where
the power imbalances between teacher and students are reduced, discussion is
invitational, and where each seeks to receive and attend to the other through
empathetic listening. Confirmation is the "act of affirming and encouraging the
best in others" (Noddings, 1992, p. 24), "while nurturing the student towards
the ethical ideal" (Beck & Cassidy, 2009, p. 58).

Bergman (2007) sums up these four dimensions working in concert as "the
best self of the educator seeks a caring relationship with the best self of the
student […] which requires receptivity and leads to engrossment, motivational
displacement, and the most competent reasoning toward as adequate a response
as possible."

OUR STUDY

The stories and examples we refer to in this chapter are data from a research
study[2] conducted in British Columbia (BC), Canada. At the time, the research
team and many of their graduate students had been studying the ethic of care in

their programs of study and were enthusiastic about wanting to deepen their understanding of educational practices of care. There was little written at the time about the enactment of care in educational settings, and much less empirical research on the topic. A group of educators from a variety of backgrounds and educational settings (elementary, secondary, alternate, post-secondary; inner-city, suburban, rural, multicultural, socioeconomically diverse) were invited to participate in a community of inquiry that was initially planned for two years, but ended up running for over four years because of the interest of the participants. The focus of our inquiry was to understand how educators sought to enact care in their classrooms, what challenges they faced in their practice, and how they addressed them.

Each participant was interviewed individually, most often at their school or workplace, to explore their views and practices of care. All the participants met once a month as a group for a few hours on a Saturday morning. The meetings in the early stages were structured, with set readings and topics from care theory for exploration. They soon evolved into group discussions of particular issues and concerns that participants raised from their practice. The audio-taped data that emerged from these sessions were rich and reflected a complexity that led us to further explorations and discussions. Among the findings of this chapter, one of the most significant was the cultivation of care practice through the community of inquiry itself, both as self-care and in enhancing participants' classroom practice. We bring you six of these participant narratives that illustrate ethical care in action and demonstrate the growth of compassionate educators working for social justice.

Teachers' Lived Experiences

Of the 14 educators who participated in the study, we feature data from six: Brooke, an elementary teacher; Ken, a secondary school counsellor; Mark, an elementary teacher; William, a secondary teacher at an independent school for high-need youth; Denise, an elementary school vice principal; and Sarah, a principal of an inner-city elementary school.[3]

Brooke: Care As a Way of Being

Brooke began her teaching career as a primary teacher and quickly became the science expert at her elementary school. At the time of the research, she was in a teacher educator role in a professional development program at a BC university.

Brooke found her way into teaching after leaving an abusive relationship, and she describes her process of recovery from this situation as life changing and one that influenced her decision to be a teacher:

> I think that because I was an underdog and found my way through that [...] I have always worked with these kinds of students, the ones who just had had so many strikes against them, had really difficult situations they found themselves in [...] And I'm not saying that I was always successful at it, but at least I did always certainly try to find alternate ways to have them be successful. Because the standard system isn't usually one that works for those kinds of kids.

Brooke felt strongly that "each child wants to be successful and that they deserve every opportunity to be successful whether socially or academically or learning new skills." This belief led her to understand the importance of developing sound relationships with her students and her colleagues:

> And so, if I found that a student was having difficulty, I wouldn't be able to assist them unless I knew them. Unless I took the time to figure out what their individual needs were. So I guess this is why I view care as very much about doing, but also getting to know each student [...] By knowing that person, by truly getting to see where they've come from, what's important to them, what they need, then I can adjust my own practice to help them achieve, help them work towards success.

In her role as a teacher educator, she has "incredibly high expectations" for herself and her students, and these standards translate into important points of influence. One anecdote demonstrates Brooke's deeper understanding of the needs of children:

> I was doing a teacher evaluation the other day and this student teacher was feeling very frustrated. He had a very difficult class that he was trying to find his way about ... and he was kicking kids out into the hallway, two in a row. And I thought ... I can't continue to be a fly on the wall, so I stepped out of my observer role, went out into the hallway to speak to these children (this little guy was just tugging at my heart), and then, after the session, I instructed all my teacher candidates that they are not to do that. They are not to send children into the hallway, that's not an avenue that they can choose to do as a teacher. For one, it was an unsafe situation because these children were quite

volatile, but more than that, at the very time that these children need a connection to someone, they are then cut off.

Brooke continued to describe other situations with her teacher candidates that illustrate both her philosophy about supporting children and her focus on laying a good foundation for her teacher candidates:

> The other day, a teacher candidate said, "Well, I have different expectations for this child—all we expect from him is that he brings his pencil." I was furious with that student teacher, and I said to her, "Why are you expecting less from that child? He is on an IEP [Independent Education Plan] because he's got behaviour problems, and that's because he hasn't been engaged in learning. Stop expecting less just because he comes from a messed-up home." I know that I need to be caring of my teacher candidates, to be patient, and to help them, but I get impatient with a system that doesn't expect that all children can be successful.

As with all of the participants in this chapter, Brooke identified many challenges, and one was what she called "the constant fight with yourself." She was referring to the tendency to "go the easy way and let things go" versus "doing the right thing." She gave an example of one of her elementary students who made a racist comment during his class presentation. She ended the presentation, informed the student that it was an inappropriate comment, and explained to the presenter that she would reflect on how best to explore it later. At the end of the day, she consulted with her teaching partner because, as Brooke explained in her interview, "It was such an important thing and I wanted to handle it correctly." The next day, she led a discussion with her students about the comment, explored the history of affirmative action (which was the issue that led to the comment), and why it was important. This led to a discussion on why the comment was inappropriate and racist. She remarked in her interview, "We ended up having this amazing conversation with our students and it was so enriching." Brooke reflected that it would have been easier to give the student a detention, or send a note home to his parents, or hand out another punishment, but she realized that she had a responsibility to educate this student and his classmates, without damaging the relationships she had built.

When asked to describe her own understanding of care theory, Brooke said:

> There are so many aspects of the world and of teaching and schools that can be very discouraging. You see children struggle academically, we see homes

and families that struggle with poverty, with abuse issues, we see a system that doesn't support teachers and their learning, and that doesn't support all children, we fight with bureaucratic structures, and it's very easy to get cynical […] I see care as a way to offer hope. For me, care is the avenue of hopefulness.

This pathway, for Brooke, also meant working with parents, colleagues, and administrators, and projecting this vision of hope: "It cannot just be your words […] it has to be a way of being. It means questioning and reflecting on one's actions, to ensure consistent alignment with the principles of ethical caring."

Ken: Belonging and Mattering

Ken was a counsellor at a secondary school at the time of the study, with 18 years of experience as a teacher, program director at an alternate school, and counsellor. He spent time describing the differences among the three schools where he had worked and how these contexts raised many questions for him about the inequities of schooling. In particular, he was struck by the close connection between socioeconomic status and academic achievement and was interested in whether care ethics might create a better learning environment for youth from lower socioeconomic families.

He described how students from poor families at his alternate school often felt like they did not belong and that they did not matter to their teachers: "It was common to hear things like 'I don't care about school' or 'That teacher doesn't really care,' or 'Why should I care?'" Ken became convinced that these experiences led to disengagement from learning. He wondered: "What can I do to create change?"

Belonging was a key concern for Ken: "If more at-risk students could feel a sense of belonging and recognition within the school community this would […] encourage them to participate more fully within it." In his own practice, he spent time getting to know his students, meeting resistance and disinterest with warmth, and initiating conversations about things that mattered to them. As he noted in his interview, "It's modelling […] you are modelling how people can interact with one another [in a healthy way]. It's not like forcing your agenda, you are just 'being.'" Ken applied Noddings's concept of confirmation through the notion of unconditional positive regard as articulated by psychologist Carl Rogers, by encouraging students to be their best selves, whatever that might be. Recognizing that his students may have limited experiences of being cared for, or caring for others, Ken created a pet-care program with students taking the responsibility for the animals. School, for these students, was becoming a place centred in relationships and conversations, rather than discipline and rules, tests and punishment. They mattered to someone.

Ken also discussed the "tyranny of the curriculum": "If an ethic of care was more central to the education curriculum, students would be able to learn things that they actually care about [and this …] would make them feel more cared for."

For Ken, practicing care followed Noddings's views on creating connections in the curriculum, caring for ideas, and the importance of fostering critical thinking. Teachers, he said, should be more flexible: "More flexibility in scheduling and perhaps less instructional classes and more self-paced ones could help individual students living in less fortunate personal and social situations."

William: Meeting Them Where They Are At

William was a teacher at an accredited independent school in British Columbia that served vulnerable youth who had dropped out or been pushed out of the traditional school system. All had been labelled as having "severe behaviour" problems at their former schools, and many faced the challenges of substance abuse, learning difficulties, mental health problems, dysfunctional home environments, and involvement in the youth justice system.

In describing the work of the school, William shared the first line of the school's vision statement: "We are a safe, respectful, and nurturing community, sensitive to each person and his or her uniqueness." He went on to say that the school was intentionally designed to "meet each student where they are at, both academically and socially:"

> We are trying to create a culture of care in the classroom, and not just the teachers understand that but all the students are aware […] that we need to create an atmosphere where people are respected for where they are at. Care, and that vision, really starts from the staff—teachers are really part of […] the community with the students, and work on building that sense of community in the class.

The culture of care is reflected throughout the school, from the physical environment of the building to the relationships that staff promote. The school has welcoming open spaces, cozy areas with couches, soft lighting, plenty of snacks available in the kitchen, and coffee and toast served in the morning, and each student is personally greeted when they come to school. "When students come in here they should feel like this is their school, and for the first time the hope is that they would be able to say, 'This is my place,'" says William.

Echoing Ken, he observed that many of their students have had "a void in their life of care," having experienced harmful relationships with the adults and bureaucrats in their lives, and a lack of predictability and consistency: "A lot of them have a real issue in [...] trusting that adults would have their best interests in mind in making decisions [...] For them to feel safe, they need to understand that they're cared for. That they are respected for who they are."

He recalled his own Grade 11 social studies teacher who was an influential role model: "[He] set a positive tone, and still had excellent boundaries with students but was always there for students [...] So, what I'm really reflecting on a daily basis is how do you set boundaries in ways that are caring?"

William observed that his students learn so much from what is modelled by the adults at the school:

> Absolutely, the curriculum is important, but I think that setting a tone of care, the relationships that are built, both by students but even by how the students watch staff relate. Even in the small actions like walking around the school, how you deal with somebody from the public, how you talk to people both in the school and outside [...] I think that sends a really clear message. It is a responsibility for sure, but we model to the students how to deal with stress, with frustration, and I think those kinds of things can be really powerful messages to kids.

William summarized his views by saying, "I feel that care is the most important part of the school experience."

Mark: Introspection and Self-Care

In contrast with the other educators featured in this chapter, Mark is a relatively new teacher. Mark's decision to become a teacher was not intentional, nor noteworthy. All he remembered was that teaching kids at camp had been fun, and when it came time to put food on the table, he thought that teaching might not be a bad career.

Mark sees himself as "a guide for the children" and is not particularly interested in "the monotonous things that you have to do like classroom set up, routines and such things."

> Ideally, I see myself as a teacher, guiding them and nurturing them in a way in which they are well, now and in the future. That they see themselves as part of something greater than just themselves, and seeing that they participate in

some kind of action outside of themselves […] not as some kind of a saint, you know, but that there is no separation between themselves and […] it's a normal part of who they are.

He continues: "The whole idea of a classroom without any ethic of care is a pretty scary thought." When pressed for why he would think so, he talked about the school becoming a factory, of encouraging children to be "smart" in the absence of critical thinking or connecting with others.

When asked what drove his vision of care, Mark emphasized starting with "care of self" and being influenced by the work of Thich Nhat Hanh. Care of self was not a matter of self-absorption, but more about self-improvement:

Say you want to look at peace in the world or you want to do something that brings about some kind of balance, then you begin with yourself and you use tools like mindfulness to first of all be at peace with yourself, to take care of yourself, and to recognize, 'Okay, maybe I'm a person with a bit of temper, or a person who gets impatient,' and you accept yourself as that, and maybe try and look at the roots of all of that […] and change for the better […] then I think you can go beyond to a wider sense […] of caring for others, for the students in your classroom, for distant others, for the natural world.

Accordingly, one cannot care for others unless one has developed the capacity to do so, in other words, is resourced. In this way, Mark was able to discern aspects about himself that were not very conducive to teaching and was willing to do the work to make those changes. He was "open to new ways of life, ways of seeing" as integral to his practice of care. He noted:

I've been able to do my job as a teacher a lot better. I mean, I still struggle, but without that kind of reflective introspection, where you are aware of yourself, aware of the stress and where it's coming from, […] without that understanding, it's just going to be very difficult.

Mark took these practices to his Grade 5 students, introducing his students gradually to attentive breathing, to modified walking meditations, and pauses in the day as a way to pay attention to others and the environment. He observed his students respecting each other without being reminded, in the way they listened to one another, and participated in discussions and activities. In his view, they were learning by doing.

Administrators Enacting Care

We had four administrators in our study, all of whom were very much aware of their role as educational leaders. From their sharing, it was apparent that they considered themselves as "leading/teaching against the grain" in reaction to leadership models that were focused more on rules, conformity, and maintaining order.

Denise: Transforming Schools

Denise described herself as coming from a dysfunctional family and greatly "influenced by struggles economically." These beginnings shaped her self-described stance as "a radical educator [...] always quite outside the box of mainstream educators," and always seeking to effect change.

Her practicum experience of working in an inner-city school in a multi-age primary classroom led her to finding a similar position in teaching. She had a mentor at university, who modelled for her the importance of having strong relationships, and the benefits of integrated curriculum and multi-age classrooms. Denise referred often to her experience in multi-age classrooms, and her "fights with neighbouring teachers" who disagreed with her approach of looking at children's needs first rather than school rules. Her innovative work in that school eventually led her to become a teacher educator at the university of her mentor, where she introduced 14 teacher candidates back into that school, transforming their views of education and helping to transform the school itself.

Much of the work in that transformation had to do with building relationships and developing a curriculum based on children's interests. The multi-age focus led to strategies such as team-teaching and long-term partnerships with parents and families. She returned again to the classroom, this time to an area populated with refugee families, continuing this focus on building a multi-age community of learners:

> Everyone at the school keeps a group of children for three years, everyone teams with at least one or two other people, and it's amazing to walk into that school. Children walk into the hallways whenever they get there, even if that's 6:30 in the morning. They don't wait for bells to come and go [...] there are couches everywhere in the hallways, there are grandmas and grandpas all over the school; it's just a real wonderful place!

Denise links this approach with the caring ethic: "When I read Noddings's work, everything that she talks about is in place in that school. And it's not just the development of a sense of belonging for kids. It is that the relationships are absolutely marked by an ethic of care, consistently."

At the time of the study, Denise had recently become vice principal at a school that had seen a rapid change in demographics, with new immigrants, predominantly people of colour, moving into more established neighbourhoods of white families. When she tried to initiate the successful multi-age model, she was met with resistance, especially among teachers who saw it as a threat to their autonomy. As Denise commented, "They just want to have things the way they are." She persisted with bringing in new practices. For example, she collected children's books in heritage languages, and invited the grandmothers of the Punjabi families who were new to the neighbourhood to come in each morning and read stories in Punjabi to their grandchildren. This disrupted the dominant thinking of the day that children should be speaking English only in school, although the practice was informed by research (Toohey, 2018) that showed the importance of young children learning their heritage language. More importantly, the school was becoming a place of community for all families.

In remembering the difficulty she had to move teachers out of their set ways of thinking, she snorted: "Educators are a product of the culture of conformity and obedience […] of math tests and homework. This is not school, and this is not learning."

We could see how Denise's philosophy of teaching was strongly influenced by her experiences of "doing things differently:"

> I hold the belief that schools should encourage personal development and growth, and this notion that all children must attain certain standards in certain curricular areas I understand is the tradition in our part of the world, but I wrestle with it because I don't believe it to be important particularly […] promoting individual and relational growth is more important.

As a teacher educator and leader in the school, she trusts that teachers come into their profession with what she calls "an intuitive caring for the relationships among individuals," and yet, in her experience, the system beats it out of them by demanding an accountability for instrumental achievement and test scores. She says, "I've come to understand that only through strong relationships will the kids really understand what their desires, wants, needs, interests, and talents are, and it's through their growth and relationships with other people that they will flourish individually as well."

Sarah: Creating Relationships One Student at a Time

Sarah was a principal of an elementary school when she joined the study. The school was designated inner city, in a suburban area that received high numbers of immigrant and refugee families, most of whom could be described as low socioeconomic status. There were over 50 languages spoken in the school population, and many students were not yet functional in English.

Sarah's most important priority, as she saw it, was creating relationships with students, "one student at a time." She did this by circulating around the school, initiating conversations, showing interest in their families—"knowing the names of their brothers and sisters, their lives, and their interests." Her accessibility to students was modelled in the way she interacted with them, breaking down the barriers between the perceived authority of the principal and the students. In the rare times she was in her office, her door was always open. Students were encouraged to drop in anytime, thus eliminating the association of a visit to the principal's office with the threat of punishment. Relationships with students extended to their families.

Some of the more powerful examples from Sarah's practice involved her handling of sensitive and difficult cases regarding what is commonly seen as "problem" behaviour. She explained that children from refugee families, in particular, brought experiences to the school that "we couldn't begin to understand." "One student had seen his father tortured and then killed in front of the family. Another had lost most of her family to war." It was important that she and the teachers understand the extreme circumstances of these children, and how they struggled to adapt to their new home. In one incident at school, a boy had chased down another boy, and "pummelled him into the ground." Sarah relates, "In these times of zero tolerance, I should have suspended this boy for the extraordinary violence." Instead, after she had attended to the injured boy, she talked to each of them to find out what had led to this incident. She discovered that the "attacker" had been instructed by his mother to protect his sister at all times: "He had seen his sister being chased by the other boy, but what he did not understand was that they were playing a game of tag!" Sarah then brought both boys together and facilitated a conversation where each heard the story of the other and came to understand what had happened. Each of the families was informed of how she had handled the incident:

> What was a remarkable follow up was that the mother of the boy who had been attacked invited the other to their house to play. This child had never been invited

to anyone's house before [...] I was blown away by this act of generosity, and it led to new friendships. This is what I mean—when everyone understands— parents, community members, staff, and, most of all, the students, you have their trust that you are working for every child in that school [...] We have to recognize our common humanity and our relationships as being at the heart of what we do in schools.

Sarah had many more stories about creating a place of safety and belonging in the school, an enormous challenge given the diverse backgrounds, languages, cultures, and experiences in the school community. She spoke about her feelings of rage and despair in working in a system that was constructed by bureaucrats. The messages from the Ministry of Education were mostly in the language of business and the economy, and the new plans emerging from the Ministry prioritized standardized testing. In standing up for children, and for educational values, Sarah exemplified that a school run on the ethic of care is run by principles rather than rules.

DISCUSSION

The six educators featured in this chapter each talked about the importance of establishing authentic relationships with each student, which involved spending time with them, listening to their frustrations, hopes, and aspirations, because, as Brooke pointed out, "You can't determine a student's needs unless you know that student." Students were viewed as individuals, not as a collective whole. Although as a school principal Sarah was responsible for hundreds of students, she was careful to engage individually with students one-on-one wherever they congregated, including having an open-door policy to her office.

Because developing relationships was considered central to their role as teachers and administrators, each willingly adjusted their curriculum to meet their students' need for academic success, rather than expecting the students to adjust to "the tyranny of the curriculum," as Ken described it. Caring for students meant "doing things differently," as Denise observed; in fact, she often felt the need to challenge the culture of conformity that she felt pervaded the school system but was antithetical to students' learning. Denise helped to establish multi-age and cross-disciplinary learning environments in her school, which gave students a greater sense of belonging.

The need for students to belong pervaded many of the interviews. William talked about creating a "culture of care" through the design of his school and the creation of student-friendly spaces so that students felt that the school was "their place." As a counsellor, Ken was concerned about creating an environment where the vulnerable students he served felt a sense of belonging and recognition. Even though Sarah acknowledged that it was a challenge for every student to feel that they mattered, she made it a priority. Mark's vision of belonging was a collective one. He sought to guide his students to think beyond themselves by becoming aware of their environment and others' needs.

The educators practiced wise actions in the best interests of their students. Sarah's approach to dealing with the fight between boys on the playground is a good example. Rather than suspending the perpetrator, she created opportunities for the boys to learn each other's stories, which led to reconciliation rather than frustration. When dealing with a student's racist comment, Brooke engaged her students in dialogue that brought understanding rather than punishment.

The interviews revealed educators who were thoughtfully introspective and self-reflective regarding their interactions with students and their goal to enact the caring ethic. Brooke described fighting with herself to "do the right thing" and not take the easy way out. Each educator identified the importance of modelling the behaviour, not just talking about it. Mark articulated the importance of self-improvement and awareness in order to care for others. William observed that even small everyday actions set a tone and communicate powerful messages.

Interestingly, each of the educators highlighted here did not keep their motivation to enact the caring ethic to themselves. As educational leaders, William, Sarah, and Denise sought ways to see ethical caring enacted throughout their schools, although Denise commented on the internal resistance she experienced and Sarah talked about her frustration dealing with external bureaucrats.

Self-care also surfaced as an important dimension to having the resourcefulness to care for others. Brooke said she sometimes she felt discouraged and even cynical. William described his school as a community where care was practiced at many different levels. Mark relied on mindfulness as a way to resource himself to care more effectively.

Overall, there was ample evidence of care theory supporting educators to develop a relational practice and to cultivate an ethical self that could contribute to a more caring school environment.

CONCLUSION

In this chapter, we set out to investigate how an ethic of care was practiced in the classrooms and schools of the teachers and administrators who studied care theory. What became clear to us at the end of the research cycle was how participants grew in their commitment to ethical caring, gaining validation and confirmation themselves through discussing their practice and their challenges with others. The feedback they were receiving from their students and from the positive change they were seeing in their schools further strengthened their resolve to continue and deepen their practice. There were enormous challenges that threatened their practice, none greater than the issues arising from the social upheaval of our times. And yet for all of our teachers and administrators in this chapter, practicing care in schools gave them hope, and as Brooke stated so well, it was "a way to offer hope."

QUESTIONS FOR CRITICAL THOUGHT

1. What are some new understandings you have gained about the ethic of care?
2. In what ways does this chapter encourage you to think more deeply about enacting the ethic of care into your classroom and school?
3. What are some of the challenges, in your view, faced by teachers in practicing a pedagogy of care, and how do these limit the enactment of care?

GLOSSARY

Ethic of care: A moral theory that conceptualizes ethical caring as distinct from natural caring. It has been described by Nel Noddings, the leading scholar on care ethics, as "creating, maintaining positive relations" (Noddings, 1992, p. 21). Following the scholarship of Carol Gilligan (1982), Noddings articulates care as a "needs and response-based ethic" (1992, p. 21) that involves an encounter or connection between the one caring or carer, and the cared-for or receiver of care. The carer perceives that there is need for care and is moved to respond with a caring act. This impulse to care becomes ethical caring in the relationship between the one who gives and the one who receives care. The cared-for participates by "receiving" the act of care through response or reciprocity. Ethical caring in these terms offers opportunities for people to connect with one another "in relationships characterized by mutuality" (Noddings, 1992, p. 18).

Mutuality: In the ethic of care, this refers to the understanding that for the act of caring to be ethical, it is important for the caring relationship to be mutual. Further, the roles of carer and cared-for are not fixed.

Reciprocity: For a caring action to be complete, the one who receives care responds by confirming that the care is received and that their needs have been met.

School culture: The environment that prevails in a school; in the formal curriculum; in the informal or hidden curriculum; and in the relationships among administrators, teachers, students, staff, and families; the social spaces; the policies and procedures—indeed, every aspect of schooling.

NOTES

1. We have not included a literature review on the enactment of ethical caring in schools, due to space limitations, but wish to acknowledge that there is a small but growing body of literature on this topic.

2. The research was funded by a grant from the Social Sciences and Humanities Research Council of Canada. The research team included principal investigator Dr. Heesoon Bai, Dr. Wanda Cassidy (co-investigator), and Dr. Kumari Beck, all from Simon Fraser University's Faculty of Education. Details of the study and further information can be obtained from the authors.

3. All names are pseudonyms.

REFERENCES

Beck, K., & Cassidy, W. (2009). Embedding the ethic of care in school policies and practices. In K. te Riele (Ed.), *Making schools different: Alternate approaches to educating young people* (pp. 55–64). Los Angeles: Sage.

Bergman, R. (2007). Caring for the ethical ideal: Nel Noddings on moral education. *Journal of Moral Education*, 33(2), 149–162.

British Columbia Teachers' Federation. (2019a). *Graduation rates in British Columbia*. Retrieved from https://bctf.ca/uploadedFiles/Public/Publications/FactSheets/GraduationRates.pdf.

British Columbia Teachers' Federation. (2019b). *Inclusive education and special needs in British Columbia*. Retrieved from https://bctf.ca/publications.aspx?id=49000.

Cassidy, W., & Bates, A. (2005). "Drop-outs" and "push-outs": Finding hope at a school that actualizes the ethic of care. *American Journal of Education*, 112(1), 66–102.

Dewey, J. (1916). *Democracy and education*. New York: Macmillan.

Freire, P. (1970). *Pedagogy of the oppressed*. New York: Continuum.

Gillespie, W. (2015). *The ethic of care and educational leadership: The caring school principal—a case study* (Doctoral dissertation). Retrieved from ProQuest Dissertations Publishing (UMI No. 3637833).

Gilligan, C. (1982). *In a different voice: Psychological theory and women's development.* Cambridge, MA: Harvard University Press.

Greene, M. (1991). Retrieving the language of compassion: The education professor in search of community. *Teachers College Record, 92,* 541–555.

Hayes, C., Ryan, A., & Zseller, E. (1994). The middle school child's perceptions of caring teachers. *American Journal of Education, 103,* 1–17.

Hoot, J. L. (2011). Working with very young refugee children in our schools: Implications for the world's teachers. *Procedia-Social and Behavioral Sciences, 15,* 1751–1755.

Jackson, P., Boostrom, R., & Hansen, D. (1993). *The moral life of schools.* San Francisco: Jossey-Bass.

Mayeroff, M. (1971). *On caring.* New York: Harper & Row.

McDowell, K. (2011). *Who cares? Who doesn't? An exploration of perceptions of care based on the experiences of secondary school students from different economic groups* (Unpublished doctoral dissertation). Simon Fraser University, Burnaby, BC, Canada.

Montabello, S. (2008). *Journeying into the heart of schools: Dwelling in time, place and intimacy* (Unpublished doctoral dissertation). Simon Fraser University, Burnaby, BC, Canada.

Noddings, N. (2012). The language of care ethics. *Knowledge Quest, 40*(5), 52–56.

Noddings, N. (1992). *The challenge to care in schools: An alternative approach to education.* New York: Teachers College Press.

Noddings, N. (1984). *Caring: A feminine approach to ethics and moral education.* Berkeley: University of California Press.

Parker, W. C. (2011). Constructing public schooling today: Derision, multiculturalism, nationalism. *Educational Theory, 61*(4), 413–432.

Rauner, D. (2000). *They still pick me up when I fall: The role of caring in youth development and community life.* New York: Columbia University Press.

Toohey, K. (2018). *Learning English at school: Identity, socio-material relations and classroom practice* (2nd ed.). Milton Keyes, UK: Multilingual Matters.

van der Putten, S. (2017). *The impact of one school community on female refugee adolescents and their sense of belonging* (Unpublished doctoral dissertation). Simon Fraser University, Burnaby, BC, Canada.

Wotherspoon, T., & Schissel, B. (2001). The business of putting Canadian children and youth "at risk." *Canadian Journal of Education, 26,* 321–339.

CHAPTER 3

Educators' Journeys of Studying Contemporary Indigenous History and Culture: Along the Road of Compassion to Reconciliation

Joanna Black

LEARNING OBJECTIVES

1. To promote understanding of and compassion for Indigenous human rights issues by imagining the creation of curricula through studying a contemporary Indigenous artist who deals with concepts of injustice.
2. To define and comprehend the role of reconciliation in our schools now, to comprehend the National Centre for Truth and Reconciliation's educational Calls to Action (62–65), and to develop ways in which to address and implement these calls to create positive effects in our classrooms today.

INTRODUCTION: THE KEY ROLE OF CULTURE, HISTORICAL KNOWLEDGE, AND EDUCATION

On June 11, 2008, former Prime Minister Stephen Harper made a formal public apology to the Canadian Indigenous population, recognizing the great harm, significant pain, and long-lasting, injurious, and devastating impact of residential schooling within Canada (Florence, 2016; Indigenous and Northern Affairs Canada, 2008). It was recognized that the enduring absence of a public apology has impeded the healing and reconciliation process between Indigenous and non-Indigenous peoples (CBC News, 2008). As Niigaan James Sinclair (2017), influential Indigenous scholar and academic at the University of Manitoba, states, we are now "waking up to Canada's 149th year of dysfunctional relationship with Indigenous peoples." It is only within the last few years that Canadians are beginning to acknowledge this **cultural genocide** that occurred within our country by **settlers** upon our Indigenous population (Truth and Reconciliation Commission of Canada [TRC], 2016, p. 3).

Canadians are being asked to seek reconciliation within our own country. What does this act of reconciliation exactly mean? Intricate and complex Indigenous–settler issues are presently generating significant questions, and both Indigenous and settler populations are in the process of meeting this challenge. Niigaan Sinclair poignantly asks us to consider, "What does reconciliation look like, feel like, and how is that embodied in our country?" (2017). To these questions, some Canadians are currently seeking answers within our communities. Yet as Ry Moran, the director of the National Centre for Truth and Reconciliation (NCTR) at the University of Manitoba, observes:

> The challenge is that many Canadians are not even up to speed on the most basic elements of indigenous perspectives on history, and this renders them ill-equipped to understand the rapid advancement of indigenous rights in the province, city and country. … We the people of Canada have created these challenges. We are responsible for fixing them. (Moran, 2016, p. A7)

Knowledge of Canadian history is indeed important. To address this, the authors of the TRC provide ways Canadians can work towards reconciliation in the form of 94 calls to action. Of these, 21 calls are directed towards educators (Moran, 2016). For four calls (62–65), the writers specifically address lack of teacher training and curricula development within kindergarten to Grade 12 public schools regarding Indigenous peoples, their history, and contemporary teachings (National Centre for Truth and Reconciliation, n.d.).

These calls directed to the educational community are not surprising, as it was an injurious educational approach mandated within residential schools that was so instrumental in causing great pain and harm to Indigenous peoples. Just as deleterious and painful educational approaches were instrumental in the wrongs inflicted upon the Indigenous, the NCTR views constructive and healing educational approaches as one of the ways to rectify the damage in order to rebuild. In other words, what caused the wounds—education—can, if changed, hopefully restore to health those in need. This chapter was inspired by the need to take positive steps. As stated in then Prime Minister Stephen Harper's public apology (CBC News, 2008), we need to be:

> … forging a new relationship between Aboriginal peoples and other Canadians, a relationship based on the knowledge of our shared history, a respect for each other, and a desire to move forward together with a renewed understanding that strong families, strong communities, and vibrant cultures and traditions will contribute to a stronger Canada for all of us. (CBC News, 2008)

THE RESEARCH METHODOLOGY

This book chapter is about my research studying workshops; for this chapter, I embarked upon setting up and examining teacher in-service training by asking participants to join seven in-service workshops held at the Winnipeg Art Gallery over one year, from October 18, 2016, to May 16, 2017. I identify myself as a white settler woman. An objective of this chapter is to engage and educate participants in Indigenous culture and history. The main objective is to help these educators use this new knowledge to develop pertinent and meaningful curricula regarding contemporary Indigenous art. Throughout these workshops, case study research was conducted to enable the examination of 30 participants' circumstances, exchanges, challenges, experiences, and curricula development. This study involved 30 kindergarten to Grade 12 Manitoba educators working in three private and seven public school divisions/boards across Manitoba. Participants comprised educators, coordinators, and art consultants within rural and urban Manitoban schools. Teachers involved were selected because they were eager and receptive to in-service training about current Indigenous art in relation to meaningful pedagogical approaches.

During this study, two people were instrumental in the sessions and helped guide the workshops. The first person, Leah Fontaine, is of Anishinaabe/Dakota/Métis ancestry, and she was a research assistant on this project. Currently, she works within higher education at the University of Manitoba in the position of Indigenous Initiatives Educator. Fontaine also teaches Indigenous art history at the School of Art at the University of Manitoba. The second person involved in this study is Allison Moore, the Winnipeg Art Gallery's Art Educator of Youth Programs. Moore wrote a blog for participants during the research (2017), documenting the workshop experiences so that all educators involved could access and use the blogs for reference, specifically for curricula development and their own teachings within classrooms. Fontaine and Moore also conducted presentations during the workshops about Indigenous art history and the WAG Indigenous collection. They also offered ongoing guidance to participants regarding their curricula development for their professional teachings within schools. All individuals in this chapter have pseudonyms except for Leah Fontaine and Allison Moore, who requested their actual names be used. This was to analyze themes that arose from this particular case-based circumstance (Best & Kahn, 1993; Merriam, 1998).

The Winnipeg Art Gallery (WAG) was chosen as a site for the research as a result of its uniqueness; moreover, gallery staff had the ability to acquire knowledge that would be difficult to obtain elsewhere as they used the WAG's art (Merriam, 1998). It is a gallery recognized for its current dedication to Indigenous art. WAG administration has and continues to embrace Indigenous culture: they are in the midst of building an Inuit Art Centre housing their large collection of over 13,000 Inuit artworks (WAG, 2017a, 2017b). Moreover, they have recently hired two Indigenous curators (Green, 2017; Isaac & Nagam, 2018; WAG, 2017c, 2017d).

Elders—who are knowledgeable and respected members of their Indigenous communities for their outstanding comprehension of their history and long-established teachings, rituals, and healing practices—participated in all seven workshops. The first workshop began with a representative, Amanda Simard, from the Treaty Relations Commission of Manitoba (TRCM), discussing Indigenous history in relation to treaty lands; she outlined the Canadian government's ignominious behaviour, including government officials' lying, cheating, and utter dishonesty, with the result that Indigenous land rights were stripped away from Indigenous populations (Friesen, 2016; Shore, 2017). This workshop was followed by a representative from the NCTR, Kaila Johnston, providing an invaluable historical overview of Indigenous history and the cultural genocide that occurred. Subsequent to this, during the next three workshops, the Winnipeg Art Gallery's collection of Indigenous art was examined under the guidance of Moore, while Fontaine additionally presented an overview of the history of Indigenous art. Three contemporary professional Indigenous artists also discussed their own professional art practices. In this chapter, I will focus on KC Adams (2016) and Lita Fontaine (sister to Leah Fontaine), who both are Winnipeg artists (see Figures 3.1 and 3.2). During the sixth workshop, educators/participants were asked to develop curricula pertaining to Indigenous art-making processes, which they shared during the final workshop. Finally, after the workshops ended, five participants were selected for one-hour interviews, chosen because they were keen, insightful, and articulate. During the analysis, qualitative content analysis was employed; a successive, iterative process revealed key art and artistic themes that were similar and recurring among the participants (Stake, 1995; Yin, 2003), and which are critical in discussions of Indigenous culture through visual art-making processes.

I am cognizant of trying to redress current power structures in place regarding concurrent homogenization of less dominant cultures within Canadian society—specifically, the Indigenous (Archer-Cunningham, 2007; Irwin, Rogers, & Wan, 1999). Central to this chapter is an explanation of art and artistic themes examined by current Canadian artists that are fundamental in discussions of teaching and learning about Indigenous culture. This is crucial, as visual art is vital as a means of communication and understanding within and about contemporary Indigenous culture (Fitznor, 2017; Toulouse, 2018) in the attempt to work toward truth and reconciliation.

ARTIST: LITA FONTAINE

Lita Fontaine has been a professional art educator working extensively in Winnipeg public schools as an artist in residence for over 25 years. Working since the early 1990s within the fine art world, she has also established herself as a notable professional artist. During her speech at the WAG workshop, Fontaine discussed some of her art as well as its relationship to education. She is of tri-cultural heritage, being Dakota, Anishinaabe, and Métis, and as a result is greatly influenced by her Indigenous heritage, which has become a foundation and reference point for her own art throughout her career.

Of the many artworks created by Fontaine and discussed in the WAG workshops, *Mom* (Figure 3.1) resonates with historical overtones, meaning that there are many references to Indigenous history, particularly concerning residential schools. Fontaine works with diverse materials from paint to fabric. I will discuss *Mom* in detail as it sheds light on this artist's themes. Fontaine depicts her mother, Anne Fontaine, who spent six years in a residential school from ages 10 to 16. The artwork is an exploration of personal family histories and trauma. Later, in her counterpart artwork, *Mom Too,* Fontaine explores the effects of the residential school system on her mother.

Mom is a montage: a small black and white picture of Fontaine's mother and fellow children in a residential school is placed inside a larger, identical picture, which is itself placed inside an even larger identical image. Thus, the image is repeated three times. By placing the pictures within a picture in repetition, the artist uses the replication of this image for a specific end, "to portray assimilation

Figure 3.1: *Mom*

Source: Lita Fontaine, 1998. Courtesy of the artist. Collection of the Winnipeg Art Gallery.

which is why the schools were created in the first place—in order to colonize the masses" (Fontaine, personal communication, July 31, 2018). Fontaine wants us not just to look, but look again at the children, some of whom are smiling while others have a more solemn expression, glancing downwards with shadows playing off a few of their young faces. Reiterations of this image are symbolic of the reverberating effects of residential school experiences.

In the book *Lita Fontaine, Sanksannica,* by McCleod and colleagues (2016), McCleod states that Fontaine's earlier collages are similar to colonial quilts and blankets. The squares delineated are, for Fontaine, indicative of unreachable worlds (2016, p. 19). Additionally, repeated polka dots in her art are symbolic of night stars and are reflective of her own Dakota spirit name, which is Stars Full of Emotions Woman, hence representing Fontaine in the image (McCleod et al., 2016, pp. 22, 48).

In other artworks, Fontaine addresses generational impact and negotiated dual identity formation, both of which are key to her work. Her sense of self in a twofold world of Indigenous and settler, her conception of reclaiming Indigenous culture, her resistance to generational impact, and her idea of constructing new, positive identities that rise from painful histories are crucial to her thematic explorations (McCleod et al., 2016, p. 20).

Interviews: Participant Dialogue

Up to the point of Fontaine's visit to the WAG to conduct her workshop, workshop participants had received information about Indigenous histories and about the broken treaties and their impact. Thus, the discussion about Fontaine's work was not surprising. During the talk that ensued with the participant educators about Fontaine's art, some people were astonished to learn about Canada's historical past in relation to treatment of the Indigenous. As one of the workshop participants, Chris, observed, some people were "in shock." Many participants stated they were not taught about Indigenous cultures. Lynn, who is herself Indigenous, asked a pertinent question: How can one teach kids if one does not know one's own history? In fact, Laurie reflected, "We have such a huge job ahead of us with this generation being the first generation ever, getting this history and getting it right ... we all need that education [about the Canadian Indigenous] and we all need to hear it together" as both Indigenous and settler students.

Laurie talked about her family shame that kept her Métis background a taboo subject, not to be discussed even within her own household. Her own father was Métis, and whenever the subject would turn to his cultural background, she observed that he always shunned these discussions by leaving the room. Similarly, Lynn's mother never taught her Indigenous language because she wanted to protect Lynn from getting hurt and ostracized. Lynn said, "I grew up and didn't want to be who I was."

Susan, who teaches kindergarten to Grade 5 art in the inner city, strongly advises educators to not shy away from difficult, painful, and complex subjects. "Eye opening" is how she described conversations with her students about Indigenous culture. Susan talked about a conceptual art piece, made by a girl from her early years class, as "insightful, passionate, and sophisticated far beyond her years." This year, she said, was the first time her pupils really talked about Indigenous experiences. She reflected, "I don't talk down to kids, I don't reach down to kids. I think I have a good sense of intuition to know when, how much is enough. ... I definitely think that teachers should not be afraid to tackle it."

The importance of studying visual art was discussed by Catherine, who stated that it enables us to see the world through someone else's eyes. Laurie exclaimed, "Anything you can write about you can explore through art. That is what excites me." Teachers across curricula areas considered teaching Indigenous culture to provide solid learning based on historical understandings, and present social and political comprehensions. To teach Indigenous cultures, a strong foundation is vital: Diane pointed out that it is essential to build on this underpinning in a way that fosters children's skills, knowledge, and creativity. Now that many people openly want to discuss and address difficult Indigenous history, many of the participants also stated the need to avoid old ways of teaching and learning. Susan and Laurie talked about how one should really think about the purpose of curricula a teacher develops and to make it meaningful in order to avoid stereotypes. Teachers should avoid merely providing clichéd activities, such as making totem poles out of toilet paper rolls or carving soapstone sculptures from soap products, which they often do with the intention of providing hands-on, experiential workshops. Instead, workshop participants wanted to foster in their children rich, historical understandings as a foundation to understanding the present through contemporary art.

The introduction to Fontaine, her background, and her struggles shed a light for participants on ways in which educators can approach teaching art in classrooms through looking through the eyes of the oppressed. Many Canadians have been dominated and persecuted; they have faced their own struggles, leaving war-torn countries throughout the world. Some have themselves experienced cultural genocide in their own lands. Rather than avoid this topic as a null curriculum (one that is not taught), teachers should make it a part of the explicit curriculum (one that is openly described) (Flinders, Noddings, & Thornton, 1986).

During the workshop discussions, participants stated they believe it is crucial to change the hidden curriculum that tells the story of the struggle of pioneers without telling the story of the devastation of the Indigenous people. One needs to hear both sides and learn what the oppressors did to the oppressed. Why do non-Indigenous settlers need to heal themselves? As Martin Luther King stated:

> According to this view [of the oppressor that King abhors], it is all right to lie with a bit of finesse. It's all right to exploit but be a dignified exploiter. It's all right to even hate, but dress your hate up into garments of love and make it appear that you are loving when you are actually hating. This type of moral and ethical relativism is sapping the very life's blood of the moral and spiritual life of our nation and our world. (Dunn, 2017)

Comprehending the duality and dichotomy of two cultures and their effects upon each other is vital to the creation of a more positive future for our Canadian society.

ARTIST: KC ADAMS

KC Adams is an Indigenous Canadian artist from the Fisher River Cree Nation who is now located in Winnipeg. Her background is Métis from Scottish and British, as well Ojibwe (Anishinaabe) and Cree ancestors. Popular culture, science fiction, and contemporary societal issues are areas she explores in her art, in which she uses diverse media, from paints and photographs to sculptural materials and prints. It was only while she was studying at Concordia University in Montreal that she began to explore her Indigenous background in her art, having been raised not knowing about her own culture—similar to many descendants of residential schooling, she was uninformed about her own background. Adams now explores, works with, and shows respect for her own ancestral past.

Perception (Figure 3.2) is a body of artworks Adams discussed during the WAG workshop and that had meaning for many participants. It consists of 130 large digital posters projected onto Winnipeg structures, hung in transit shelters, and placed on the city's billboards in 2015. It is a large-scale public artwork that is a political critique of the way in which our current society views Indigenous people. In this series of artworks, Adams actively confronts marked societal prejudice, racism, bigotry, and societal stereotypes regarding the Indigenous.

Each artwork in *Perception* consists of two Indigenous portraits of the same person juxtaposed against each other: on the left side is the negative portrayal with racial comments; on the right side is another portrayal of the same person along with that person's Indigenous names and background. The art emphasizes the dichotomy between the way people are viewed by others in settler society and the way in which the subjects perceive themselves. Adams contrasts the stereotyped image of the Indigenous person—a Westernized societal cliché—with the realistic and more intimate life experience of that same person (Samphir, 2015). In so doing, she points out the typical stereotypes with which Indigenous people are forced to contend.

Interviews: Participant Dialogue

Adams's artworks are very contemporary in that she not only creates digital photographs but also displays them outside the traditional art gallery setting. Moreover, she works with contentious, highly sensitive issues about settler attitudes towards Indigenous people. For Laurie, Adams's theme in *Perception* was a contrast to the more traditional, painterly Indigenous artists' thematic explorations created by such professionals as Norval Morrisseau and Jackson Beardy or

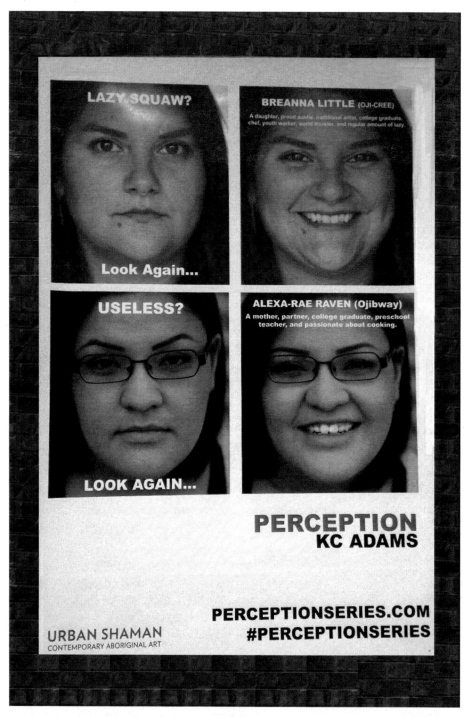

Figure 3.2: *Perception*

Source: KC Adams. Digital photograph. Taken from an art installation on Winnipeg street bus shelters by Joanna Black, 2015. Used by permission.

the well-recognized printmaker Daphne Odjig. Laurie noted that this contrast between older and more modern Indigenous artworks does not mean contemporary Indigenous art is not Indigenous art just because it is so dissimilar to more established artists. Contemporary art is moving away from expressing Indigenous legends and beliefs that were so much a part of the art of the past and is moving towards an examination of such essential and urgent life themes for Indigenous people today as colonialization and its impact upon all Canadians, and the politics of trauma and reconciliation.

For all participants, exploring contemporary themes with their students who are confronting current societal issues is fundamental; they believe teachers should be addressing these crucial concepts within schools. Challenge is also important, and indeed, teaching about contemporary Indigenous art is often difficult and thought provoking, evidenced by the participants' assertions in which they found it opposes traditional viewpoints. For instance, Laurie asserted:

> Indigenous is still being created and it has evolved. That's a great starting place. But look at it where it comes to from that! [We need to look] … at art as inspiring change, making people think, and at the political action, right? It's resistance as turning things on its mirror, turning things around, and showing that mirror back.

In her art, Adams delves into the lens of stereotypes and clichés. Laurie herself recounted her experience of racism as a Métis person:

> They whispered, how they [would say] I think she's Métis, [because] she wears the shawl. And so, these stories and talk about [these things] like the hiding of who you are. And that shame and then looking at that symbolism of a shawl, right? What you can unpack with that artistically [is something I would like to explore.]

Many of the 30 workshop participants decided to write and to teach curricula that related to those things they learned during the WAG workshops about current and topical issues that they found relevant and pressing. Adams's and Fontaine's inspirations were fundamental in showing participants ways to approach curricula regarding their students' experiences and backgrounds that is sensitive to experiences of both settler and Indigenous children.

TWO EXAMPLES OF CURRICULA DEVELOPMENT

Curricula Designed by Diane Foster

Diane Foster, a white, middle-class art educator, teaches special education, English as an Additional Language (also known as EAL), and other programs in her middle and high school from Grades 7 to 12 at an inner-city school in Winnipeg. During the workshops, she read books about Indigenous teachings. She also studied the medicine wheel and the TRC's recent calls to action. Foster decided to team up with the teacher of Native Studies within her school to develop new curricula for her Indigenous students regarding the theme of identity. Her approach, she states, was very pragmatic because she realized many of her Indigenous pupils knew little about their own culture.

The first activity Foster undertook with her pupils was mask-making—a simple, easy starting point, designed to allow her pupils to delve into and examine their own specific Indigenous culture and identity. Her students used plaster bandages to create the mask, which they then painted—a very traditional lesson plan Foster was familiar with teaching. Foster built upon the knowledge her students acquired for her next project. A collage study followed: youth were asked to create an artwork using an assemblage of different materials, from paint and newspaper clippings to computer text.

Foster made a collage work and used it as an exemplar (see Figure 3.3) during her teaching. For this unit plan, she addressed historical teachings. Before making collages, students learned about residential schools, including the one

Figure 3.3: Uncover the Truth About Residential Schools

Source: Diane Foster. An example of collage created by Diane for teaching at the middle and secondary school level. Used by permission.

located within five miles of the WAG and their own school. She noted that few of the workshop participants were aware of its existence.

Foster was affected by Fontaine's art, and in particular by her use of imagery repetition. Throughout the collage shown in Figure 3.3 is frequently recurring text: "Uncover the truth about residential schools." Additionally, the number 62 is repeated throughout her work: this number is a direct referral to the TRC's call to action to make age-appropriate curriculum regarding Indigenous culture. Repeated painterly work depicts specific images: brown elm tree trunks, green grass, and dragonflies. Foster had found in talking to her students that she needed to "uncover the truths" about residential schools because many of her Indigenous students lacked understanding of what transpired in these schools and its impacts.

Of import to Foster was a discussion during the WAG workshop in which participants talked about the significance of metaphors and symbols in teaching and learning about art. Specifically, during these sessions she remembered the talk about abundant elm trees in Winnipeg—there has and continues to be an elm bark beetle invasion, and its infiltration is currently threatening the existence of the beautiful elm cover that shades this prairie city. WAG workshop participants developed the idea of the symbolism of this harmful insect representing the invasion of settlers; also, the WAG participants liked the notion of strong elm trees being representative of Indigenous cultures. Therefore, Foster used this symbolism in her own collage and asked her students to consider using symbols in their own art.

For Foster's exemplar (Figure 3.3), she explored the Dutch elm disease and its deleterious effects. In her discussion, she talked about the beetle imagery transforming into dragonflies, seen on the right of the artwork. The beetle signifies the beginning of understandings of the cultural genocide that occurred; the dragonflies, for her, represent a metamorphosis, and thus, new beginnings. She has hope. As Foster stated, "We're really trying to make a new beginning ... [where it was] so negative in the initial intrusion and now the beginning is becoming a positive [one]." She discussed how in this artwork the depiction is of a dead forest metamorphizing into a reborn one. Thus, the idea of new growth and new beginnings in the art imagery is important: she is optimistic.

Curricula Designed by Susan Smith

Susan Smith, a white, middle-class settler, is a visual artist herself and teaches kindergarten to Grade 5 visual art and dance in the position of a resource educator at an inner-city school in the north end of Winnipeg, which has a large Indigenous population. She received grant money to design programing support for Indigenous Elders to visit her school. Throughout the school and her board/division, Canada's 150th birthday was celebrated and, as a consequence, Smith had her students address this theme in their own artworks. As she stated, she is not shy about addressing aspects of Canadian history that are not positive and need to be addressed: one of these is the treatment of Indigenous people and the residential schools. Another is the ways in which **colonization** affects all Canadians—both settlers and Indigenous peoples.

Smith devised curricula for her Grades 3 to 5 students, asking them to create 150 paintings, which she displayed at the end of the year in a school board/division student art display for the annual exhibition called *Arts in the Park*. To address Canada's birthday as a theme in art, Smith taught about Canadian treaties, the 94 calls to action, and the impact of these upon her students and their families. Many of her pupils have grandparents and great-grandparents who are residential school survivors, and Smith has recently provided opportunities in her classes for youth to have open discussions about these topics. She stated that before this year, she had never heard her pupils address these ideas. Smith found that "some of my students are finally coming up in front of the whole class, even saying, 'You know my grandparent, my aunties …' and it's been very healthy for them."

In preparation for the art-making process, Smith taught her students about contemporary Indigenous artists and their artwork—artists such as Christi Belcourt, Jaime Black, KC Adams, and Sonny Assu. She asked that all her pupils address the theme of residential schooling, and she also solicited them to specifically think about repercussions for Indigenous youth attending these schools. Smith stated she was amazed at how thoughtful her students were regarding this process. Using questions about her pupils' own Indigenous backgrounds fostered rich conversations in Smith's classes: unlike Diane Foster's experience, Smith found her pupils knew all sorts of historical details. For instance, Smith talked about a child who knew that Indigenous children were used in experiments for malnutrition, and other young people said that they knew residential youth were intentionally not fed properly. Smith responded by saying to her very young students that the Canadian government had indeed made, as she stated, "serious mistakes."

Figure 3.4, created by one of Smith's students, is part of the 150-canvas project. This artwork is realistic, painted in blue tones depicting a child crying. This youth is standing in a helpless position, looking at the viewer. Above her head to the left is an image of a residential school, and to her right is her family. The school is depicted with sombre browns and black tones, and in contrast to this is her smiling family illustrated with rich, colourful, saturated hues. Smith observes

Figure 3.4: Untitled

Source: Artwork created by one of Susan Smith's students from the early years class about residential schools. Publicly displayed at Kildonan Park, Winnipeg, Manitoba, and at the student art contest *Imagine a Canada.* Used by permission.

how her students have changed. Before this, they were reluctant to speak about their own pasts and histories. Now, they are markedly different, far more open, more detailed, and more able to talk about their Indigenous backgrounds.

CONCLUSION

Teachers involved in the WAG workshops reflected upon their experience with in-service training. They expressed their naivety and the fact that they believed they lacked necessary knowledge about Indigenous culture before taking the

WAG workshops. However, all found that taking these workshops was help-ful and extremely informative. They delineated three issues that arose from this experience:

1. knowledge acquisition,
2. changing from the standard, traditional, colonial teaching approaches to the teaching of Indigenous culture, and
3. lack of time for proper preparation.

All WAG participants observed that, prior to planning, curricula teachers should undertake research, gain historical knowledge, and acquire a founda-tional background regarding past Indigenous issues and current Indigenous art-ists. Some teachers continued to augment their knowledge and stated they would move forward in developing their teachings after the WAG workshops ended. Of utmost importance, they believed, is that teaching Indigenous history provides a foundation for studying Indigenous culture and art. For instance, Diane asserted that she learned a considerable amount by using the history as scaffolding and making the teaching cross-curricular. She asserted that one needs to connect it to "people's individual symbolism so that students own it themselves. ... You're scaffolding on Indigenous history and having a starting point that everybody can relate to." It is recommended that educators be given time to acquire this pertinent and much-needed knowledge.

Participants expressed that teaching in the old ways should be avoided. Spe-cifically, they advised that educators should steer away from kitschy and standard traditional teachings such as having children make Navajo blanket look-alikes and totem pole sculptures.

Another key issue was the lack of time teachers have for this necessary learn-ing; they need more hours in the day to learn about Indigenous culture and develop curricula. Some participants found solutions. A few initiated effective outreach to other teachers within their school. Within some school boards/di-visions, Indigenous educators have created strong unit plans; though they do not address art educational issues, they have provided a strong historical foun-dation for learning about Indigenous issues. These can be used by art teachers to build up their own programs. Some WAG workshop participants co-taught and co-developed Indigenous unit plans, finding that relying on other teach-ers' skills and knowledge about Indigenous culture made it easier—provided these co-workers were knowledgeable and sensitive to current Indigenous issues. In-service training also addresses the lack of time teachers have; however, all participants shared that their school board/divisions did not provide vital and necessary training regarding Canadian Indigenous culture. They found that having the WAG workshop sessions made it far easier to acquire skills and knowledge within the hectic demands of teaching. Thus, it is recommended that all school boards within Canada undertake in-service on Indigenous culture for their teachers, inviting Indigenous Elders and Indigenous people to speak to educators and students within our schools.

Many benefits from experiencing the WAG workshops were described by all participants. Firstly, participants found that dealing with diverse, politically relevant subject matter inspired by Indigenous contemporary artists was extremely effective. Participants stated that the approaches utilized in the WAG workshops worked. These methods were constructive and valuable. Specifically, they reflected that it is important to examine contemporary artists; study topical, current, and pertinent themes in the artworks; and not shy away from historical, sociological, and political content. Lilly stated, "We work with teenagers, they're passionate and political—they have ideas and opinions, and they're just learning that there's a world out there. I think that is probably the most beautiful way of tapping into [their ideas] through those contemporary artists [and the ideas they bring to light]." The workshops were a model for ways to approach the development of meaningful, topical curricula.

Secondly, all participants stated that teaching about current Indigenous art is important. As one educator, Steve, stated: "[This is] one of the reasons I love art. I just shut my door and ask some tough questions and have interesting conversations. It becomes known, you know, as the room where interesting things happen!" As a result of the workshops, some participants found that they were turning away from teaching art with the sole purpose of creating pretty objects.

Thirdly, some teachers were hesitant to teach highly contentious, hard-hitting, topical ideas, but learned that their students can not only handle them but can even appreciate them. After developing and teaching curricula about Indigenous art, their students of all ages, from kindergarten to Grade 12, were able to delve into difficult material. The teachers are aware of the provocative issues current Indigenous artists bring to the forefront of their art, and by teaching this material, they are confronting highly contentious and difficult materials. They discovered that even young children can handle this subject matter and do so with appreciation and insight. Participants also observed that these controversial, provocative, questioning, and relevant Indigenous issues are not only of import, but that children are also drawn to these crucial concepts because they are all effected by the settler–Indigenous issues that Canada faces today.

Diane observed, "What stood out for me was the connection … trying to reclaim space for identity. … And in a sense, I feel like the topic and the bigger picture is a struggle that we all are involved with. So I connected with it on a personal level." WAG participants overwhelmingly advise teachers not to shy away from teaching this important subject matter.

Lastly, and most significantly, teachers talked about the value of teaching these curricula: their Indigenous students opened up to them. Students who formerly were ashamed of their Indigenous backgrounds were now willing to talk about their pasts and were amenable to addressing what they had previously kept hidden. A number of participants felt that addressing contentious Indigenous culture called for teaching about political activism. They were teaching about broken promises, ethics, and integrity, and they were giving students a voice. They asked, "Where do we go from here?"

Teachers in the WAG workshops expressed the need for experiencing more hands-on art-making, the need for hearing about more Indigenous contemporary artists' discourses regarding their own works, and the need for exposing themselves to teachers' best practices in their development of curricula. Importantly, WAG participants talked about the concept of reconciliation. There is a need to confront vast complexities and hard truths in order for all Canadians—Indigenous and non-Indigenous—to begin to heal. They speak of the importance of analyzing ways to work towards healing the relationships between Indigenous and settler cultures. They talk about the fact that this healing process involves acquiring further knowledge and having many more informed discussions based on inclusive points of view between the conquerors and the conquered. Learning about both views is of utmost importance in order to investigate and acknowledge the complex, intertwined lives of both the Indigenous and the settlers and the ways in which they are affected by each other. To reference Martin Luther King again, he advises that a better society is formed from justice and change built by people working together (Dunn, 2017). To do this in such a way as to create genuine and collective change, we must begin to construct a more restorative path, built on respect and trust.

QUESTIONS FOR CRITICAL THOUGHT

1. Canadians are being asked to seek reconciliation within our own country. What does this act of reconciliation mean for us as educators and for our students who are both settlers and Indigenous?

2. What can we do to foster people's knowledge about Indigenous cultures, while avoiding clichés and stereotypes, in order to promote a process and culture of understanding and compassion? Specifically, how can you as an educator provide relevant contemporary curricula that promote a caring discourse in order to speak to the TRC's calls to action (62–65), as mandated by the National Centre for Truth and Reconciliation (n.d., pp. 69–72)?

3. What are the ways in which you can combine Indigenous historical knowledge with contemporary visual art to convey complex themes and concepts regarding Indigenous culture in the curricular fields you teach?

GLOSSARY

Colonization: Political and social control by one group over another group of people. The purpose is for the controlling group to economically take advantage of the oppressed group through the exploitation of resources in order to acquire dominance and, most importantly, procure wealth. Both dominated peoples and oppressors are affected by this process.

Cultural genocide: Destruction of social, creative, and spiritual structures and practices that lead to identity formation. The result is the annihilation of people's sacred, artistic, political, and social knowledge and its structures that stops the passing of this learning and understandings to future generations.

Settlers: Non-Indigenous people who arrived from another country and live in a new land. They became citizens where Indigenous people reside.

NOTE

Research on Contemporary Indigenous Art and Education is supported by grants from the University of Manitoba's University Indigenous Research Program (UIRP) and the Faculty of Education's Research Development Fund (RDF). The assistance of these bodies is gratefully acknowledged. I also wish to acknowledge the generous help and support of both Leah Fontaine, artist/educator of Anishinaabe/Dakota/Métis ancestry, and Allison Moore, professional artist and educator.

REFERENCES

Adams, KC. (2016, November 24). *KC Adams at the Winnipeg Art Gallery*. A workshop at the Winnipeg Art Gallery, Winnipeg, Manitoba.

Archer-Cunningham, K. (2007). Cultural arts education as community development: An innovative model of healing and transformation. *New Directions for Adult & Continuing Education*, 116, 25–36. https://doi.org/10.1002/ace.274.

Best, J., & Kahn, J. (1993). *Research in education*. Boston, MA: Pearson Education Company.

CBC News. (2008, June 11). Prime Minister Stephen Harper's statement of apology. *CBC News*. Retrieved from http://www.cbc.ca/news/canada/prime-minister-stephen-harper-s-statement-of-apology-1.734250.

Dunn, T. (2017, January 13). 27 Martin Luther King Jr. quotes to remember under the new president [Blog post]. Retrieved from http://www.upworthy.com/27-martin-luther-king-jr-quotes-to-remember-under-the-new-president.

Fitznor, L. (2017, February 24). *Laara Fitznor at the Winnipeg Art Gallery*. A workshop presentation at the Winnipeg Art Gallery, Winnipeg, Manitoba.

Flinders, D. J., Noddings, N., & Thornton, S. J. (1986). The null curriculum: Its theoretical basis and practical implications, *Curriculum Inquiry*, 16(1), 33–42.

Florence, M. (2016). *Fighting Canada's wrongs; Residential schools—The devastating impact on Canada's Indigenous Peoples and the Truth and Reconciliation Commission's findings and calls for action*. Toronto: James Lorimer & Company.

Friesen, J. (2016, March 21). *Canadian treaty education: An historical overview*. Paper presented at the meeting for Winnipeg Art Galleries and Museum Educators, The Manitoba Museum, Winnipeg, MB.

Green, R. E. (2017, November 12). Winnipeg Art Gallery presses on with Inuit Art Centre, new exhibition. *The Globe and Mail*. Retrieved from https://www.theglobeandmail.com/arts/art-and-architecture/winnipeg-art-gallery-presses-on-with-inuit-artcentre/article36526533.

Indigenous and Northern Affairs Canada. (March 2008). *Statement of apology to students of Indian residential schools*. Retrieved from http://www.aadnc-aandc.gc.ca/eng/1100100015644/1100100015649.

Irwin, R. L., Rogers, T., & Wan, Y. (1999). Making connections through cultural memory, cultural performance, and cultural translation. *Studies in Art Education*, 40(3), 198–212.

Isaac, J., & Nagam, J. (2018). Insurgence/resurgence [Blog post]. Retrieved from https://www.wag.ca/art/exhibitions/upcoming-exhibitions/display,exhibition/206/insurgence-resurgence.

McCleod, A., Ningewance, P. M., Warren, D., Fontaine, L., & Lebedinskaia, N. (2016). *Lita Fontaine, Sanksannica*. Altona, MB: Art Gallery of Southwestern Manitoba.

Merriam, S. B. (1998). *Case study research in education: A qualitative approach*. San Francisco: Jossey-Bass Inc.

Moore, A. (2017). Contemporary Indigenous art and education project at the Winnipeg Art Gallery [Blog post]. Retrieved from https://indigenousartfocusgroup.wordpress.com/blog.

Moran, R. (2016, December 22). True reconciliation takes hard work. *The Winnipeg Free Press*, p. A7.

National Centre for Truth and Reconciliation. (n.d.). *Truth & reconciliation: Calls to action.* Winnipeg: University of Manitoba Press.

Samphir, H. (2015, March 31). KC Adams: Perception, imagery and the fragility of prejudice. *Canadian Dimension*. Retrieved from https://canadiandimension.com/articles/view/kc-adams-perception-imagery-and-the-fragility-of-prejudice.

Shore, F. J. (2017). *Threads in the sash: The story of the Métis people.* Winnipeg: Pemmican Publications.

Sinclair, N. (2017, December). *Notes from a lecture on Indigenous perspectives of reconciliation.* Presented at the meeting at the Canadian Museum for Human Rights, Winnipeg, MB.

Stake, R. (1995). *The art of case study research.* Thousand Oaks, CA: Sage Publications.

Toulouse, P. R. (2018). *Truth and reconciliation in Canadian schools.* Winnipeg: Portage and Main Press.

Truth and Reconciliation Commission of Canada. (2016). *A knock on the door: The essential history of residential schools.* Winnipeg: University of Manitoba Press.

WAG (Winnipeg Art Gallery). (2017a). *Inuit art centre.* Retrieved from http://inuit.wag.ca.

WAG (Winnipeg Art Gallery). (2017b). The Pagan (1996) by Lita Fontaine. Retrieved from http://wag.ca/art/collections/canadian-art/display,contemporary/54213.

WAG (Winnipeg Art Gallery). (2017c). WAG and artist/curator Jaimie Isaac awarded Canada Council Grant for Aboriginal curatorial residency [Press release]. Retrieved from http://wag.ca/about/press/media-releases/read,release/437/wag-and-artist-curator-jaimie-isaac-awarded-canada-council-grant-for-aboriginal-curatorial-residency.

WAG (Winnipeg Art Gallery). (2017d). Winnipeg Art Gallery and University of Winnipeg announce scholar and curator Dr. Julie Nagam as first chair in history of Indigenous Arts in North America [Press release]. Retrieved from http://wag.ca/about/press/media-releases/read,release/452/winnipeg-art-gallery-and-university-of-winnipeg-announce-scholar-and-curator-dr-julie-nagam-as-first-chair-in-history-of-indigenous-arts-in-no.

Yin, R. (2003). *Case study research: Design and methods.* Thousand Oaks, CA: Sage Publications.

CHAPTER 4

Straight Teacher Allies: Lessons from Compassionate Educators

Leigh Potvin

LEARNING OBJECTIVES

1. To describe strategies that teachers can use to queer mathematics and science curricula.
2. To understand the role that teachers can play in supporting human rights issues in schools.

INTRODUCTION: ANTI-HOMOPHOBIC, ANTI-OPPRESSIVE, AND QUEERING PEDAGOGIES

This chapter focuses on research completed to explore the experiences of straight teacher allies working in K-12 schools in Ontario in the spring and summer of 2016. The purpose of the research is to expand and elaborate on understandings of allies and their experiences as leaders of anti-homophobia initiatives in schools.

An increasingly common way for straight teachers to confront homophobia and transphobia is through LGBTQ+ ally and activism work in schools. Some straight teachers are active supporters of Gay Straight Alliances (GSAs), which are student-led anti-homophobia groups in schools. Others deliver anti-homophobia or queer curriculum and/or organize school-based anti-homophobia events or activities (LaPointe, 2016; Russell, 2011). Activism guided by queer pedagogies serves not only to disrupt homophobia but also to confront **heteronormativity** and **heterosexism** in schools (Britzman, 1995; Bryson & de Castell, 1993; Luhmann, 1998). Heteronormativity is the normalization of heterosexual privilege (Driskill, Finley, Gilley, & Morgensen, 2011; Fischer, 2013; Martino, 1999; Rodriguez, 2007) evident in school dances and health/sex education curriculum, among other aspects of school life. Heterosexism presumes the superiority and naturalness of heterosexuality (Finley, 2011; Ingraham & Saunders, 2016; Meyer, 2007; Pinar, 1998; Walton, 2006). These concepts are essential to understanding why challenging the hegemony of heterosexuality is important for shifting school culture.

Both heteronormativity and heterosexism are key concepts explored by queer theorists (Ingraham & Saunders, 2016; Pinar, 2007; Rodriguez, 2007; Rodriguez & Pinar, 2007). The goal of queer theory is to move away from a paradigm where heterosexuality is normalized and homosexuality is marginalized (Luhmann, 1998; Pinar, 1998). Heteronormative assumptions lead to beliefs about homosexuality that deny it the same level of agency as heterosexuality. Homophobia would see its end, Halperin (1997) argues, if this traditional binary of subject (hetero) and object (homo) could be replaced with a broader, systemic queer ideology that dismantles homophobia, heterosexism, and heteronormativity. Strategic resistance to homophobia, guided by **queer pedagogies**, is more effective than ad hoc anti-homophobia efforts because such resistance requires a shift away from heteronormativity (Halperin, 1997; Rasmussen, 2004). Martino encourages teachers to "move beyond a dominant liberal pedagogy to encourage students to think about what we take for granted as 'normal' and 'natural'" (1999, p. 147). Queer pedagogies provide teachers with models they can examine and then apply to queer politics and content in their classrooms and lesson plans (Britzman, 1995; Bryson & de Castell, 1993; Kumashiro, 2002). Teachers with queer pedagogies are often guided by theory that values, alongside deeply reflective teaching practices, a multiplicity of identities and lived experiences. Many anchor their teaching practice in a compassionate approach—that is, in a place of genuine care for students and their well-being.

I present anti-homophobia and queering approaches in schools as connected, but distinct, concepts (Britzman, 1995; Bryson & de Castell, 1993; Kumashiro, 2004). In the context of this chapter, anti-homophobia stances resist regressive gender-based oppression. Queer pedagogies also resist those forces but, additionally, re-envision schools as places for multiple perspectives and identities (Goldstein, Russell, & Daley, 2007). Participants in this research who have a more developed background in critical pedagogies, especially in feminism and anti-racism, tend to extend their ideas of allyship beyond a desire to help or fix the current problems. In other words, participants with a strong critical pedagogical and anti-oppressive foundation have started to engage in a queering of their school context (Kumashiro, 2004). This extension beyond anti-homophobia efforts often involves a re-envisioning of the current curriculum as well as a re-examination of the school context itself. Participants such as Cameron, Julia, Lucy, and Emily (all names are pseudonyms) also see the nuances of intersectionality (Cho, Crenshaw, & McCall, 2013; Crenshaw, 1991).

Kumashiro (2004) highlights four different approaches to anti-oppressive education, which participants in this chapter move among: (1) improving the experiences of oppressed/marginalized students; (2) changing the way people conceive of difference; (3) challenging power and privilege and their social implications in society and schools; and (4) acknowledging and discussing the challenges associated with anti-oppressive education. Anti-homophobia education often focuses on improving the experiences of marginalized and oppressed peoples, whereas queering education/educational contexts involves challenging the structures of power and privilege in society. Both are important parts of a whole; however, they involve different work. Leaving the eradication of prejudice to teachers, principals, and the school system is a grand request that is achievable but requires the support of other people. Educators can and should be part of the process of challenging straight privilege, but they cannot be the only line of offence.

RESEARCH DESIGN AND METHODS

The research was guided by narrative inquiry, which Connelly and Clandinin identify as a collaborative process that involves "mutual storytelling and re-storying" (1990, p. 4). They identify four stages of narrative inquiry that often overlap and can exist simultaneously for the researcher and participant: living, telling, retelling, and reliving. The experiences that participants gain from living, telling, retelling, and reliving are translated and discussed in an interview experience. Narrative inquiry helps frame this chapter and the storying of the participants' experiences. Stories of experience are more widely accessible to a broader range of readers and also allow advocates and activists the opportunity to reflect on the political nature of the work they do (Barone, 2009).

Participants

This chapter is drawn from a larger study (Potvin, 2017, 2018) and includes some of the participants and data from a larger body of work. The 16 participants in the overall research study are from various regions across Ontario: six participants are from Northern Ontario (districts of Sudbury, Thunder Bay, and Greenstone [Longlac, Geraldton]); two are from Toronto; four are from the Greater Toronto Area; one is from Ottawa; and three are from Central Ontario (Peterborough, Durham Region). Participants range in age from 25 to 60 years. Their teaching and ally experiences are varied, some with two years of teaching experience and others with more than 25 years of experience. Of the 16 participants, two are vice principals (both elementary level), one is a student support person (SSP),[1] two are occasional teachers (OTs), and the remaining 11 are full-time classroom teachers (three elementary and eight secondary). All the participants identify as straight, cisgender (men assigned male at birth, women assigned female at birth) and all but one participant identify as white. Pseudonyms are used throughout this chapter.

LESSONS LEARNED

Kumashiro (2002, 2004) suggests that teachers should build instructional strategies atop an anti-oppressive pedagogy. In other words, anti-oppressive pedagogies—in this case, queer pedagogies—are not add-ons to an otherwise heteronormative curriculum or pedagogical approach. Using self-reflexivity, educators can infuse all curriculum with a queer and anti-oppressive pedagogy by disrupting knowledge (Kumashiro, 2004). I explore this idea by engaging with participants' narratives and experiences with mathematics curriculum, health and physical education curriculum, and in extra-curricular contexts. I arrived at these categories through the responses and experiences of the participants, who frequently connected the ideas we were discussing (straight privilege, anti-homophobia, queering curriculum) back to their experiences with mathematics and health and physical education. I focus on those here because of their relevance to the participants, but also to educators who may be reluctant to see how anti-oppressive education or queering practices fit in the mathematics curriculum. The health and physical education curriculum was top-of-mind for many participants because of the roll-out of a new (and for some controversial) curriculum that was ongoing during data collection.

Mathematics Curriculum

Simon, a student support professional (SSP) and GSA leader, reflected upon the shift in classroom practices he has observed over the last couple of decades. As an SSP, he works one-on-one with students who need learning support in the classroom; he also moves between several classrooms where students require his support, and as such, he observes many classroom teachers in a day. In response to my question about what barriers he thinks exist for LGBTQ+ youth and their allies in schools, he said:

> I think there have been some gains in the last 15 years, but there is a lot of work to be done. Right? For example, the board needs to provide ongoing training regarding human rights issues and make the interconnection between several areas. I think they are lacking the interconnection between Indigenous issues, Indigenous education, and LGBTQ+ issues. And some other components [such as] why are students not successful in the classroom? If they are not able to make those connections, teachers and staff are not able to move forward. I mean, to receive training of a half hour on Indigenous issues and talk about treaties in 15 minutes, that's crap. It needs to be embedded in the professional development component to such an extent that when you are teaching mathematics you are going to be taking into consideration LGBTQ+ issues.

Simon suggested infusing curriculum with queer pedagogy that avoids the trappings of a one-off approach that could compartmentalize or tokenize important social justice issues, such as LGBTQ+ rights. As an example, one-off days can be problematic because they fail to authentically integrate queer identities and politics into the mainstream (Yep, 2002). The approach Simon suggested enables teachers of all subjects to integrate queer content into their lesson planning and activities, while also highlighting the importance of intersectionality (Cho, Crenshaw, & McCall, 2013; Crenshaw, 1991). Teachers are often required to be mindful of the multiple forms of oppression (and privilege) that exist in classrooms and schools. However, for many people in schools, LGBTQ+ students represent a moral issue where homosexuality is viewed as immoral—a perspective that is not applied to Indigenous students or Indigenous studies.

While Simon suggested that it is important to integrate queer content into all subjects, including mathematics, some practitioners in my study identified related obstacles. Madison, a secondary school mathematics teacher and GSA leader in Southeastern Ontario, finds including queer content, let alone a queer pedagogy, in her mathematics classes a challenge. She said the curriculum itself does not elucidate a critical or queer focus:

> The [mathematics] curriculum? Not so much. Although I think there was one year where I was showing them graphs that had been published, it was surveys

about bullying and the content touched on gender and sexuality and bullying that targeted those. But I wouldn't say I make a point to put it into my curriculum. It would be more like just in terms of the general respect that I expect from students and students in my class. That's how it [anti-homophobia] would come up in my class.

Madison makes a strong critique of the mathematics curriculum, or at least her interpretation of it. If the integration of queer content and pedagogy presents a challenge to Madison and others in her position, I suggest that more curriculum options with stronger leadership should be explored. It is often the case that mathematics (and science) are viewed, frequently by the teachers themselves, as being outside the realm of social justice (Rands, 2009). A queer pedagogy can guide classroom experience but doing so is left up to the disposition or pedagogical leanings of the individual teacher. So while pedagogy is essential to queering schools and disrupting knowledge, formalizing the curriculum is also crucial.

Similarly, Andrew, a mathematics teacher in Northern Ontario, responded to the notion that it is difficult to integrate queer content into mathematics. He said, "It is a little bit harder. I think it's mostly a cop out [when people say that], but I think it is a bit harder." Andrew is deeply committed to activism, particularly to the environment, labour, race, and gender equity. He related a story about a significant moment in his mathematics teaching:

So, there's a bunch of the questions that—if you look in the textbook—assume a gender binary. So, to make a committee, the committee needs to have this many girls, how many different ways can you have a committee with x number of boys, right? And it assumes a clear gender binary. So anyway, I was super busy one day, I looked through some old files I got from someone else, I just grabbed one, and I was like, "Okay, I'm going to throw that on the Smartboard, we're going to do a couple of questions and then we'll work on it."

Shortly after delivering the main part of the lesson, he grew uncomfortable and decided to take action. He apologized to the class, acknowledging that he had been in a hurry that day and had grabbed a lesson he had used many times before but that he realized now was problematic. He wanted to relay to his students that he was aware that there were more than two genders despite what the mathematics problem presented. He also committed aloud to his students that he would do better next time and not use that kind of problem again. At the end of his class, a student approached him:

I had this student come up to me [who said,] "Thank you so much for doing that, I don't see myself on one end of this binary or another and I really appreciate that [you acknowledged gender exists outside of boy and girl] and I've never had another teacher [in] this school who would do that or would have said that." Which I know wasn't the case, because I know a bunch of the other teachers [who would have said the same thing], but clearly it had never come up. [The student said,] "Thank you so much, this was so meaningful to me." [They were] just glowing because of this stupid little thing that I had said.

Here, Andrew reflects on what seemed to him like an insignificant act on his part. In fact, he felt ashamed when he made a deal of the gender binary in the math problem, and yet his action was so meaningful for one of his students. This Grade 12 student had never in all their years at school had a teacher acknowledge that gender exists beyond the traditional binary. Andrew's simple disclaimer and public acknowledgement was poignant for the student in his class. His acknowledgement demonstrates a deep level of engagement in his practice as a teacher, and, yet, it seems unfortunate that this should be such a revolutionary act for him as an educator and for his student in their scholastic life. This example points to how deeply rooted the dominant gender narrative is in schools and the ways that curriculum expectations can clearly guide teachers.

Andrew and Madison provided insights into the ways that the mathematics curriculum can be queered with deliberate intent, without being labour intensive. Andrew identified the ways that heteronormative and cisgender privilege exist unchecked in the mathematics curriculum. Madison and Andrew both illustrated how the mathematics curriculum can be filled with content that reflects gender diversity. LGBTQ+ identities can be integrated into mathematics and science curricula as readily as they can be into social sciences and humanities and health and physical education curricula (Kumashiro, 2002; Luhmann, 1998; Pinar, 1998). Rands warns, however, that queering mathematics should not involve an "Add-Queers-And-Stir" method (2009, p. 184), but rather one that envisions new possibilities. Andrew's desire to move beyond the gender binary in his combinatorics class reflects an important step in the right direction; however, Rands suggests, "Mathematical Inqu[ee]ry pushes teachers and students to take the level of interrogation one step further" and to question, for example, conceptions of gender and family—and even to solve problems with variables one may not know (2009, p. 187). Although the mathematics curriculum currently may not have clearly articulated anti-homophobic or queer content, the health and physical education curriculum does—a reality that is a source of controversy and top-of-mind for participants.

Health and Physical Education Curriculum

The health and physical education (HPE) curriculum in Ontario was revised in 2010 for the first time since 1998. However, the curriculum was pulled shortly after its release because of the controversy around the sexuality curriculum. It was further revised and published in 2015, but it is under fire once again. Most curriculum subject areas are updated on a three- to five-year revision cycle to ensure their relevance.[2] However, the Ontario Ministry of Education policy of curriculum review is process-oriented, which means there is no hard-and-fast rule or timeline for curricula to be updated. Critics of the HPE curriculum (in 2010) suggested that the new curriculum promoted alleged deviant sexual behaviour, pre-marital sex, age inappropriate content, and "gay sex."[3] The so-called controversial pieces of the curriculum exist within the examples used to illustrate the intended learning. For example, in Grade 3, gender identity and sexual orientation are included as examples of "invisible differences." Other invisible differences include cultural values, skills, and learning abilities. These invisible differences sit in contrast to visible differences, which are outlined in the Grade 3 curriculum as hair colour, height, and eye colour.[4] Teachers, however, are not required to use the examples the curriculum provides. Every participant in this chapter referenced the 2015–2016 rollout of the updated HPE curriculum in their interviews without prompting. For the majority of participants in this chapter, backlash from some parent communities was at the forefront of their minds.

Jennifer is an elementary teacher in a relatively large Southern Ontario school board. The school where she teaches has a student population of mostly new Canadian students from South Asian Muslim and Sikh families. She discussed the way she teaches relationships as part of the (now controversial) Grade 3 HPE curriculum:

> K-8 is teaching the new sex/health unit at the same time. Grade 3, I'm in Grade 3 this year, and it's easy breezy—we're talking about family and what makes a family, like it's—"oh sweet!" We're about love and feeling safe, okay, good.

Before the curriculum update, Jennifer incorporated her anti-homophobic pedagogy into the HPE curriculum. Part of her approach includes teaching about same-sex families, something that she thinks some members of the parent community could consider controversial. Because of the new curriculum changes, she can continue to teach the curriculum content in a way that honours and includes LGBTQ+ families with greater institutional support for her approach. The staff at the school, including Jennifer, had not received any substantive complaints from parents about the Grade 3 curriculum delivery at the time of our interview. The principal had received a couple of phone calls from the parents, but Jennifer said that upon discussing the changes with the principal, parent concerns were assuaged.

Trueman, a new and inexperienced teacher, teaches full-time at a Francophone Catholic school board in Southern Ontario. He chooses to hide his own beliefs and values about LGBTQ+ equity from his school community for fear of repercussions. This is a professional move he noted is prudent for him as a young teacher seeking stable, full-time employment in a province with few full-time teaching opportunities. He articulates his view of the HPE curriculum and how it fits into the school where he works:

> [It's] a kind of an example of how things [related to LGBTQ+ issues/people] are touchier subjects because really I don't know if you've read it [the HPE curriculum], but I've gone through it and really nothing is offensive, like anybody who was all up in arms was dumb and didn't read it. That's my opinion. But we still have to have like a whole training session about it. They [board officials/administration] told us since the start of the year, "Nobody teaches that curriculum until we tell you guys what to do" and "Don't touch it." [Then they said,] "Oh well, the Bishops are still going through it." So, I guess there's no sense of urgency there and now they've told us to just teach it as we've taught it in previous years without approaching the new material. Because it's … it's all taboo. Like, don't do that.

This example demonstrates the influence that school leadership and policy-makers have over the teachers in their schools. New teachers who are concerned about job security may be particularly inclined to maintain the status quo in terms of equity and human rights issues for fear of backlash. If the status quo in schools and classrooms does not honour or uphold equity measures and human rights, then social justice–oriented teachers might be stopped in their tracks. In other words, schools should create environments both inside and outside classrooms that strive for equity so as to encourage students and teachers to advocate for human rights. Having noted this, it is worth considering Trueman's additional comment: "Realistically, I could teach it however I'd like, and I don't think there'd really be any repercussions, but yeah, still that's the kind of politics around it." It is hard to reconcile these two quotations because his actions conform to the directives of the administration. Trueman highlighted and mirrored

Callaghan's (2007) work on Catholic school systems in Canada. In it, Callaghan argues that Catholic schools position their policies relative to the directives of the Vatican and what she calls "Catholic homophobia," more generally. As a result, LGBTQ+ people in Catholic schools keep their identity hidden. Furthermore, Callaghan writes that "Catholic spokespersons seem more concerned with condemning homosexuals themselves than the harassment of homosexuals" (2007, p. 5).

Extra-Curricular School-Based Activities

Straight teacher allies often participate in extra-curricular commitments related to their gender and equity activism in addition to their curricular and pedagogical ones. Many participants run GSAs, participate in union committees, organize schoolwide celebrations, and/or run workshops for students or staff. The nature of the activities depends upon school culture, gaps in school services, and individual commitment to equity.

Cameron problematized the effectiveness of the one-off, celebratory days in discussing some of the barriers for allies in schools. He said, "We [teachers] put up a poster that says [a classroom or school is] a safe space, and therefore, it is. And we don't actually do anything to make the space safe." This reflection implies Cameron's belief that anti-homophobia initiatives need to be more deliberate and active.

Julia focused simultaneously on her work as a classroom teacher and as a leader in her school. She is dedicated to examining how her activism fits into initiatives at the board level and how her anti-oppressive/queer pedagogy guides her teaching. One of her initiatives is to expand the influence of the Rainbow Club in her school. She relies on the assistance of staff from the district's school board office to help her implement meaningful programming, especially amongst Grades 4 to 6 classes where a lot of gender-based bullying occurs. She explained:

> You've got kids in the school calling each other faggot, calling each other gay in a way that's mal-intended. The obvious thing is to do some work. And so, this isn't a barrier, but there are administrators who would be uncomfortable with the idea of bringing somebody like that in without maybe checking with the parents first. To me, you know, this is a basic human right—we don't have to check with the parents to be teaching how to be kind to each other, how to be decent to each other.

Like Simon, Julia emphasized the importance of LGBTQ+ activism as a human rights issue. Her convictions are reflected in her queer, anti-oppressive pedagogy. Her pedagogy resists the dominant and potentially regressive narrative about queer issues in schools. Julia explained what Rainbow Week, one of the initiatives of the Rainbow Club, at her urban elementary school includes:

> Monday of Rainbow Week we have a transgender author coming who writes children's books, and he is going to read from two of his books. His name is S. Bear Bergman[5] ... he's a career author but also comedian and presenter, and his thing is talking about transgender [issues]. I think the transgender piece is really important because particularly for the primary grades kids who are not yet questioning their sexuality but they might already be questioning their gender identity.

Julia's approach, which is to start teaching students about their gender through the work of well-known trans author S. Bear Bergman, is unique. Her approach demonstrates that she has a profound understanding of how to introduce her elementary school-aged students to queer content and pedagogy. Julia achieves this in ways that are both relevant to the students' development and age appropriate. She resists the tendency to equate sex with gender or to conflate them. Julia also reflected on the school board policies that are shaping not only her school's culture and context, but the culture and context of the schools in the entire school district as well:

> We are in the [school board] now implementing all-gender washrooms in all the schools, and we certainly did have students who are not adhering to what might be the extreme [...] binary, traditional gender expressions. And we need for everyone to be okay with that, so I think that that's a great way to start the week.

Julia's awareness of and connection to the student population in her school guides the anti-oppressive work that she does, including Rainbow Week. For Julia, Rainbow Week evolved out of what she views as limitations to Day of Pink.

In Lucy's school, staff participation and leadership (beyond her own involvement) in school-based initiatives can be challenging. She explained the role she often assumes in the schools where she has worked:

> We did a few kinds of workshops and things, but we had to really drag teachers in to help and all they would do was supervise. There was, it almost became the tip of the tokenism then moved out to the level of "Okay, those are the teachers that deal with the gay stuff and the sexism stuff" and "I'm [principal] just going to keep hiring supply teachers that make sexist jokes to kids" or "I'm going to

continue to teach novels that don't support the existence of the LGBTQ+ students or people in society." So, I did feel like every school I go to there's one or two people, and then we become the activists and everyone else thinks, "Okay, just like we have a volleyball coach we have a 'take care of these marginalized students' area."

Anti-oppressive educational initiatives in schools, for Lucy, are frequently aggregated with other extra-curricular commitments. Administration and staff often perceive that if they have one or two staff members who are "champions" for marginalized students, then they do not have to worry about that kind of work themselves. Lucy highlights that "One of the hardest things is to get everybody to just do some—a little bit of this work, you know? Stop calling them ladies and gents or don't make deprecating comments about people?" Here, she implies that she thinks it should be the collective responsibility of the entire staff to ensure that LGBTQ+ equity initiatives and that LGBTQ+ students themselves are valued and feel safe at school.

Madison described other initiatives at her school that extend beyond Day of Pink and when student participation in the GSA is low:

[Our school board hosts] a board-wide day of workshops for kids, as well as a board-wide school dance at a central location for all the kids and the GSAs. So, we do all those events. I would say in past years, it's been nice that we had GSA kids that were interested in being part of [the GSA]. [They'd] have a table, and they'd put face paint on kids with rainbow colours and whatever. [In years where the GSA is more teacher-led] where we don't have the kids coming out to meetings, [staff] put up posters, and we encourage staff and kids to wear pink and make sure it's on our Twitter feed—wear pink to support blah, blah, blah. So, I would say it ends up being teacher-led in those years where you just can't get the support from the kids, but we definitely do [events like Day of Pink]. My favourite thing is that my board puts a school bus in the Pride parade every summer. And kids are welcome to walk with us.

Madison's use of "blah, blah, blah" is notable in the disregard she showed for common school-based activism such as wearing pink. Frequently, activities like Day of Pink (and wearing pink) are used as an example of the progressive nature of a school. Consequently, it is noteworthy that the people organizing them (like Madison) seem to question the limits of their effectiveness.

I would not suggest abandoning activities such as Day of Pink altogether, but rather, acknowledging that they are one component of what should be a more macro, holistic approach to queering schools and school communities. Like Julia, Madison highlighted the way her activism complements school board initiatives, as well as those among the broader community, for LGBTQ+ people. Beneficial opportunities to share ideas and connect with other allies are possible, even in years where student participation may be lower at the school where she works. She also indicated the usefulness of institutional training for LGBTQ+ allies.

CONCLUSION

In this chapter, straight teacher allies demonstrate their adaptability and responsiveness to LGBTQ+ topics in their classrooms and school-based activities, even though many have little-to-no formal training on gender equity or human rights. They implement strategies that are useful for new teachers and teacher candidates to consider. While many of the participants organize activities for Day of Pink or, in other cases, Rainbow Week, most of them situate this work at the tip of the proverbial iceberg. More needs to be done, and some participants address this by infusing their classroom content with anti-homophobic and queer lessons guided by a compassionate stance. Most of the participants in this chapter see the curriculum as a living document in which there is room for it to be infused with more queer content. For Cameron and Julia, this means reading children's books and watching films with queer content. Instead of viewing the inclusion of queer content in the curriculum as controversial or as a nuisance, the participants in this study view the curriculum as an opportunity for social justice advocacy and compassion. For Simon, educators can include queer and Indigenous perspectives; indeed, it is their responsibility as educators to do so. Stefan also highlighted the importance of human rights and the interconnected or intersectional nature of oppression. He understands, as does Lucy, that privilege and oppression live in schools, as they do in the rest of society, and that educators must do their best to teach youth (and sometimes colleagues) about it.

Almost all of these educators make queer or anti-homophobic perspectives part of their classrooms and are often the only person in their school to do so. By taking up this social justice work, they often feel further isolated from their colleagues and wary of parents and administration. However, the fact that infusing queer content and anti-homophobic perspectives is at the discretion of teachers is problematic. For teachers such as Lucy and Jennifer, presenting a queer curriculum to their students runs the risk of parent backlash, particularly from vocal, conservative religious communities. They balance their professional responsibil-ity to respect people's faith backgrounds with their conviction that the rights of LGBTQ+ people must be upheld and honoured. Participants often under-take anti-homophobia initiatives that seek to resist the dominant narratives, but they do not consistently envision or create new ways for their schools to respond to anti-homophobic initiatives. Those who do challenge the dominant narra-tive, particularly by focusing on their own privilege, espouse values that seek to queer school spaces. In my research, teachers who challenge heteronormativity and heterosexism seem to be infusing their routines with anti-oppressive educa-tion practices, particularly a discourse that highlights the importance of human rights and places its focus on students who have experienced oppression or mar-ginalization (Kumashiro, 2004).

The participants in this chapter are the primary individuals leading LGBTQ+ equity initiatives in their schools. What would happen if those teachers left their school? How are new, inexperienced teachers to know that honouring LGBTQ+ rights and identities is the rule rather than the exception? Institutional, and not just individual, leadership must become the norm. Unfor-tunately, many teacher allies engage in equity and activism work in classrooms and schools with very little educational background, training, or support. School boards and administrators need to support LGBTQ+ youth (and their allies) to ensure not only the drafting, but also the implementation, of safe school policies. The convergence of religious identities (particularly conservative, fundamental-ist stances) presents an active challenge to the anti-oppressive position of many of these activists and degrades the existence of LGBTQ+ people. Teachers fear parent backlash even in circumstances where no such resistance has yet occurred.

QUESTIONS FOR CRITICAL THOUGHT

1. How can you prepare yourself to integrate human rights and LGBTQ+ content throughout your classroom activities and/or your extra-curricular commitments?
2. Consider Trueman's position as a new teacher concealing his political be-liefs to secure employment. How do you plan to balance the practical need for employment with your own private and/or political beliefs?
3. Imagine you are in a teaching placement or position and you are expected to teach a contentious curriculum with a high profile in public (such as the HPE curriculum in Ontario). How do you honour the curriculum and the human rights of your students while recognizing the potential for familial and/or administrative backlash?

GLOSSARY

Heteronormativity: The normalization of heterosexual privilege.

Heterosexism: The presumed superiority or naturalness of heterosexuality.

Queer pedagogies: Educators who are guided by a teaching philosophy that values, alongside deeply reflective teaching practices, a multiplicity of identities and lived experiences, particularly those educators who work towards honouring a proliferation and representation of identities in their curriculum and classrooms.

NOTES

1. Also known as an educational assistant (EA), or a teachers' assistant (TA), these educational professionals support students with individual education plans and/or other unique learning needs in the classroom and/or school environment.

2. The Ontario Ministry of Education does not hold itself to specific timelines for curriculum review. In practice, it happens every three to five years, but the ministry emphasizes process (not specific timeframes) on its website. See http://www.edu.gov.on.ca/curriculumreview/process.html.

3. See, for example, http://www.campaignlifecoalition.com/index.php?p=Sex_Ed_Curriculum.

4. http://www.edu.gov.on.ca/eng/curriculum/elementary/health1to8.pdf. At the time of publication, the health and sexual education curriculum has once again become contentious under the Conservative government in Ontario. As such, this iteration of the curriculum is no longer readily available online.

5. S. Bear Bergman, trans activist and author, can be found at http://www.sbearbergman.com.

REFERENCES

Barone, T. (2009). Narrative researchers as witnesses of injustice and agents of social change? *Educational Researcher*, 38(8), 591–597. https://doi.org/10.3102/0013189X09353203.

Britzman, D. P. (1995). Is there a queer pedagogy? Or, stop reading straight. *Educational Theory*, 45(2), 151–165. https://doi.org/10.1111/j.1741-5446.1995.00151.x.

Bryson, M., & de Castell, S. (1993). Queer pedagogy: Praxis makes im/perfect. *Canadian Journal of Education/Revue canadienne de l'éducation*, 18(3), 285–305. https://doi.org/10.2307%2F1495388.

Callaghan, T. D. (2007). Contra/Diction: How Catholic doublespeak in Canadian Catholic secondary schools furthers homophobia. *Canadian Online Journal of Queer Studies in Education*, 3(1).

Cho, S., Crenshaw, K. W., & McCall, L. (2013). Toward a field of intersectionality studies: Theory, applications, and praxis. *Signs*, 38(4), 785–810. https://doi.org/10.1086/669608.

Connelly, F. M., & Clandinin, D. J. (1990). Stories of experience and narrative inquiry. *Educational Researcher*, 19(5), 2–14.

Crenshaw, K. (1991). Mapping the margins: Intersectionality, identity politics, and violence against Women of Color. *Stanford Law Review*, 43(6), 1241–1299. https://doi.org/10.2307/1229039.

Driskill, Q. L., Finley, C., Gilley, B., & Morgensen, S. L. (2011). Introduction. In Q. L. Driskill, C. Finley, B. Gilley, & S. L. Morgensen (Eds.), *Queer Indigenous studies: Critical interventions in theory, politics, and literature* (pp. 1–31). Tucson: University of Arizona Press.

Finley, C. (2011). Decolonizing the queer Native body (and recovering the Native bull-dyke): Bringing 'sexy back' and out of Native studies' closet. In Q. L. Driskill, C. Finley, B. Gilley, & S. L. Morgensen (Eds.), *Queer Indigenous studies: Critical interventions in theory, politics, and literature* (pp. 32–42). Tucson: University of Arizona Press.

Fischer, N. L. (2013). Seeing "straight," contemporary critical heterosexuality studies and sociology: An introduction. *The Sociological Quarterly*, 54(4), 501–510. https://doi.org/10.1111/tsq.12040.

Goldstein, T., Russell, V., & Daley, A. (2007). Safe, positive and queering moments in teaching education and schooling: A conceptual framework. *Teaching Education*, 18(3), 183–199. https://doi.org/10.1080/10476210701533035.

Halperin, D. M. (1997). *Saint Foucault: Towards a gay hagiography*. New York: Oxford University Press.

Ingraham, C., & Saunders, C. (2016). Heterosexual imaginary. In *The Wiley Blackwell encyclopedia of gender and sexuality studies* (pp. 1–4). Hoboken, NJ: Wiley-Blackwell. https://doi.org/10.1002/9781118663219.wbegss762.

Kumashiro, K. K. (2004). *Against common sense: Teaching and learning toward social justice*. New York: Routledge.

Kumashiro, K. K. (2002). *Troubling education: "Queer" activism and anti-oppressive pedagogy*. New York: Routledge.

LaPointe, A. A. (2016). Queering the social studies: Lessons to be learned from Canadian secondary school gay-straight alliances. *The Journal of Social Studies Research*, 40(3), 205–215. https://doi.org/10.1016/j.jssr.2015.07.004.

Luhmann, S. (1998). Queering/querying pedagogy? Or, pedagogy is a pretty queer thing. In W. Pinar (Ed.), *Queer theory in education* (pp. 141–155). Mahwah, NJ: Lawrence Erlbaum Associates.

Martino, W. (1999). "It's okay to be gay": Interrupting straight thinking in the English classroom. In W. J. Letts IV & J. T. Sears (Eds.), *Queering elementary education: Advancing the dialogue about sexualities and schooling* (pp. 137–150). Lanham, MD: Rowman & Littlefield.

Meyer, E. (2007). "But I'm not gay": What straight teachers need to know about queer theory. In N. M. Rodriguez & W. Pinar (Eds.), *Queering straight teachers: Discourse and identity in education* (pp. 15–29). New York: Peter Lang.

Pinar, W. F. (2007). Introduction: A queer conversation, toward sustainability. In N. M. Rodriguez & W. Pinar (Eds.), *Queering straight teachers: Discourse and identity in education* (pp. 1–14). New York: Peter Lang.

Pinar, W. F. (1998). Introduction. In W. F. Pinar (Ed.), *Queer theory in education* (pp. 1–39). Mahwah, NJ: Lawrence Erlbaum Associates.

Potvin, L. (2018). Gay/straight alliances: The need for straight support in schools. *Canadian Association of Principals Journal: Hot Topics in Education*, Spring, 12–14.

Potvin, L. (2017). *More than pink shirts and posters: Beyond the limits of anti-homophobia education* (Unpublished doctoral dissertation). Lakehead University, Thunder Bay, ON, Canada.

Rands, K. (2009). Mathematical inqu[ee]ry: Beyond "Add-queers-and-stir" elementary mathematics education. *Sex Education*, 9(2), 181–191. https://doi.org/10.1080/14681810902829646.

Rasmussen, M. L. (2004). Safety and subversion: The production of sexualities and genders in school spaces. In M. Rasmussen, E. Rofes, & S. Talburt (Eds.), *Youth and sexualities: Pleasure, subversion, and insubordination in and out of schools* (pp. 131–152). New York: Palgrave MacMillan.

Rodriguez, N. M. (2007). Preface: Just queer it. In N. M. Rodriguez, & W. Pinar (Eds.), *Queering straight teachers: Discourse and identity in education* (pp. vii–xii). New York: Peter Lang.

Rodriguez, N. M., & Pinar, W. (2007). *Queering straight teachers: Discourse and identity in education*. New York: Peter Lang.

Russell, G. M. (2011). Motives of heterosexual allies in collective action for equality. *Journal of Social Issues*, 67(2), 376–393. https://doi.org/10.1111/j.1540-4560.2011.01703.x

Walton, G. (2006). H-cubed: A primer on bullying and sexuality diversity for educators. *Our Schools, Our Selves*, 15(2), 117–126. Retrieved from https://www.researchgate.net/publication/242517856_H-.

Yep, G. A. (2002). From homophobia and heterosexism to heteronormativity: Toward the development of a model of queer interventions in the university classroom. *Journal of Lesbian Studies*, 6(3–4), 163–176. https://doi.org/10.1300/J155v06n03_14.

CHAPTER 5

Closing the Gaps: A Compassionate View of Mental Health beyond the Medical Model

Christina Luzius-Vanin and Alana Butler

LEARNING OBJECTIVES

1. To explore the various insights that the critical perspectives of disability studies, neurodiversity, and Mad Studies provide on the unique complexities that students with mental health challenges and diagnosis experience.
2. To understand the teacher's position as social support for all students and explore various empowerment intervention strategies that can be used to support students living with mental health challenges or diagnosis.

INTRODUCTION

Mental health and wellness has become a topic of current interest in Canadian schools (Canadian Mental Health Association, 2018a; Ministry of Education, 2013). It has been reported that almost half (49 percent) of Canadians will experience some form of mental health "disorder" in their lifetimes (Canadian Mental Health Association, 2018b). A longitudinal study by Kessler and colleagues (2007) determined that the first onset of mental disorders typically occurs before the age of 18. The most recently available statistics show that

10 to 20 percent of Canadian youth are affected by a mental illness or disorder, and approximately 5 percent of male youth and 12 percent of female youth between the ages of 12 and 19 have experienced a major depressive episode (Canadian Mental Health Association, 2018a). It is estimated that 1 percent of Canadian youth over the age of 16 will develop schizophrenia (Canadian Mental Health Association, 2018b). Suicide is the leading cause of death among 15-to-24-year-old youth. The 2017 Ontario Student Drug Use and Health Survey (OSDUHS) surveyed 11,435 Ontario students from Grades 7 to 12. The data showed that about 40 percent of students experienced moderate to severe psychological distress in the past year (Centre for Addiction and Mental Health, 2018a). The researchers determined that female students were twice as likely as males to experience poor mental health (Centre for Addiction and Mental Health, 2018b).

Despite the prevalence of mental illness among students, there is still a stigma associated with disclosing and seeking treatment for mental health challenges. Stigma refers to any characteristic that is deeply discrediting to the individual (Goffman, 2009). Mental illness is stigmatized because of its association with violence and suicide in the media. Media analyses show that most news reporting on the topic of mental health is negative. McGinty, Kennedy-Hendricks, Choksy, and Barry (2016), in a sample of 400 newspaper articles from 1995 to 2014, found that 55 percent of the news reports associated mental illness with interpersonal violence or suicide and that only 14 percent of news reports described positive stories of recovery or treatment. The Mental Health Commission of Canada (2012) reported that almost 40 percent of news articles about mental illness focus on danger, violence, and criminality, while only 12 percent of articles take an optimistic perspective. Sampogna and colleagues (2017) argue that stigma can be perpetuated by large-scale reporting of criminal incidents involving those with a documented mental illness.

In spite of the negative news media coverage, there have been positive examples of the media being utilized to reduce the stigma around mental health challenges (Cheng et al., 2016; Scholz, Crabb, & Wittert, 2014). Anti-stigma campaigns are dynamic and work across systems to bring out community and eventually societal change. Cheng and colleagues (2016) found that mass media campaigns endorsing mental health and psychiatric services can affect health care–seeking behaviour and utilization of health care services.

Mental health has been an important emerging topic in educational discourse as educational practitioners, researchers, and administrators try to develop an understanding of how school personnel can support the well-being of our school community and support individual students who are experiencing specific mental health challenges. There must be an understanding of what the educator's roles and responsibilities are when supporting the well-being, social development, and learning of all students, including those living with mental health challenges. In most provincial education acts, teachers have been tasked with *in loco parentis* provisions, which means that teachers are sometimes called to act in the place of a parent. Teachers are responsible not only for the education of our students but also for their overall well-being and social inclusion within our school communities. Noddings (2013) argues for an ethic of care in schooling that approximates maternal care. The caring relationship is central to the teacher-child relationship. In her seminal work on the subject, Noddings (2013) articulated a framework for care called circles and chains. Caring is a part of natural relationships within a family circle. Teachers and students may form chains of caring relationships in the school environment. Fostering an ethic of care for the mental health of students will help to ensure that school communities are inclusive.

A gap in the existing literature is that scholarly material addressing mental health in school environments has not engaged with critical perspectives arising out of **neurodiversity** and **Mad Studies** advocacy that seek to empower those with mental health challenges (McWade, Milton, & Beresford, 2015). This chapter will examine the issue of mental health and schools from Zimmerman's conception of **empowerment**, which is concerned with "identifying capabilities instead of cataloging risk factors and exploring environmental influences on social problems instead of blaming victims" (1995, p. 570). Through this empowerment framework, interventions centre on increasing wellness, gaining access to knowledge, developing skills, collaborating with professionals, and reducing challenges (Zimmerman, 1995).

First, this chapter will provide a brief overview of current approaches to addressing mental health issues in schools. Next, the chapter will explore how marginalized populations face disproportionate mental health challenges in school. The chapter will then explore how current approaches to addressing mental health in schools are restricted to a medicalized model that does not take into account perspectives arising from critical disability studies, neurodiversity, and Mad Studies. Last, the chapter will propose ways for teachers and school administrators to empower their students through inclusive mental health and wellness policies and practices.

CURRENT APPROACHES TO MENTAL HEALTH IN SCHOOLS

There is varying research on effective evidence-based approaches to mental health support in Canadian schools. Characteristics of effective mental health programs include approaches that are long-term, focus on universal and early intervention, are sensitive to cultural or gender-based differences, and offer multiple integrated elements within programming (Browne et al., 2004). Wei, Kutcher, and Szumilas (2011) emphasize the importance of a comprehensive mental health school program that is informed by evidence-based approaches that create a continuum of care networks through mental health promotion, prevention, and treatment.

The Mental Health Commission of Canada (2013) created a mental health literacy strategy for Canadian schools that aimed to decrease stigma and frame mental health within a continuum of conditions ranging from depression to psychosis. The mental health literacy strategy also included information about early onset of disorders so that adequate mental health supports can be identified earlier on. Best practices highlight the effectiveness of integrating mental health literacy in everyday classroom discussions by teachers who have achieved literacy in mental health (Kutcher, Bagnell, & Wei, 2015; Kutcher, Wei & Morgan, 2015; Manion, Short, & Ferguson, 2013). Mental health promotion strategies include collaborative school and community partnerships to create a positive culture of well-being and inclusion for all students (Rowling, 2012). Preventative programs aim to forestall various mental health challenges, such as depression and anxiety (Manion, Short, & Ferguson, 2013). Evidence shows that early screening and identification along with early intervention strategies can be an effective prevention tool (Browne et al., 2004; Manion, Short, & Ferguson, 2013).

Research studies have also identified gaps in Canadian school-based mental health supports. Sixty-four percent of students in one study reported that there was a lack of mental health resources available in their school (Bowers, Manion, Papadopoulos, & Gauvreau, 2013). Very few schools provide comprehensive evidence-based services across a continuum of mental health distress and diagnosis (Manion, Short, & Ferguson, 2013). Although accessibility to onsite services improves ongoing participation in the pursuit of mental well-being, there is always a risk of a breach in confidentiality for students who receive treatment in their school communities (Browne et al., 2004). There are Canadian examples of accessible mental health services, which offer collaborative services that connect the school and mental health service providers. Rousseau, Measham, and Nadeau (2013) describe a collaborative health care initiative in Montreal involving school, clinic, and community partnerships to support refugee children suffering from PTSD. The diverse teams include a range of health care professionals, social workers, school personnel, and community organizations who work collaboratively to support the needs of the children.

CURRENT MENTAL HEALTH TRAINING FOR TEACHERS

One of the most critical gaps in the provision of support for children with mental health challenges is the lack of training received by teachers. Only 31.5 percent of students believed that their teachers were prepared to address the mental health needs of the school (Bowers, Manion, Papadopoulos, & Gauvreau, 2013). Whitley, Smith, and Vaillancourt (2013) argue that teachers may play a key role in the prevention of mental disorders by providing adequate early intervention support for sufferers.

Rodger and colleagues (2014) conducted a study of syllabi from 700 Bachelor of Education courses across Canada to assess their mental health literacy content across four criteria: (1) listed mental health in the course title; (2) included words related to mental health; (3) described supports available; and (4) provided information about fostering supportive relationships with those suffering mental distress. The researchers found that only 104 syllabi listed at least one criterion for mental health literacy, 84 syllabi met two criteria, 23 met three criteria, and only 2 met all four criteria. Rodger et al. (2014) concluded that only two courses met the criteria for a mental health literacy course. Their findings demonstrate that Bachelor of Education programs lack courses in mental health literacy.

A study of 3,900 Canadian teachers found that although teachers identified mental health as a critical issue in their schools, 87 percent of them reported that there was a lack of adequate teacher training in mental health (Canadian Teachers' Federation, 2012). Sixty-eight percent of the teachers stated that they had received no training in mental health. Andrews, McCabe, and Wideman-Johnston (2014) surveyed 75 high school teachers, and the results indicated that, although teachers believed that dealing with mental health challenges was within the scope of their jobs, they felt unprepared to address these challenges. Over 90 percent of the survey respondents indicated that they agreed that mental diagnosis would affect dropout rates and academic achievement (Andrews, McCabe, & Wideman-Johnston, 2014). Only 36 percent of the survey respondents stated that they were confident in their knowledge of mental health challenges and resource support.

In addition to the lack of training, another challenge is that current mental health training for teachers focuses on a medicalized model that treats mental illness as an aberration and fails to include scholarly contributions from critical disability advocates. Contemporary approaches that challenge the medical model include neurodiversity and Mad Studies.

MENTAL ILLNESS AND MARGINALIZED PERSONS

For educators working with marginalized groups, such as the poor, racialized, recent immigrant, refugee, disabled, and Indigenous populations, providing mental health supports is even more critical. In their quantitative study of 150 homeless Toronto youth, Kirst, Frederick, and Erickson (2011) found that 84 percent of the sample had not completed high school. Twenty-four percent of the sample also experienced concurrent substance abuse and mental illness. Isaranuwatchai and colleagues (2014), in a quantitative analysis of the 2010 Ontario Student Drug Use and Health Survey (OSDUHS), found that self-ratings of poor mental health were associated with moderate-to-high illicit drug use in high school. Moreover, students with disabilities have a higher risk of anxiety and depressive disorders (Canadian Mental Health Association, 2018b). And students with physical or intellectual disabilities are at greater risk of being bullied and ostracized in school, both of which contribute to depression and anxiety (Malboeuf-Hurtubise et al., 2017).

As an intergenerational impact of collective trauma, Indigenous persons worldwide experience higher rates of mental health issues (Boksa, Joober, & Kirmayer, 2015; Nelson & Wilson, 2017). Notably, this manifests itself in higher suicide rates. Indigenous Canadians have suicide rates that are twice the national average, with females more likely than males to attempt or commit suicide (Centre for Addiction and Mental Health, 2018a). The suicide rate of Indigenous youth is five to six times higher than the national average and among Inuit youth is eleven times the national average (Centre for Addiction and Mental Health, 2018a). Indigenous populations also experience higher rates of alcoholism and substance abuse, all related to mental health (Nelson & Wilson, 2017).

Slaunwhite (2015) used data from the Canadian Community Health Survey to show that Canadians with an annual income of less than $30,000 experienced higher rates of mental health distress. In the Canadian Community Health Survey, low-income individuals reported barriers to mental health care that include accessibility to quality mental health care and fear of stigma or further marginalization. Children and youth in low-income households experience higher levels of stress, which contributes to poor mental health (Centre for Addiction and Mental Health, 2018a).

New immigrants to Canada, particularly those who are racialized, may experience mental health distress as a consequence of adapting to a new culture and a labour market that may not recognize their foreign-earned credentials (Ward, Bochner, & Furnham, 2006). Moreover, refugee children in Canada may have experienced or witnessed traumatic events that have deleterious effects on their long-term mental health (Rousseau, Measham, & Nadeau, 2013).

CRITICAL DISABILITY, NEURODIVERSITY, AND MAD STUDIES

Critical disability scholars contend that the discursive framing of mental health conditions is ableist. Ableism refers to structural and social systems that normalize able-bodied persons and relegate the differently abled as deficient. Devlin and Pothier (2008) argue that the language of disability is problematic because it is "othering." Mental health conditions are labelled "disorders" and the colloquial usage of the terms *crazy* and *insane* further contributes to the stigmatization of those who experience mental health challenges.

The term *neurodiversity* is credited to an Australian disabilities activist named Judy Singer who, in her 1998 honours thesis, first articulated the idea that neurological differences form a differentiated social identity, called neurodiversity. Since Singer first introduced the term, it has undergone a variety of metamorphoses and is now more broadly understood as "a solidarity network of movements fighting for radical acceptance of all types of human diversity, under a broad range of 'anti-normalism'" (McWade, Milton, & Brersford, 2015). The neurodiversity crusade arose as an extension of the disability rights movement to include those individuals with neurological differences. McGee (2012) posits that neurodiversity is also a response to the rise of neoliberalism over the past few decades. Neoliberal ideology as manifested by practice has shifted responsibility for mental health care to the family network and away from government support. The demands created by neurologically diverse populations may challenge the existing conceptualizations of personhood. Neurodiversity is a political discourse that puts forth the contention that social categories such as race, gender, ethnicity, and sexual orientation should be extended to include those for whom neurological predispositions are non-normative. Neurodiversity includes a range of non-normative mental conditions ranging from autism to bipolar "disorder" and schizophrenia.

Mad Studies represents another critical challenge to existing discourses about mental health in schools. Existing mental "disorders" are classified according to criteria from the *Diagnostic and Statistical Manual of Mental Disorders* (DSM-V) developed by the American Psychiatric Association. There have been historical changes in conditions once deemed "abnormal" or "deviant" that are now accepted as "normal"; the most notable is the classification of homosexuality, which the American Psychiatric Association officially classified as a sociopathic personality disturbance in 1952 and did not remove from the DSM until 1973 (American Psychiatric Association, 2013).

Mad culture and Mad Studies developed out of the work of activists who challenged the treatment-focused method of addressing mental health challenges (Reville & Church, 2012; Schrader, Jones, & Shattell, 2013). The term *madness* was reclaimed in an effort to challenge the control that the medical model holds on the descriptions and labelling of mental states (Schrader, Jones, & Shattell, 2013). The medical model focuses on treating various socially constructed mental illnesses and prescribes interventions that are typically pharmaceutical to correct the "deviant" individuals (Rashed, 2016).

The psychiatric survivors movement (sometimes referred to as psychiatric consumer/survivor/ex-user movement) evolved from the efforts of a group that was critical of the coercive methods and perspectives within mainstream literature on mental health (Chamberlain, 1978; Schrader, Jones, & Shattell, 2013). Characterizing mental variances as impairment has contributed to sanism—or mentalism—which is the systematic discrimination against those diagnosed with a mental health disorder (Poole et al., 2012). Mad Studies advocates counter sanism by making the perspectives, histories, and experiences of those who are deemed mad central to their advocacy (LeFrançois, Beresford, & Russo, 2016).

The problem of sanism is that it can encourage low expectations from others, such as teachers and mental health professionals, related to everything from academic achievement to social functioning. The labelling of those with mental health conditions as incompetent, irrational, or violent and requiring constant supervision is a consequence of sanism (Chamberlain, 1990). Similar to neurodiversity, Mad advocates argue that mental variations are diverse identities; they criticize the medical model for marginalizing those with mental "disorders" (Beresford, Nettle, & Perring, 2010).

SHARED EXPERIENCES OF MENTAL HEALTH USERS IN EDUCATIONAL CONTEXTS

The social stigma and negative experiences post-secondary students have with formal school accommodations for mental health challenges have been well documented in the literature (Collins & Mowbray, 2005; Martin, 2010; Mowbray, Bybee, & Collins, 2001; Salzer, Wick, & Rogers, 2008). Salzer, Wick, and Rogers's (2008) study found that 56 percent of their participants who received accommodations in school reported feeling embarrassment, shame, or a fear of stigma from teachers. Forty-two percent reported that they had negative experiences when asking for or receiving accommodations. In a separate study, 63 percent of participants noted that they did not disclose their condition to educational staff (Martin, 2010). Fifty-five percent of students decided not to disclose for fear of being discriminated against. Collins and Mowbray (2005) also found that post-secondary students feared stigmatization and perceived there to be a lack of supportive programming when they registered for accommodations. Moses (2010) found that 44.6 percent of the study's participants felt rejected or devalued by some of their peers, while 10 percent felt socially isolated. Moreover, 34.8 percent of participants indicated that they were either discriminated against or stigmatized by some of their school teachers, counsellors, or staff (Moses, 2010). Arguably, Mad Studies can help us to open a space within our educational discourses for reconceptualizing how educators support and accommodate students in our classrooms.

EDUCATOR AS A "NATURAL" SUPPORT AND MENTOR

Educators' positions *in loco parentis* situate teachers as natural supports and mentors for all students, including those with mental health challenges and diagnoses. For educators to effectively fulfill roles as "natural" supports and mentors, there must be a clear understanding of what it means to be a natural support for students and diversify educational knowledge of mental health and experiences to include the expertise of neurodiversity and Mad Studies, mental health service users, and empowerment research.

Individuals build trust, membership, and companionship by interacting within social networks. "**Natural caregivers**" are individuals whom a person naturally seeks out to receive informal advice as well as emotional and instrumental support (Israel, 1985). "**Natural mentorship**" is an organic relationship that can develop within the extended family, school, and community between a caring non-parental adult and a young person (Schwartz & Rhodes, 2016). Mentors provide continual guidance, support, and instruction, and they encourage mentees to develop competence, autonomy, and character (DuBois & Karcher, 2014; Rhodes, 2002). Mentoring support includes instrumental support, such as the development of skills, and emotional support through listening, acceptance, and validation, as well as companionship (Cohen & Wills, 1985). Hamilton and Darling's (1996) study found that teachers often partake in instrumental and functional mentorship roles as they continuously challenge students to set high goals for themselves, assist them in developing a plan to meet these goals, and foster the necessary skills to achieve them.

From the perspective of Noddings's (2013) framework of caring, educators' positions as social supports create a relational ethic of caring between teachers and students with mental health challenges or diagnoses. Educators serving *in loco parentis* are social supports to, and "natural mentors of," students. In order to address their position in relation to students who are experiencing mental health challenges, teachers must become familiar with two aspects of practice. First, educators must be willing to implement classroom strategies that help facilitate an inclusive learning environment. Second, educators must support students in their social roles as community school members. Educators/mentors who seek the full development of learners with mental health challenges will investigate and address the disruptions to academic and social functioning.

EMPOWERMENT FRAMEWORK: MENTAL HEALTH AND EMPOWERMENT

Empowerment is a process that includes active participation where individuals gain greater control of their lives, acquire rights, and reduce marginalization. Empowerment also centralizes the individual's strengths and existing support systems (Peterson, 2014; Zimmerman, 1995). As a support and mentor for students experiencing mental health challenges, educators must be informed about mental and instructional strategies to support these learners. In addition, educators should also understand how to empower these students. Research has examined empowerment as a multi-dimensional construct that includes individual agency, access to resources, and an understanding of individual rights (Chamberlain, 1997; Clark & Krupa, 2002; Nelson, Lord, & Ochocka, 2001; Peterson, 2014; Zimmerman, 1995). Empowerment interventions build a strength-based framework that aims to facilitate an individual's abilities while exploring how the environment influences an individual's challenges and social problems (Zimmerman, 1995). Educators hold a level of power over their students and their students' successes within their school system. Thus, they must understand how their positions in the school's systems, as well as school systems themselves, can either contribute to or negate the empowerment processes that support student success in education and overall quality of life.

Empowerment within community mental health settings was developed from the service user movement in the 1970s. It reshaped power theory to create strength-based interventions focusing on enhancing life experiences within the community through environmental approaches and de-professionalization (Clark & Krupa, 2002). Empowerment research within a mental health context argues that there needs to be a shift from a pathological, exclusive paradigm of care to a collaborative, inclusive research approach that supports individuals within their own communities (Corrigan, 2002). Empowerment interventions utilize empowerment conditions to increase wellness, improve access to knowledge, develop skills, collaborate with professionals, and reduce problems (Zimmerman, 1995). Empowering conditions include access to basic needs, resources, and advocacy, and peer support, including personal motivation, supportive relationships, and responsive communities (Nelson, Lord, & Ochocka, 2001; Onken et al., 2002). Integrating empowering conditions within community interventions results in a more empowered and inclusive environment for all members.

EMPOWERMENT INTERVENTIONS

The reflective, individualized, and participatory nature of empowerment provides educators, school staff, and communities with the individualized insight needed to fulfill their responsibilities as social supports and mentors for students with mental health challenges and diagnoses. Empowerment theory will allow school communities to provide a space to voice shared experiences among those with varying mental health challenges and diagnoses, which will assist individual students in navigating the challenges they face when interacting within our educational institutions. During a literature review of effective empowerment interventions for service users, four key strategies were found for successful empowerment in the community:

1. emphasizing process to cultivate empowerment;
2. choosing, controlling, and independence;
3. participating in meaningful ways as contributing citizens; and
4. creating responsive and accepting communities.

Emphasizing Process to Cultivate Empowerment

Every student's school and learning experiences are unique. Each learner has different interests, past experiences, and learning preferences. The educational discourses on growth mindset emphasize the importance of risk-taking in the learning process. Similarly, rehabilitation empowerment research emphasizes the importance of using a process structure that focuses on growth, learning, and allowing mental health service users to make mistakes (Doround, Fossey, & Fortune, 2015; Frese, Knight, & Saks, 2009). Educators should recognize that students living with mental health challenges and diagnoses are experiencing a lot of changes. In addition to sharing in the learning and developmental challenges that their peers are experiencing, they are learning what it means to them (and to others) that they have a particular mental health disorder. They are also learning what supports work for them in varying contexts. Educators should work with students with mental health challenges and diagnoses to explore how they are best supported in their classrooms.

Empowerment focuses on strength-based approaches that foster personal resilience and coping techniques (Cook et al., 1996; Corrigan, 2002; Stromwell & Hurdle, 2000). Empowerment processes develop a growth mindset regarding how individuals support themselves practically, where individuals constantly re-evaluate their unique needs, capabilities, and what resources are accessible to them (Doround, Fossey, & Fortune, 2015; Frese, Knight, & Saks, 2009). As a result, students take an active position where they are allowed to voice their concerns and make decisions and mistakes. What is important to keep in mind is that through this process, students are learning how to support themselves as students and learners. This means students may not always use accommodations effectively or appropriately. It is important that educators do not take these moments personally, but instead seize them as learning experiences for students. This approach builds student resiliency within a growth mindset that focuses on the ability to improve academic ability by incremental learning. It acknowledges how, in theory, a particular support may seem ideal but may not be effective for all students or may not take all students' unique needs into consideration. This approach also addresses how different environmental factors influence the success of supports in different contexts. With this in mind, the supports educators provide for students must be flexible, continually assessed, and adaptive. They must be able to grow as contexts and student needs change.

Choosing, Controlling, and Independence

Choice, control, and independence are necessary to successful empowerment interventions (Clark & Krupa, 2002; Cook et al., 1996; Frese, Knight, & Saks, 2009; Onken et al., 2002). Empowerment interventions focus on building autonomy through a self-directed journey where mental health service users lead and control their own path to recovery, as well as make choices about how their supports are developed and implemented (Cook et al., 1996; Frese, Knight, & Saks, 2009; Onken et al., 2002). Successful recovery involves providing mental health service users with multiple opportunities and options for making choices and building decision-making skills that support their own recovery journey (Onken et al., 2002). Effective opportunities for making choices provide mental health service users with options that align and evolve with their fluctuating goals and needs (Onken et al., 2002). Along with providing mental health service users with choice and control, empowerment research in mental health emphasizes the importance of developing interpersonal skills to enable individuals to become interdependent with their social networks and natural supports (Stromwell & Hurdle, 2000). Therefore, through choice, control, and independence, mental health service users are able to create and act within partnerships with their "natural supports."

In an educational context, students and teachers work together to develop classroom interventions, accommodations, and modifications that enable students to fully participate socially and function academically. Teachers thus position themselves as "natural" mentors who assist students in making decisions by using knowledge they have as "learning experts" and student supports. As a result, students take an active position where they are allowed to voice their concerns and make decisions on an ongoing basis. In this partnership, the teacher provides continual opportunities for students to make choices, as well as develop skills to strengthen their decision-making abilities and agency.

Participating in Meaningful Ways as Contributing Citizens

Empowerment rehabilitation research emphasizes the importance of mental health service users being engaged in meaningful participation within their support system and communities (Corrigan, 2002; Frese, Knight, & Saks, 2009; Onken et al., 2002). Enabling mental health service users to develop and define their own sense of meaning, purpose, and goals is crucial for building meaningful participation in society (Onken et al., 2002). Varying opportunities and options that are aligned with personal goals are also crucial to enable mental health service users to engage meaningfully within their communities. In order to ensure that educators are empowering students in a meaningful way, it is important that the students' personal goals dictate how they participate as community members and within their classroom and school supports. It is necessary for teachers and school staff to collaborate with students to co-develop goal-oriented supports and student roles within our schools and classrooms.

Outcomes of empowerment within a community include well-developed social support systems, a sense of belonging, a meaningful contributing role in the community, a space to advocate for individual rights, and better community supports (Doround, Fossey, & Fortune, 2015; Stromwell & Hurdel, 2000). To enable students to build strong social networks, it is vital that mental health service users have interdependent, supportive, and accepting relations; access to different types of communication and social contact; as well as opportunities to experience a balance of solitude and togetherness (Onken et al., 2002). To build interdependency, it is vital that mental health service users are able to help and support others through participating as community citizens within meaningful and socially respected roles (Doround, Fossey, & Fortune, 2015).

Creating Responsive and Accepting Communities

Responsive and accepting communities are created by equitable relationships between all members of a community, ongoing respect, and understanding (Nelson, Lord, & Ochocka, 2001; Onken et al., 2002). Responsive and accepting communities are not static. They are open to new information or strategies, and they focus on "natural" supports and self-help (Nelson, Lord, & Ochocka, 2001; Onken et al., 2002). Responsive communities provide accessible resources and models that are supported by individuals, communities, and peers (Onken et al., 2002). These responsive communities provide a space for mutual peer supports, where service users can share experiential knowledge, skills, and social learning (Frese, Knight, & Saks, 2009). By allowing the voices of peer support leaders and service users in educational settings, school personnel would gain insights into the complexities that students with mental health challenges and diagnoses are experiencing in hopes of becoming continuously responsive to the needs of students.

CONCLUSION

There is a common understanding in education that educators are not mental health professionals and that they are unable to act as therapist or to administer any mental health treatments to individuals who are experiencing mental health difficulties. It is important to emphasize that educators are not responsible for mental health treatment or diagnosis. However, much discourse on mental health in school has earmarked the mental health of students as a problem that needs to be solved. Educators' positions on mental health—and their aim to "solve" the problem—has led educational practitioners, administrators, and researchers to address mental health generally within a notion of wellness and mindfulness. Further, they have begun to develop preventive school-wide initiatives to maintain positive mental health in our school communities. As a result, educational practitioners, researchers, and administrators have centred on examining predominant mental health challenges that everyone experiences, such as academic stress, anxiety, and depression. They have aimed their attention at how school personnel and educators can mediate these challenges within our school population. We must ask ourselves if these preventive and wellness initiatives are enough. Are they inclusive of, and do they support, all students in our educational institutions?

Thus far, medical perspectives have dominated educators' understanding of the identity, experiences of, and interventions for students living with a mental health disorder. These perspectives can blur the roles of medical and educational practitioners, which is problematic. As mentioned above, educators are not qualified to practice medical treatments. Additionally, if we allow medical knowledge to dominate narratives about students who experience mental health disorders and to inform the ways in which we intervene, then we limit ourselves to seeing these students' identities and experiences from a pathological and deficit perspective. Medical perspectives, treatments, and practitioners are not the only ways to support individuals living with mental health disorders. Mental health service users and survivors of mental health services argue that the notion that only individuals with highly specialized training can help, support, or understand mental health users is problematic (Jones & Brown, 2013). The *in loco parentis* position of educators, however, situates teachers in a position of natural support and mentoring for all students, including those with mental health difficulties. For educators to effectively fulfill their roles as natural supports and mentors, they must understand what it means to be a natural support for students. Further, they must diversify their knowledge of mental health and experiences to include the expertise of neurodiversity and Mad Studies, mental health service users, and empowerment research.

QUESTIONS FOR CRITICAL THOUGHT

1. Who have we left out of the discussion on mental health in schools? What mental health experiences have we neglected? What must we include in our discussion about supporting students with mental health challenges or diagnoses in education?

2. What do educators need to know to support students with mental health difficulties? In what ways are you equipped to support students with mental health difficulties or diagnoses in your classroom? What resources are at your disposal?

3. How could you use any one of the critical perspectives (disabilities studies, neurodiversity, or Mad Studies) or empowerment intervention strategies, to support students with mental health difficulties or diagnoses in your classroom?

GLOSSARY

Empowerment: A process that includes active participation where individuals gain greater control of their lives, acquire rights, and reduce marginalization. Empowerment centralizes the individual's strengths and existing support systems. Empowerment interventions build a strength-based framework that aims to facilitate an individual's abilities while exploring how the environment influences an individual's challenges and social problems.

Mad Studies: Mad Studies and culture developed out of activists' efforts to challenge the treatment-focused method of addressing mental health challenges. Madness was reclaimed by critical disability advocates to challenge the control that the medical model holds over the descriptions and labelling of mental states.

Natural caregiver(s): Individuals within a person's social support network whom they naturally seek out to receive informal advice as well as emotional and instrumental support.

Natural mentorship: An organic relationship that can develop within the extended family, school, and community between a caring non-parental adult and a young person.

Neurodiversity: A political discourse that maintains that social categories such as race, gender, ethnicity, and sexual orientation should be extended to include those for whom neurological predispositions are non-normative.

REFERENCES

American Psychiatric Association. (2013). *Diagnostic and statistical manual of mental disorders (DSM-5)*. Arlington, VA: American Psychiatric Association.

Andrews, A., McCabe, M., & Wideman-Johnston, T. (2014). Mental health issues in the schools: Are educators prepared? *The Journal of Mental Health Training, Education and Practice*, 9(4), 261–272.

Beresford, P., Nettle, M., & Perring, R. (2010). *Towards a social model of madness and distress?: Exploring what service users say.* York, UK: Joseph Rowntree Foundation.

Boksa, P., Joober, R., & Kirmayer, L. J. (2015). Mental wellness in Canada's aboriginal communities: Striving toward reconciliation. *Journal of Psychiatry & Neuroscience*, 40(6), 363–365.

Bowers, H., Manion, I., Papadopoulos, D., & Gauvreau, E. (2013). Stigma in school-based mental health: Perceptions of young people and service providers. *Child and Adolescent Mental Health*, 18(3), 165–170.

Browne, G., Gafni, A., Roberts, J., Byrne, C., & Majumdar, B. (2004). Effective/efficient mental health programs for school-age children: A synthesis of reviews. *Social Science & Medicine*, 58(7), 1367–1384.

Canadian Mental Health Association. (2018a). *Mental health resources in schools.* Retrieved from https://ontario.cmha.ca/documents/mental-health-resources-in-schools.

Canadian Mental Health Association. (2018b). *Fast facts about mental illness.* Retrieved from https://cmha.ca/about-cmha/fast-facts-about-mental-illness.

Canadian Teachers' Federation. (2012). *Understanding teachers' perspectives on student mental health: Findings from a national survey.* Ottawa: Canadian Teachers' Federation.

Centre for Addiction and Mental Health. (2018a). *Half of female students in Ontario experience psychological distress, CAMH study shows.* Retrieved from https://www.newswire.ca/news-releases/half-of-female-students-in-ontario-experience -psychological-distress-camh-study-shows-689075651.html.

Centre for Addiction and Mental Health. (2018b). *Mental illness and addiction: Facts and statistics.* Retrieved from https://www.camh.ca/en/driving-change/the-crisis-is-real/mental-health-statistics.

Chamberlain, J. (1997). A working definition of empowerment. *Psychiatric Rehabilitation Journal*, 20(4), 43–46.

Chamberlain, J. (1990). The ex-patients' movement: Where we've been and where we're going. *The Journal of Mind and Behavior*, 11(3/4), 323–336.

Chamberlain, J. (1978). *On our own: Patient-controlled alternatives to mental health system.* New York: McGraw-Hill.

Cheng, J., Benassi, P., De Oliveira, C., Zaheer, J., Collins, M., & Kurdyak, P. (2016). Impact of a mass media mental health campaign on psychiatric emergency department visits. *Canadian Journal of Public Health*, 107(3), 303–311.

Clark, C. C., & Krupa, T. (2002). Reflections on empowerment in community mental health: Giving shape to an elusive idea. *Psychiatric Rehabilitation Journal*, 25(4), 341–349.

Cohen, S., & Wills, T. A. (1985). Stress, social support, and the buffering hypothesis. *Psychological Bulletin*, 98(2), 310.

Collins, M. E., & Mowbray, C. T. (2005). Higher education and psychiatric disabilities: National survey of campus disability services. *American Journal of Orthopsychiatry*, 75(2), 304–315.

Cook, J. A., Pickett, S. A., Razzano, L., Fitzgibbon, G., Jonikas, J. A., & Cohler, J. J. (1996). Rehabilitation services for persons with schizophrenia. *Psychiatric Annals*, 26(2), 97–99.

Corrigan, P. W. (2002). Empowerment and serious mental illness: Treatment partnerships and community. *Psychology Quarterly*, 73(3), 217–228.

Devlin, R. F., & Pothier, D. (2008). *Critical disability theory: Essays in philosophy, politics, policy, and law.* Vancouver: UBC Press.

Doround, N., Fossey, E., & Fortune, T. (2015). Recovery as an occupational journey: A scoping review exploring the links between occupational engagement and recovery for people with enduring mental health issues. *Australian Occupational Therapy Journal*, 62, 378–392.

DuBois, D. L., & Karcher, M. J. J. (Eds.). (2014). *Handbook of youth mentoring.* Thousand Oaks, CA: Sage Publications.

Frese, F. J., Knight, E. L., & Saks, E. (2009). Recovery from schizophrenia: With views of psychiatrists, psychologists, and others diagnosed with this disorder. *Schizophrenia Bulletin*, 35(2), 370–380.

Goffman, E. (2009). *Stigma: Notes on the management of a stigmatized identity.* New York: Simon and Shuster.

Hamilton, S. F., & Darling, N. (1996). Mentors in adolescents' lives. In K. Hurrelmann & S. Hamilton (Eds.), *Social problems and social contexts in adolescence: Perspectives across boundaries* (pp. 199–215). New York: Aldine de Gruyter.

Isaranuwatchai, W., Rinner, C., Hart, H., Paglia-Boak, A., Mann, R., & McKenzie, K. (2014). Spatial patterns of drug use and mental health outcomes among high school students in Ontario, Canada. *International Journal of Mental Health and Addiction*, 12(3), 312–320.

Israel, B. A. (1985). Social networks and social support: Implications for natural helper and community level interventions. *Health Education Quarterly*, 12, 65–80.

Jones, N., & Brown, R. L. (2013). The absence of psychiatric c/s/x perspectives on academic discourse: Consequences and implications. *Disability Studies Quarterly*, 33.

Kessler, R. C., Angermeyer, M., Anthony, J. C., de Graaf, R., Demyttenaere, K., Gasquet, I., & Ustün, T. B. (2007). Lifetime prevalence and age-of-onset distributions of mental disorders in the World Health Organization's World Mental Health Survey Initiative. *World Psychiatry*, 6(3), 168–182.

Kirst, M., Frederick, T., & Erickson, P. G. (2011). Concurrent mental health and substance use problems among street-involved youth. *International Journal of Mental Health and Addiction*, 9(5), 543–553.

Kutcher, S., Bagnell, A., & Wei, Y. (2015). Mental health literacy in secondary schools: A Canadian approach. *Child and Adolescent Psychiatric Clinics of North America*, 24(2), 233–244.

Kutcher, S., Wei, Y., & Morgan, C. (2015). Successful application of a Canadian mental health curriculum resource by usual classroom teachers in significantly and sustainably improving student mental health literacy. *The Canadian Journal of Psychiatry*, 60(12), 580–586.

LeFrançois, B. A., Beresford, P., & Russo, J. (2016). Destination mad studies. *Intersectionalities*, 5(3), 1–10.

Malboeuf-Hurtubise, C., Lacourse, E., Taylor, G., Joussemet, M., & Ben Amor, L. (2017). A mindfulness-based intervention pilot feasibility study for elementary school students with severe learning difficulties: Effects on internalized and externalized symptoms from an emotional regulation perspective. *Journal of Evidence-Based Complementary & Alternative Medicine*, 22(3), 473–481.

Manion, I., Short, K. H., & Ferguson, B. (2013). A snapshot of school-based mental health and substance abuse in Canada: Where we are and where it leads us. *Canadian Journal of School Psychology*, 28, 119–135.

Martin, J. M. (2010). Stigma and student mental health in higher education. *Higher Education Research & Development*, 30(3), 259–274.

McGee, M. (2012). Neurodiversity. *Contexts*, 11(3), 12–13.

McGinty, E. E., Kennedy-Hendricks, A., Choksy, S., & Barry, C. L. (2016). Trends in news media coverage of mental illness in the United States: 1995–2014. *Health Affairs (Project Hope)*, 35(6), 1121–1129.

McWade, B., Milton, D., & Beresford, P. (2015). Mad studies and neurodiversity: A dialogue. *Disability & Society*, 30(2), 305–309.

Mental Health Commission of Canada. (2013). *School-based mental health in Canada: A final report*. Retrieved from https://www.mentalhealthcommission.ca/sites/default/files/ ChildYouth_Schol_ Based_ Mental_Health_Canada_Final_ Report_ ENG_O.pdf.

Mental Health Commission of Canada. (2012, February 2). Canadian news media regularly stigmatize people with mental illness. Retrieved from https://www. newswire.ca/news-releases/canadian-news-media-regularly-stigmatize-people-with-mental-illness-509548941.html.

Ministry of Education (Ontario). (2013). *Foundations for a healthy school: Promoting well-being is part of Ontario's achieving excellence vision.* Toronto: Queen's Printer for Ontario.

Moses, T. (2010). Being treated differently: Stigma experiences with family, peers, and school staff among adolescents with mental health disorders. *Social Science & Medicine,* 70(7), 985–993.

Mowbray, C. T., Bybee, D., & Collins, M. E. (2001). Follow-up client satisfaction in a supported education program. *Psychiatric Rehabilitation Journal,* 24(3), 237–247.

Nelson, G., Lord, J., & Ochocka, J. (2001). Empowerment and mental health community: Narratives of psychiatric consumers/survivors. *Journal of Community & Applied Social Psychology,* 11, 125-142.

Nelson, S. E., & Wilson, K. (2017). The mental health of indigenous peoples in Canada: A critical review of research. *Social Science & Medicine,* 176, 93–112.

Noddings, N. (2013). *Caring: A feminine approach to ethics & moral education.* Berkeley: University of California Press.

Onken, S. J., Dumont, J. M., Ridgway, P., Dornan, D. H., & Ralph, R. O. (2002). *Mental health recovery: What helps and what hinders? A national research project for the development of recovery facilitating system performance indicators.* Prepared for National Technical Assistance Center for State Mental Health Planning, National Association of State Mental Health Program Directors.

Peterson, A. N. (2014). Empowerment theory: Clarifying the nature of high-order multidimensional constructs. *American Journal of Community Psychology,* 53, 96–108.

Poole, J. M., Jivraj, T., Arslanian, A., Bellows, K., Chiasson, S., Hakimy, H., Pasini, J., & Reid, J. (2012). Sanism, "mental health" and social work/education: A review and call to action. *Intersectionalities,* 1, 20–36.

Rashed, M. A. (2016). In defence of madness: The problem of disability. *Journal of Medicine and Philosophy,* 44(2), 150–174.

Reville, D., & Church, K. (2012). Mad activism enters its fifth decade: Psychiatric survivor organization in Toronto. In E. Shragge, J. Hanley, & A. Choudry (Eds.), *Organize! Building from the local for global justice* (pp. 189–201). Toronto: PM Press.

Rhodes, J. E. (2002). *Stand by me: The risks and rewards of youth mentoring relationships.* Cambridge, MA: Harvard University Press.

Rodger, S., Hibbert, K., Leschied, A., Pickel, L., Stepien, M., Atkins, M., & Vandermeer, M. (2014). Shaping a mental health curriculum for Canada's teacher education programs: Rationale and brief overview. *Physical & Health Education Journal,* 80(3), 28–39.

Rousseau, C., Measham, T., & Nadeau, L. (2013). Addressing trauma in collaborative mental health care for refugee children. *Clinical Child Psychology and Psychiatry,* 18(1), 12–136.

Rowling, L. (2012). *Australian perspectives on findings from the national SBMHSA scan, survey and review.* Paper presented at the 3rd National Symposium for Child and Youth Mental Health, Calgary, AB.

Salzer, M. S., Wick, L. C., & Rogers, J. A. (2008). Familiarity with and use of accommodations and supports among postsecondary students with mental illness. *Psychiatric Services*, 59(4), 370–375.

Sampogna, G., Bakolis, I., Evans-Lacko, S., Robinson, E., Thornicroft, G., & Henderson, C. (2017). The impact of social marketing campaigns on reducing mental health stigma: Results from the 2009–2014 Time to Change programme. *European Psychiatry*, 40, 116–122.

Scholz, B., Crabb, S., & Wittert, G. A. (2014). "We've got to break down the shame": Portrayals of men's depression. *Qualitative Health Research*, 24(12), 1648–1657.

Schrader, S., Jones, N., & Shattell, M. (2013). Mad pride: Reflections on sociopolitical identity and mental diversity in the context of culturally competent psychiatric care. *Issues in Mental Health Nursing*, 34, 62–64.

Schwartz, S. E. O., & Rhodes, J. E. (2016). From treatment to empowerment: New approaches to youth mentoring. *American Journal of Community Psychology*, 58, 150–157.

Slaunwhite, A. K. (2015). The role of gender and income in predicting barriers to mental health care in Canada. *Community Mental Health Journal*, 51(5), 621–627.

Stromwell, L. K., & Hurdle, D. (2000). Psychiatric rehabilitation: An empowerment-based approach to mental health services. *Health & Social Work*, 28(3), 206–213.

Ward, C., Bochner, S., & Furnham, A. (2006). Stress, coping, and adjustment. In C. Ward, S. Bochner, & A. Furnham (Eds.), *The psychology of culture shock* (pp. 71–98). London: Routledge.

Wei, Y., Kutcher, S., & Szumilas, M. (2011). Comprehensive school mental health: An integrated "school-based pathway to care" model for Canadian secondary schools. *McGill Journal of Education*, 46(2), 213–229.

Whitley, J., Smith, J. D., & Vaillancourt, T. (2013). Promoting mental health literacy among educators: Critical in school-based prevention and intervention. *Canadian Journal of School Psychology*, 28(1), 56–70.

Zimmerman, M. A. (1995). Psychological empowerment: Issues and illustrations. *American Journal of Community Psychology*, 23(5), 581–599.

CHAPTER 6

The Compassionate Language Educator: Understanding Social Issues in Canadian Schools

Francis Bangou, Stephanie Arnott, Carole Fleuret, Douglas Fleming, and Marie-Josée Vignola

LEARNING OBJECTIVES

1. To provide a space to think about current issues in language education and disrupt the mechanisms that may prevent language teachers from becoming compassionate educators.
2. To generate new insights into how research and educative practices can be transformed to reimagine language teaching and learning.

INTRODUCTION

We live in an open and wired world defined in part by massive flows of information and people travelling across borders. In that regard, Canada has long been known globally for its progressive technological and immigration laws and the cultural diversity of its population. According to the latest Canadian Census (Statistics Canada, 2016), 21.9 percent of the nation's population is foreign-born (the highest percentage in 85 years), and it is estimated that immigrants could represent up to 30 percent of the Canadian population by 2036. Increasingly, these newcomers speak a diversity of languages. In fact, between 2011 and 2016, the number of people who report a native language other than Canada's official languages (French and English) rose by 13.3 percent. Moreover, in 2016 almost

20 percent reported speaking more than one language at home. Besides transforming Canadian society, these trends force the nation to ask critical questions pertaining to multilingual students' education and belonging.

Undoubtedly, within this context, developing the necessary competencies in French and English (the two official languages of Canada) is crucial to helping multilingual learners function successfully in today's Canadian society. Such a reality also forces language educators and researchers to constantly think about how to become compassionate educators who respectfully attend to the needs of these learners.

To guide readers through this reflexive journey, we will call on our experiences as second language (L2) teacher educators and researchers to think about current issues in language education and explore how to disrupt mechanisms that may prevent language teachers from becoming compassionate educators. Ultimately, we will generate new insights into how research and educative practices can be transformed to reimagine language teaching and learning.

This chapter is divided into five sections. The first section focuses on the challenges associated with becoming technology-enhanced language educators capable of attending to a mobile, ever-changing, and open-ended educational world. In the second section, the author explores how his experiences with teacher candidates in Canada have informed his teaching practices with groups of experienced English as a Second/Foreign Language (ESL/EFL) teachers from Western Chinese provinces as part of a three-month summer professional development project. More specifically, he describes how demystifying the "native speaker" has contributed to **equity** within this program. The third section is devoted to the experiences of allophone[1] students in Francophone schools in Ontario and explores how stereotypical representations of **bi-plurilingualism** can be disrupted to promote equity and success for these learners. The fourth section interrogates the capacity of French as a Second Language (FSL) teachers in Canada to become agents of change, while in the fifth section, the author examines the new linguistic reality for both **French Immersion** students and student teachers and proposes the use of a language portfolio that can help improve French language proficiency.

TEACHER EDUCATION IN TECHNOLOGY-ENHANCED LANGUAGE EDUCATION (FRANCIS BANGOU)

It is now recognized that digital technologies have transformed many aspects of our lives, including how we teach, communicate, and learn. Consequently, traditional teaching and learning practices are no longer adapted to the needs of today's learners, who increasingly do not feel stimulated in the classroom and who run the risk of moving away from the educational system (C21 Canada, 2012, 2015). It is not surprising, then, that curricula in numerous countries have been updated to ensure that pedagogical practices are in line with the societal, cultural, and technological demands of the 21st century.

This requirement has been articulated by the non-profit organization Canadians for 21st Century Learning and Innovation (C21 Canada), which recently developed a learning framework for Canada's public education systems whereby "personalized access to teachers highly skilled in 21st Century learning skills and research-based learning environments is a universal right of every Canadian learner" (2012, p. 4). It is, therefore, crucial for language teachers to possess these same competencies, as they are at the forefront of educating future generations. Such competencies include (1) the capacity to apply creative and innovative thought processes; (2) the capacity to adapt to ever-changing and complex environments; and (3) the capacity to appreciate diversity, disorder, and ambiguity (C21 Canada, 2012, 2015). Undoubtedly, within such reforms, digital technologies appear to be key enablers in achieving such competencies. Unfortunately, research shows that both pre- and in-service L2 teachers often feel under-prepared for integrating digital technologies into their practices, as they frequently struggle to enact what they have learned in their teacher education programs once they enter the classroom (Son & Windeatt, 2017). Consequently, L2 teachers fall short of providing instruction that fosters the literacy skills that students need to succeed in a complex information-based society. This shortcoming may also be due to the absence of appropriate conceptual and methodological resources to work within the complex, ambiguous, and ever-changing reality of integrating such technologies into a language classroom. In that regard, Roy argues that novice teachers often find it a challenge "to cope in a highly differentiated atmosphere, with the result that they experience great difficulties, friction, and stress" (2003, p. 5).

Hence, experts have problematized not only the appropriateness of teacher education in Technology Enhanced Language Education (TELE) but also the research practices used to help L2 teachers integrate digital technologies into their practices (Johnson, 2013). If we agree that most of the challenges faced by TELE teachers nowadays are complex, ambiguous, ever-changing, and unpredictable, then "teacher preparation deserve[s] a different kind of theoretical attention that would not merely seek regularities and order but be able to see learning opportunities in irregular spaces and moments, and in discontinuous flashes rather than in continuities" (Roy, 2003, p. 5). In that regard, Deleuze and Guattari's pragmatics (1987) seem to propose alternative conceptual and methodological vehicles in line with ever-changing and intricate phenomena. Indeed, Deleuze and Guattari created concepts to disturb reality, stimulate thinking, and allow for the creation of new possibilities for life and innovation. One of the most widespread Deleuzo-Guattarian concepts in education is the rhizome (Deleuze & Guattari, 1987). In botany, a *rhizome* refers to a root that grows horizontally by constantly establishing new connections and interconnections through experimentations in a particular context. Deleuze and Guattari used the image of the rhizome to disturb traditional linear, static, and reproductive thinking and bring to the fore rhizomatic thinking, which is non-linear, unpredictable, interconnected, experimental, and emergent.

An increasing number of Canadian scholars and educators have adopted Deleuze and Guattari's concept of a rhizome to transform education. For instance, Cormier (2012, 2016), developed the concept of **rhizomatic learning** in part to guide the design of a MOOC (Massive Open Online Course) aimed at helping students to work in complex domains where there are no best or set answers to problems. Faced with uncertainty and lack of responses from external sources, learners within the MOOC experimented together with possible solutions, and in this way, the community became the curriculum. In L2 education, Waterhouse (2016) developed the concept of rhizocurriculum to help us think differently about the relationships between teacher and students in ESL classrooms and see learning possibilities in irregularities.

The concept of the rhizome has also been used to experiment with the complexity of becoming a technology-enhanced L2 educator and to guide the design of an online course. This has been done with the aim of helping language teachers experiment with the integration of digital technologies into their practice, as well as the aforementioned 21st-century competencies (Bangou & Vasilopoulos, 2018). So far, findings suggest that becoming a technology-enhanced L2 teacher may be more complex and multifaceted than the acquisition and application of teaching and technological skills. Findings also highlight the need for a pedagogy that promotes creative intricacies, multimodal communication, ambiguity, and experimentation.

This section has focused on the necessity of rethinking and redesigning L2 teacher preparation in TELE to address the need of today's L2 learners. It also suggests a pedagogy based on the rhizome that fosters 21st-century competencies associated with creativity, complexity, uncertainty, and disorder. Such pedagogy also contributes to broader shifts in language education that support the need for methodologies and pedagogies capable of attending to the social, cultural, and educational world that is mobile, ever-changing, and open-ended.

EQUITY AND INTERNATIONAL ESL TEACHER PROFESSIONAL DEVELOPMENT (DOUGLAS FLEMING)

Since 2015, groups of experienced ESL/EFL teachers from rural and remote areas in Western Chinese provinces have taken part in three-month summer professional development (PD) projects at the Faculty of Education of a large Canadian university. These teachers work on improving their communicative teaching practices and English-language proficiency while living in the city for the summer.

I have placed questions of equity in the forefront of my work as an L2 teacher educator. My goal in this regard has been to assist the general education teacher candidates in my care in developing their understandings of how interlocking systems of domination, power, and privilege pervade L2 school curricula, educational beliefs, and teaching practices, so that they can critically evaluate various educational practices and construct viable strategies for inclusive pedagogy.

A theme that runs through all the courses I teach is an emphasis on teachers' responsibilities to critically reflect on their own personal assumptions and "to take into account the diverse histories, values, beliefs and bodies of the students who enter into today's classrooms" (Dei et al., 2000, p. 172). By challenging our assumptions and presuppositions about our students and ourselves, we can reformulate our understanding of the world (Atherton, 2011).

Given the fact that most teacher candidates are white (my own personal racial identity), I start my courses with Peggy McIntosh's well-known reflection that "as a white person, I realized I had been taught about racism as something which puts others at a disadvantage, but had been taught not to see one of its corollary aspects, white privilege, which puts me at an advantage" (McIntosh, 2005, p. 109).

As Sleeter notes, equity work by teachers, both white and of colour, can be successful when teachers "explicitly acknowledged racism in students' lives, helping them learn to critique and navigate its manifestations" (2016, p. 1065). The expansion and growth of English as an international language has increased the need to have teachers teaching the language in foreign-language contexts. This has also resulted in a marked increase in the number of non-native English-speaking teachers (NNESTs). At the international level, in fact, the number of NNESTs is now far greater than the number of native-speaking teachers of English (Brown, 2000). Due to a shortage of qualified English teachers and the need to improve the level of English in the public sector, governments have undertaken various initiatives, such as participation in PD courses abroad (Zhou & Shang, 2011).

In China, ESL educational reform has included a shift from a model of pedagogy based on traditional grammar-based teaching approaches and transmission of content to a focus on student-centred approaches based on communicative language learning (Zhang, Li, & Wang, 2013). In order to help implement this reform, the Chinese government sends veteran teachers abroad for three months to take PD courses, such as the one I manage at my institution.

As Firth and Wagner (1997) argue, the notion of the "native speaker" sets up an impossible and monolingual ideal that represents most speakers of English as deficient. Even though some scholars, such as Reyes and Medgyes (1994), argue that "native" and "non-native" teachers both have their positive places in L2 teaching, Amin (2000) and Kumaravadivelu (2016) clearly document that non-native teachers of English (such as themselves) are usually viewed as inferior to those considered native. Phillipson (1992) goes even further by attacking the very notion of a native speaker as a "fallacy" that has led to a hierarchy within the profession. This has been closely linked to the discourse that English is owned by those born and raised within the linguistic mainstream of an Anglo-American circle (Canagarajah, 1999; Norton, 1997).

The native speaker fallacy has set up a hierarchy specifically for veteran ESL/ EFL teachers who participate in the summer PD projects. This is concretely felt in terms of pay, status, and working conditions. The fallacy has encouraged the use of foreign "experts" and standardized tests such as the Gaokao. It has also reinforced neo-colonialism through the privileging of "first world" accents and dialects.

To counter this prevailing discourse, our project draws upon multilingual teaching faculty to represent the diversity of the Canadian linguistic landscape: the majority are speakers of French, Spanish, and Farsi who have taught and worked in English. Likewise, to counter the potential of a unidirectional dissemination of knowledge from (Western) teacher to learner (from the periphery), the curriculum is designed in close consultation with Chinese universities, funding agencies, and diplomatic officials. The projects are constantly redesigned and adapted to the unique professional and linguistic needs and goals of the Chinese teachers themselves.

As is continually emphasized in the lecture content and workshop facilitation, the participants are encouraged to evaluate (the multiplicity of) dominant trends within current L2 teaching theory and classroom practice so that they can determine for themselves the most useful approaches for their own teaching contexts.

In ways that are similar to the classes I teach with Canadian teacher candidates, my goal with these veteran ESL/EFL teachers from China is to develop their understandings of how interlocking systems of domination, power, and privilege pervade L2 school curricula, educational beliefs, and teaching practices, so that they can critically evaluate various educational practices and construct viable strategies for inclusive pedagogy. I want them to critically reflect on their own personal assumptions and reject the native speaker fallacy under which they labour.

ALLOPHONE LEARNERS IN THE FRANCOPHONE SCHOOLS OF ONTARIO (CAROLE FLEURET)

In Ontario, school populations are increasingly heterogeneous, as noted by Citizenship and Immigration Canada (2016). According to the same organization, more than 200,000 immigrants arrived in 2015, many of whom settled in Ontario. In 2006, out of 13 million Ontarians, there were 3.2 million allophones—people who did not speak French, English, or an Indigenous language. The school community welcomes students from, for example, Asia, Africa, and the Middle East.

The Ontario Ministry of Education (MOE) created programs[2] to support students in their learning of French in Francophone schools. However, the support provided remains parsimonious; conducted by the school board, it is measured in minutes and is based on emerging needs that are determined by a diagnostic assessment. The transition to regular class is not easy for the student who must understand a language they are learning and in which they are being taught. Such a context can only lead to linguistic insecurity and to the endangerment of an identity that is not recognized in the classroom: "denying languages already known to the speaker for ideological reasons prevents the rapid development of French language skills and increases linguistic insecurity, lack of identification in the functioning and appropriation processes in the target language" (Auger, 2013, p. 4, my translation).

Furthermore, although English and French are Canada's two official languages, the prevailing sociolinguistic context of French, namely its minoritization, reinforces the emphasis placed on the context of learning the language of schooling—that is, the language learned at school and by the school (Verdelhan-Bourgade, 2002). Indeed, the history that undeniably links French and English in Ontario remains very prevalent today (Fleuret, Bangou, & Ibrahim, 2013). As a result, children of newcomers to Canada experience a double or even triple minorization when learning or perfecting their knowledge of French (Gérin-Lajoie & Jacquet, 2008) and their social integration and academic success are undermined. Before the turn of the century, Heller (1999) had already criticized such homogenizing processes. Indeed, within such context little room is left for other languages, including English, which, according to Labrie (2007) is being denied in Ontario's Francophone schools. In short, apart from French, there is really no space for other languages within the Francophone schools of Ontario.

Thus, we have a real problem: how can stereotypical representations of bi-plurilingualism be deconstructed to reduce social inequalities and promote better success for allophone students?

This question does not call for an immediate answer because, as we can imagine, the context is very complex. However, it is intended to promote reflection on what we can do, in the short term, to better meet the needs of these students. What we mean here is to work in parallel on the training of teachers with regard to this reality and the representations of individuals. The idea is not just to speak about languages, but to use them!

In L2 education, in the wake of Cummins's seminal work (1979), numerous researchers have clearly underlined the contribution of learners' language repertoires in the acquisition of the language of schooling (Auger, 2013; Fleuret, Bangou, & Ibrahim, 2013). The idea here is to recognize the knowledge acquired by the student in their language of origin and to allow them to use it to promote transfer from one language to another through a cognitive back-and-forth. As Lahire reminds us (2008, p. 57, my translation), and what schools too often forget, is that "the relationship to socially constructed language is at the heart of academic failure." In other words, the view of the linguistic objects under study must be symbolically represented by the student, and these representations may differ from one society to another. It is, therefore, important that the student can rely on what is "already there" (Beacco & Coste, 2017, my translation) and on their previous experiences.

Given the heterogeneity of school populations, which remains our reality today, the way we must look at the teaching of French in Francophone schools in Ontario inevitably requires a didactic renewal that would allow students to make the most of their multi-literacy repertoires by adopting an inclusive and non-discriminatory perspective. This renewal inevitably involves a change in the pre- and in-service training of teachers, who would shift away from their role as experts and allow students to become experts in their own right.

FRENCH AS A SECOND LANGUAGE EDUCATION IN CANADA (STEPHANIE ARNOTT)

Language education in Canadian schools (kindergarten to Grade 12) is typically organized around Canada's two official languages, English and French. English-language school boards must offer FSL programs to give students the chance at becoming proficient in both official languages. Four different types of FSL programs exist (Red Deer Public Schools, 2014).

First, the majority of students currently learn FSL through a class commonly referred to as "basic" or Core French (CF), where they learn *about* French while attempting to acquire basic communication skills, language knowledge, and an appreciation of Francophone culture practiced in Canada and around the world. CF is typically the minimum FSL programming that Canadian English-language school boards are mandated to offer. After assessing that students were not reaching high levels of proficiency through the CF program, educational stakeholders attempted to redesign CF and devised a second FSL program called Intensive French (IF). Based on the neurolinguistic approach (Netten & Germain, 2012), an IF program reorganizes a middle school year (typically Grade 5 or 6) so that students have one intensive five-month period of literacy-based FSL study and, subsequently, continue in the regular CF program.

A third Canadian FSL program that is internationally renowned is **French Immersion (FI)**. Emerging in the 1960s as a promising way to teach the majority language (i.e., French) to Anglophones in Quebec, FI has since developed into the most highly sought-after FSL program in Canada. In FI, French is a subject of study and is also the language of instruction in at least two other content areas (see next section). A fourth FSL program format called Extended French (EF) has emerged as a way for schools to provide continued French learning opportunities for FI and CF students alike, but with fewer hours of French instruction (both language and content).

Since 2000, studies of FSL education in Canadian schools have shown a clear bias towards the FI program (Arnott, Masson, & Lapkin, 2019). Demand for FI programs is also on the rise (Canadian Parents for French, 2017). Consequently, English school boards are under pressure to offer more FI programming, resulting in a need for more FI teachers. While recent inquiries show promising insights into the present supply-and-demand challenges in FSL (see, for example, ACPI, 2018; Masson et al., in press), the debate is ongoing as to the extent to which this is an individual problem (where eligible teachers lack adequate French proficiency to teach FI), a system problem (where more incentives are needed to increase potential FI teacher mobility), or both.

Nonetheless, existing research has documented a persistent trend of FSL teacher attrition across all four program formats, attributed primarily to a chronic lack of community- and school-based support for FSL teachers, including a lack of resources for FI teachers, no classrooms dedicated to CF, CF teachers excluded from school planning meetings, and CF cancelled to accommodate other school priorities (Lapkin, Mady, & Arnott, 2009; Lapkin, McFarlane, & Vandergrift, 2006). This systemic lack of support is most prevalent in the CF program, where the majority of Canadian students learn French. Equally troubling in this respect is the well-documented trend of student attrition from CF, linked primarily to students' perceived lack of proficiency and grammar-oriented pedagogy, as well as to students having developed negative attitudes towards French and their language learning experience in schools (Arnott, in press).

Recently, noteworthy developments in the field of additional language education related to teaching, learning, and assessment highlight the potential for FSL teachers as individuals to make significant changes to FSL education in schools. In 2001, the Council of Europe published the **Common European Framework of Reference (CEFR)**, which was designed to provide European countries with a "transparent, coherent and comprehensive basis for the elaboration of language syllabuses and curriculum guidelines, the design of teaching and learning materials, and the assessment of foreign language proficiency" (Council of Europe, 2001). The mass uptake of the CEFR in Europe has led Canadian language education stakeholders to take notice, resulting in the widespread endorsement and implementation of the CEFR for language education across Canada (Council of Ministers of Education, 2010). In FSL in particular, research has shown the potential for the adoption of CEFR strategies to positively impact students' French language confidence and reorient the FSL classroom towards a more action-oriented approach (Rehner, 2014, 2017).

Still, there remains great debate on the degree to which the CEFR can and should be adapted to suit pan-Canadian needs and interests, particularly in regards to the colonial subtexts at play related to adopting a European framework for organizing Canadian language programs (Arnott et al., 2017). Research has shown that FSL teachers are limited in their ability to be compassionate educators when working conditions devalue the subject matter they are teaching, when they are treated like second-class citizens, and when promising professional development is disregarded due to the politicization of its European roots. It is equally evident that meaningful change in FSL education in Canada requires a significant paradigm shift at multiple levels of schooling (e.g., system, classroom, individual). In this vein, complexity (Larsen-Freeman, 2016) and post-structural (Deleuze & Guattari, 1987) perspectives on L2 education might be worth considering, as they show potential for learning more about how these systems interact in both productive and transformative ways (Waterhouse & Arnott, 2016).

FRENCH IMMERSION TEACHER TRAINING OF NON-NATIVE SPEAKERS OF FRENCH (MARIE-JOSÉE VIGNOLA)

French Immersion (FI) is a type of FSL program where French is the language of instruction used to teach school subjects for at least 50 percent of instructional time. It is possible to start FI at different points in the school cycle. The main goal of FI programs is to enable students to achieve functional bilingualism— a linguistic competence that allows them to access post-secondary studies in French and work in a bilingual or Francophone environment, provided that they continue to improve their skills in French (Roy, 2017).

The first FI programs were started in Quebec in the 1960s, a Franco-dominant context where English was a minority. The FI program aimed to improve FSL learning while ensuring learning of school subjects and English, the first language (L1) of the FI students of that time (Genesee, 1983). This form of FSL education spread rapidly across Canada in a linguistic context different from that of Quebec, including Anglo-dominant regions where French was a minority language. FI programs are now available in all Canadian provinces and territories (except Nunavut).

In the early years of FI in and outside of Quebec, teachers were mainly native speakers of French who taught native speakers of English. However, the linguistic reality has changed for both FI teachers and students. Concerning FI teachers, a recent pan-Canadian consultation conducted by the Association Canadienne des Professionnels de l'Immersion (ACPI, 2018) notes that a majority of FI teachers (54 percent) speak English as their first language (L1). The level of French proficiency (i.e., the language in which they teach) also emerged as an issue that concerned a large portion of participants in the consultation (63 percent), with over half of them expressing worry about the future of FI programs.

This reality of being a non-native speaker of French and teaching in FI has also been investigated in the teacher education context (Bayliss and Vignola, 2000, 2007). How should teacher educators address the fact that many FI student teachers are simultaneously language learner role models for their students and language learners themselves? How can FI student teachers maintain, develop, and improve their proficiency in French?

This new linguistic reality has also presented itself in the FI student population with the evolution of the sociopolitical context in Canada. At the beginning of FI, the target audience was mostly English speakers, and French was their L2 (Hayday, 2015). Researchers have recognized that "the dramatic increase in ethnic diversity in Canada's urban centers calls into question the notion of a monolithic culture in the school community" (Swain & Lapkin, 2005, p. 169). Indeed, more and more FI students speak an L1 that is a minority language (ML), one that is not an official language in Canada and does not have the same status.

The concepts of knowledge transfer and linguistic interdependence (Cummins, 1994) have helped to explain the experiences of English-speaking students learning FSL in FI programs. For instance, as Genesee (1983) argues, most studies have shown a high level of achievement in French-language school subjects and that students rapidly catch up in terms of their English-language skills. However, Reyes and Vignola (2015) point out that ML students in FI face a complex learning situation. In some cases, they are integrated into the school system in a kind of double immersion when they have to learn Canada's two official languages almost simultaneously (Taylor, 1992); they are also at risk of experiencing "subtractive trilingualism," that is to say, a progressive loss of their L1 (Olshtain & Nissim-Amitai, 2004).

The challenge is to adapt to this linguistic diversity while teaching Canada's second official language, which in reality can be a learner's L3 or L4. What space is given to ethnolinguistically diverse FI students? How is it possible to support and develop students' proficiency in French (the official L2) when there are so many L1s in FI classes? How is it possible to "allow for the use of multiple L1s in the classroom and celebrate the diverse cultures represented" (Swain & Lapkin, 2005, p. 182)?

A source of inspiration can be found in work from the field of sociocultural theory. Johnson writes that "a sociocultural perspective … recognizes that learning is not the straightforward appropriation of skills and knowledge from the outside in, but the progressive movement from external, socially mediated activity to internal mediational control by individual learners, which results in the transformation of both the self and the activity" (2009, p. 2). Johnson and Golombek elaborate that, for internalization to happen, "it takes prolonged and sustained participation in social activities that have a clear purpose (*goal-directed activities*) within specific social contexts" (2011, p. 3).

One proposal from recent research that could facilitate transformation and internalization is the use of a tool called "the language portfolio." Proposed as a significant part of the implementation of the Common European Framework of Reference (CEFR) (Council of Europe, 2001), language portfolios have been used by Canadian FI students (Mandin, 2010), student teachers (Arnott & Vignola, 2018), and teachers (Turnbull, 2011). The portfolio is a reflection and a self-assessment tool on language practice that allows for a realistic action plan to be developed in order to improve language proficiency. It can provide a space to reflect on a linguistic profile as well as on the native/non-native speaker dichotomy, and on what Johnson and Golombek call the "native speaker myth" (2011, p. 6). Its use by both FI student teachers and students would be a way to create an area of mutual empathy, communication, compassion, and sharing in the process of improving French as a language of teaching and learning. This is just one way that is proposed; it is necessary to reflect on this matter further in order to find other solutions.

CONCLUSION

The main goals of this chapter were to address current issues associated with language education in Canada and trouble the machineries that may affect the capacity of educators to address the needs of multilingual learners with compassion. Drawing on multiple theoretical perspectives (e.g., complexity theory, Deleuzo-Guattarian perspectives, critical theory, sociocultural theory), we have highlighted diverse elements (e.g., discomfort with uncertainty, uniform representations and practices, hyper-valorization of the native speaker) that may prevent L2 teachers and teacher educators from becoming compassionate educators. In addition, new insights were generated on how L2 research and educative practices can be partially renewed through pedagogies of uncertainty, use of language portfolios and learners' multi-literacy repertoires, critical thinking, and paradigmatic changes.

QUESTIONS FOR CRITICAL THOUGHT

1. As a pre- or in-service teacher, how does your relationship to uncertainty affect your capacity to become a compassionate educator?
2. What does it mean from a personal perspective to do crucial equity education in second language education?

3. How are policies ready for a didactic renewal that would allow students to make the most of their multi-literacy repertoires, in an inclusive and non-discriminatory way, and what choices would you have to make?
4. Can compassionate educators alone transform FSL teaching and learning in Canada?
5. How can we rethink French Immersion teacher training with regard to both student teachers' and FI learners' linguistic repertoires?

GLOSSARY

Bi-plurilinguism: A plurality of autonomous languages, whether two (bilingual) or many (multilingual) (Garcia & Wei, 2014, p. 11).

The Common European Framework of Reference (CEFR): A framework used to describe six stages of additional-language proficiency (two at the "basic user" stage, two at the "independent user" stage, and two at the "proficient user" stage); it describes what learner-users can do in their additional languages in four modes of communication, reception, production, interaction, and mediation, each in the oral and in the written form. Descriptors were originally developed for five communicative language activities (written and oral reception, written and oral production, and oral interaction) at all six stages of proficiency. Tests have been created to assess learners' competencies in different languages at each stage. A portfolio component (the European Language Portfolio) mediates use of the CEFR through language passports, dossiers, and biographies. The CEFR recommends an action-oriented approach to language teaching—namely real-life, task-based activities organized around students meeting "Can Do" goals.

Equity: Based on the notion that people who have been systematically denied financial and cultural resources because of their subject positions must make use of measures that give them access to the same opportunities as those within dominant spaces in society. Equity is thus distinct from equality, since the latter is based on the simple notion of "a level playing field" that perpetuates privilege. For a detailed discussion of the differences between these two concepts in terms of education, see Jonathan Kozol (1991).

French Immersion (FI): A type of FSL program where French is the language of instruction used to teach school subjects (mathematics, social sciences, visual arts, etc.) to non-native speakers of French for at least 50 percent of instructional time. It is possible to start FI at different points in the school cycle: the first year of elementary school (Early Immersion), between Grades 1 and 6 (Middle Immersion), or in Grades 6 or 7 (Late Immersion). The main goal of FI is to enable students to become functionally bilingual. French Immersion has had great success since its inception in 1965. It is offered in all Canadian provinces and territories (except Nunavut).

Rhizomatic learning: A way to conceive learning and teaching based on the Deleuzo-Guattarian concept of rhizome. Such a perspective promotes interconnectedness between learners, educators, and the world. It also advances learning experimentations within a curriculum that is not pre-set and constantly transformed according to circumstances. For more information, see http://davecormier.com/edblog/2011/11/05/ rhizomatic-learning-why-learn.

NOTES

1. People who did not speak French, English, or an Indigenous language.
2. The first one, called *Actualisation linguistique en français* (ALF) (Ministry of Education, 2010a), is aimed at students from families where French is not the predominant language and who have limited knowledge of it. The *Programme d'appui aux nouveaux arrivants* (PANA) targets learners who come from a country where French is the language of public administration and who "cannot [...] follow the regular curriculum for linguistic, cultural or academic reasons" (Ministry of Education, 2010b, p. 3, my translation).

REFERENCES

ACPI (Association Canadienne des Professionels de l'Immersion). (2018). Rapport final: Consultation pancanadienne. *Le Journal de l'Immersion*, 40(2), 6–31.

Amin, N. (2000). *Negotiating nativism, minority immigrant women ESL teachers and the native speaker construct* (Doctoral dissertation). Ottawa: National Library of Canada/ Bibliothèque Nationale du Canada.

Arnott, S. (in press). Giving voice to our core French students: Implications for attrition and the discourse on the benefits of learning FSL in Ontario. *McGill Journal of Education*.

Arnott, S., Brogden, L. M., Faez, F., Peguret, M., Piccardo, E., Rehner, K., Taylor, S. K., & Wernicke, M. (2017). The Common European Framework of Reference (CEFR) in Canada: A research agenda. *Canadian Journal of Applied Linguistics*, 20(1), 31–54.

Arnott, S., Masson, M., & Lapkin, S. (2019). Exploring trends in 21st century Canadian K-12 FSL research: A research synthesis. *Canadian Journal of Applied Linguistics, 22*(1), 60–84.

Arnott, S., & Vignola, M. J. (2018). The Common European Framework of Reference (CEFR) in French Immersion teacher education: A focus on the language portfolio. *Journal of Immersion and Content-Based Language Education*, (Special Issue), 6(2), 321–345.

Atherton, J. (2011). *Learning and teaching: Critical reflection*. Retrieved from http://www.learningandteaching.info/learning/critical1.htm.

Auger, N. (2013). *Vers une prise en compte du plurilinguisme/plurinormalisme à l'École française?* Paper presented at the 19th International Congress of Linguists, Geneva, Switzerland.

Bangou, F., & Vasilopoulos, G. (2018). Disrupting course design in online CALL teacher education: An experimentation. *E-learning and Digital Media*, 15(3), 146–163.

Bayliss, D., & Vignola, M. J. (2007). Training non-native second language teachers: The case of Anglophone FSL teacher candidates. *The Canadian Modern Language Review*, 63(3), 371–398.

Bayliss, D., & Vignola, M. J. (2000). Assessing language proficiency of FSL candidates: What makes a successful candidate? *The Canadian Modern Language Review*, 57(2), 217–244.

Beacco, J.-C., & Coste, D. (2017). *L'éducation plurilingue et interculturelle: La perspective du Conseil de l'Europe*. Paris, France: Éditions Didier.

Brown, H. D. (2000). *Principles of language teaching and learning* (4th ed.). Toronto: Pearson.

C21 Canada. (2012). *Transformer les esprits: L'enseignement public du Canada–Une Vision pour XXIe siècle*. Retrieved from http://www.c21canada.org/wp-content/uploads/2012/11/C21-Shifting-Minds3.0-FRENCH-Version.pdf.

C21 Canada. (2015). *Shifting minds 3.0: Redefining the learning landscape in Canada*. Retrieved from http://www.c21canada.org/wp-content/uploads/2015/05/C21-ShiftingMinds-3.pdf.

Canadian Parents for French. (2017). *French as a second language enrolment statistics 2011-2012 to 2015-2016*. Retrieved from https://cpf.ca/en/researchadvocacy/research/enrolmenttrends.

Canagarajah, A. S. (1999). *Resisting linguistic imperialism in English teaching*. Oxford, UK: Oxford University Press.

Citizenship and Immigration Canada. (2016). *Canada facts and figures: Immigrant overview permanent residents*. Retrieved from https://open.canada.ca/data/en/dataset/1d3963d6-eea9-4a4b-8e4a-5c7f2deb7f29.

Cormier, D. [dave cormier] (2012, March 26). *Embracing uncertainty—
Rhizomatic learning* [Video File]. Retrieved from https://www.youtube.com/
watch?v=VJIWyiLyBpQ.

Cormier, D. (2016). *Making the community the curriculum: A rhizomatic learning companion.*
Retrieved from https://davecormier.pressbooks.com.

Council of Europe. (2001). *A common European framework of reference for languages*:
Learning, teaching, assessment. Cambridge, UK: Cambridge University Press. Retrieved
from https://www.coe.int/en/web/common-european-framework-reference-languages/
?desktop=true.

Council of Ministers of Education of Canada. (2010, January). *Working with the Common
European Framework for Languages in the Canadian context: Guide for policy-makers and
curriculum designers.* Toronto, ON: Council of Ministers of Education of Canada.

Cummins, J. (1994). Primary language instruction and the education of language minority
students. In C. F. Leyba (Ed.), *Schooling and language minority students: A theoretical
framework* (pp. 3–46). Los Angeles, CA: Evaluation, Dissemination and Assessment
Center.

Cummins, J. (1979). Linguistic interdependence and the educational development of
bilingual children. *Review of Educational Research, 49*(2), 222–251.

Dei, G., James, I., Karumanchery, L., James-Wilson, S., & Zine, J. (2000). Representation
in education: Centring silenced voices, bodies, and knowledge. In Dei, G., James,
I., Karumanchery, L., James-Wilson, S., & Zine, J. (Eds.), *Removing the margins:
The challenges and possibilities of inclusive schooling* (pp. 171–196). Toronto: Canadian
Scholars' Press.

Deleuze, G., & Guattari, F. (1987). *A thousand plateaus: Capitalism and schizophrenia*
(B. Massumi, Trans.; original work published 1980). Minneapolis: University of
Minnesota Press.

Firth, A., & Wagner, J. (1997). On discourse, communication and (some) fundamental
concepts in SLA research. *Modern Language Journal, 81*, 285–300.

Fleuret, C., Bangou, F., & Ibrahim, A. (2013). Langues et enjeux interculturels: Une
exploration au cœur d'un programme d'appui à l'apprentissage du français de
scolarisation pour les nouveaux arrivants. *Canadian Journal of Education, 36*(4), 280–298.

Garcia, O., & Wei, L. (2014). *Translanguaging: Language, bilingualism and education.*
Basingstoke, UK: Palgrave.

Genesee, F. (1983). Bilingual education of majority-language children: The immersion
experiments in review. *Applied Psycholinguistics, 4*, 1–46.

Gérin-Lajoie, D., & Jacquet, M. (2008). Regards croisés sur l'inclusion des minorités en
contexte scolaire francophone minoritaire au Canada. *Éducation et francophonie, 36*(1),
25–43.

Hayday, M. (2015). *So they want us to learn French: Promoting and opposing bilingualism in English-speaking Canada*. Vancouver: UBC Press.

Heller, M. (1999). Quel(s) français et pour qui? Discours et pratiques identitaires en milieu scolaire franco-ontarien. In N. Labrie & G. Forlot (Eds.), *L'enjeu de la langue en Ontario français* (pp. 129–165). Sudbury, ON: Prise de parole.

Johnson, K. (2009). *Second language education*. New York: Routledge.

Johnson, K., & Golombek, P. (2011). *Research on second language teacher education*. New York: Routledge.

Johnson, K. E. (2013). Trends in second language teacher education. In A. Burns & J. C. Richards (Eds.), *Second Language Teacher Education* (pp. 20–30). New York: Cambridge University Press.

Kozol, J. (1991). *Savage inequalities*. New York: Broadway Books.

Kumaravadivelu, B. (2016). The decolonial option in English teaching: Can the subaltern act? *TESOL Quarterly*, 50(1), 66–85.

Labrie, N. (2007). La recherche sur l'éducation de langue française en milieu minoritaire pourquoi? In Y. Herry & C. Mougeot (Eds.), *Recherche en éducation en milieu minoritaire francophone* (pp. 1–14). Ottawa: University of Ottawa Press.

Lahire, B. (2008). *La raison scolaire: École et pratiques d'écriture, entre savoir et pouvoir*. Rennes, France: Presses universitaires de Rennes.

Lapkin, S., MacFarlane, A., & Vandergrift, L. (2006). *Teaching French in Canada: FSL teachers' perspectives*. Ottawa: Canadian Teachers' Federation.

Lapkin, S., Mady, C., & Arnott, S. (2009). Research perspectives on Core French: A literature review. *Canadian Journal of Applied Linguistics*, 12, 6–30.

Larsen-Freeman, D. (2016). Classroom-oriented research from a complex systems perspective. *Studies in Second Language Learning and Teaching*, 6(3), 377–393.

Mandin, L. (2010). Language portfolio: Graduates of immersion programs are revealed. *The Canadian Journal of Applied Linguistics*, 13(1), 104–118.

Masson, M., Larson, E. J., Desgroseilliers, P., Carr, W., & Lapkin, S. (in press). *Supply and demand of French as a second language (FSL) teachers in Canada*. Ottawa: Office of the Commissioner of Official Languages (OCOL).

McIntosh, P. (2005). White privilege: Unpacking the invisible backpack. In P. Rothenberg (Ed.), *White privilege: Readings on the other side of racism* (2nd ed., pp. 109–113). New York: Worth Publishing.

Ministry of Education of Ontario. (2010a). *Le curriculum de l'Ontario de la première à la huitième année (révisé): Actualisation linguistique en français*. Retrieved from http://www.edu.gov.on.ca/fre/curriculum/elementary/alf18curr2010.pdf.

Ministry of Education of Ontario. (2010b). *Le curriculum de l'Ontario de la première à la huitième année: Programme d'appui aux nouveaux arrivants*. Retrieved from http://www.edu.gov.on.ca/fre/curriculum/elementary/appui18curr.pdf.

Netten, J., & Germain, C. (2012). A new paradigm for the learning of a second or foreign language: The neurolinguistics approach. *Neuroeducation*, 1(1), 85–114.

Norton, B. (1997). Language, identity, and the ownership of English. *TESOL Quarterly*, 31(3), 409–429.

Olshtain, E., & Nissim-Amitai, F. (2004). Being trilingual or multilingual: Is there a price to pay? In C. Hoffmann & J. Ytsma (Eds.), *Trilingualism in family, school and community* (pp. 30–50). Clevedon, UK: Multilingual Matters.

Phillipson, R. (1992). *Linguistic imperialism*. Oxford, UK: Oxford University Press.

Red Deer Public Schools. (2014). *Review of delivery of French as a second language (FSL) programmes K-12 in Canada: Core French, Extended French, Intensive French*. Red Deer, AB: Red Deer Public Schools.

Rehner, K. (2017). *The CEFR in Ontario: Transforming classroom practice*. Retrieved from https://transformingfsl.ca/en/resources/the-cefr-in-ontario-transforming-classroom -practice.

Rehner, K. (2014). *French as a second language (FSL) student proficiency and confidence (Pilot project, 2013-2014)*. Retrieved from https://www.curriculum.org/fsl/wp-content/ uploads/2015/12/Student_Proficiency_Full_Report.pdf.

Reyes, T., & Medgyes, P. (1994). The non-native English speaking EFL/ESL teacher's self-image. *System*, 22(3), 353–367.

Reyes, V., & Vignola, M. J. (2015). Les élèves de langue minoritaire trilingues dans un programme canadien d'immersion française. *Revue d'éducation/Education Review*, 4(2), 22–27.

Roy, K. (2003). *Teachers in nomadic spaces: Deleuze and curriculum*. New York: Peter Lang Publishing.

Roy, S. (2017). *L'immersion française au Canada: Guide pratique d'enseignement* (3rd ed.). Montreal: Chenelière Éducation.

Sleeter, C. (2016). Wrestling with problematics of whiteness in teacher education. *International Journal of Qualitative Studies in Education*, 29(8), 1065–1068.

Son, J.-B., & Windeatt, S. (2017). *Language teacher education and technology: Approaches and practices*. New York: Bloomsbury.

Statistics Canada. (2016). *Census profile*. Retrieved from https://www12.statcan.gc.ca/ census-recensement/2016/dp-pd/prof/index.cfm?Lang=E.

Swain, M., & Lapkin, S. (2005). The evolving sociopolitical context of immersion education in Canada: Some implications for program development. *International Journal of Applied Linguistics*, 15(2), 169–186.

Taylor, S. (1992). Victor: A case study of a Cantonese child in early French immersion. *The Canadian Modern Language Review*, 48(4), 736–759.

Turnbull, M. (2011). *The Canadian language portfolio for teachers*. Ottawa: Canadian Association of Second Language Teachers.

Verdelhan-Bourgade, M. (2002). *Le français de scolarisation: Pour une didactique réaliste.* Paris, France: Presses Universitaires de France.

Waterhouse, M. (2016). Telling stories of violence in adult ESL classrooms: Disrupting safe spaces. *TESL Canada Journal/Revue TESL du Canada, 33*(10), 20–41.

Waterhouse, M., & Arnott, S. (2016). Affective disruptions of the immigrant experience: Becomings in official language education research in Canada. *International Multilingual Research Journal, 10*(1), 121–136.

Zhang, D., Li, Y., & Wang, Y. (2013). How culturally appropriate is the communicative approach with reference to the Chinese context? *Creative Education, 4,* 1–5. https://doi.org/10.4236/ce.2013.410A001.

Zhou, H., & Shang, X. (2011). Short-term volunteer teachers in rural China: Challenges and needs. *Frontiers of Education in China, 6*(4), 571–601.

CHAPTER 7

"I Just Want My Teachers to Care about Me": Compassion through Care with Refugee Students in High School Classrooms

Doug Checkley and Sharon Pelech

LEARNING OBJECTIVES

1. To begin to develop an understanding of some of the challenges faced by refugee students coming to Canadian classrooms and to identify some of the additional pressures that can be faced by high school–aged refugee students, while recognizing that each student's journey is unique.
2. To explore how a focus on care for refugee students can serve to develop trusting relationships between teachers and students, and to start gaining strategies to demonstrate care and ensure that care is received.

INTRODUCTION

Within this chapter, we hope to invite beginning educators to consider some common lived experiences of refugee students who have come to Canada, and to begin thinking about how to support these students through the concept of care. This chapter will focus on supporting high school–aged arrivals, who often face additional challenges to that of younger refugee students in navigating their entry into Canadian schools, while also frequently supporting their families

(McWilliams & Bonet, 2016). Although the focus of this chapter is on some of the obstacles unique to high school–aged refugees, the approach of care ethics and strategies recommended in order to demonstrate care are applicable to supporting refugee students of all ages.

The number of refugees worldwide is increasing (UNHRC, 2016) and will continue to increase (Dryden-Peterson, 2016), as will the number of high school–aged students being resettled in Canada (Government of Canada, 2015). A refugee, as defined by the United Nations High Commissioner on Refugees, is a person who

> owing to well-founded fear of being persecuted for reasons of race, religion, nationality, membership of a particular social group or political opinion, is outside the country of his [sic] nationality and is unable or, owing to such fear, is unwilling to avail himself of the protection of that country; or who, not having a nationality and being outside the country of his former habitual residence as a result of such events, is unable or, owing to such fear, is unwilling to return to it. (UNHCR, 2011, p. 14)

Based on this definition, the term *refugee* encompasses many cultures from around the world which, of course, makes the generalization of the refugee experience a difficult task. There are, however, commonalities to the experience of being displaced, trauma associated with that displacement, and expectations placed on teenage individuals upon arrival in Canada (McWilliams & Bonet, 2016). This chapter aims to raise awareness about some of those commonalities, and we hope that this awareness can help build empathy for students' experiences. We also call on teachers to explore what their students' personal and unique refugee experiences have been in order to co-develop an approach to support individual students. This approach is grounded in Nel Noddings's care ethics (2012a) and aims to recommend how to build trusting relationships through demonstration and acceptance of care. We hope, through exploring the concept of care ethics and offering suggested strategies in this chapter, that we can assist beginning teachers in supporting refugee students in their classrooms in order to improve their experience in Canadian schools.

CHALLENGES FACED BY REFUGEE STUDENTS

This section explores some of the challenges associated with the refugee experience in order to help raise awareness of the unique obstacles some refugee students face. Drawing on Nel Noddings's concept of care, we argue that it is essential, in developing a caring relationship with students, to understand where our students come from, what their experiences have been, and where they hope to go. The following examples outline some shared commonalities amongst refugees, but it is imperative to remember that each student's experience, including refugee students, is unique and therefore must be investigated individually.

Pre-Resettlement Experiences

Although it is well documented that many refugee youth demonstrate enthusiasm for academic success upon arrival in North America, refugee students can also carry with them a plethora of experiences that can create obstacles to their academic success, their opportunity to graduate, and their opportunities for post-secondary education (MacNevin, 2012). Amongst refugees, as with immigrant populations, there is often a belief that education—particularly post-secondary education—is the key to a new life free from poverty, persecution, and fear. This should come as little surprise, as the value of education is one often put forth by educational systems themselves (McWilliams & Bonet, 2016).

Refugee students expect to succeed in school and build a better life for themselves and their families, and this expectation is well warranted. The desire to succeed in school and be prepared to undertake post-secondary education is, however, not without complications. One of the major differences between refugee students in North America and immigrant students is their experience prior to arrival. Immigrants generally come to Canada from their families' home country. Refugee students, however, have generally spent a period of time in an additional asylum country, closer to home than to their new country. Dryden-Peterson (2016) defines this as the **pre-resettlement experience**, and although limited research has been done with regard to these experiences, it is clear that they are diverse and unique to individuals and small groups. Within these pre-resettlement experiences, the time frame spent in pre-resettlement, access to education, quality of education, and consistency of education are all varied. Some students will have been born in refugee camps and will have spent their entire life in a pre-resettlement camp before coming to Canada, while others may have spent only minimal time there before being resettled. Within the pre-resettlement experience spectrum, some refugees are grouped in camps while others are fully integrated into another country. Therefore, some students may have had access to regular educational systems, while other students may have been educated by whoever was available within their own camp population.

With this understanding, we can better realize that some students who have arrived in Canada may have had the following: limited or no access to education, gaps when teachers were not available, education under untrained individuals, and limited access to educational resources.

Furthermore, refugee students often bring with them experiences of war, violence, loss, and the residual effects of prolonged physical and economic hardships. This experienced trauma results in difficulties associated with both physical and mental health (McBrien, 2005; McWilliams & Bonet, 2016). Within our own teaching experience, the vast majority of our refugee students had witnessed the loss of an immediate family member, often by violent or preventable means, prior to their arrival in Canadian high schools. Classroom teachers will not necessarily be trained to counsel students about their experienced traumas, nor will they be expected to; but an awareness of students' lived realities prior to arriving in the classroom helps to establish and demonstrate care. Strategies for investigating past experiences and demonstrating care will be explored in a later section.

High School–Aged Arrival

The interrupted and often inconsistent nature of pre-resettlement education can create obstacles to the appropriate placement of students in high school classrooms (Dryden-Peterson, 2016). For students in general, course placement is usually dependent on age and previous assessment. With refugee students, administrators need to consider age, language level, previous content knowledge, and need, but students are also often limited to what courses are available to them. This becomes complicated in schools with limited opportunity to provide sheltered language-focused classes (like ESL). As a result, refugee students are often placed in classes that are age appropriate but that require greater literacy skills from them than what they currently possess. Moreover, the curriculum in those classes assumes past knowledge from previous grades, which they do not necessarily have. Additionally, there may be little information available about the students' past academic work. If transcripts and report cards are unavailable, students can also be placed below levels they are capable of.

If the students arrive at the age for high school, they may be faced with language and cultural differences, and also with school system differences. They often need to learn to navigate a whole new system of curriculum, styles of pedagogy, and teacher expectations. Teachers can often incorrectly assume that their refugee students are either content with their level of understanding or unengaged because they are quiet in the classroom (Dryden-Peterson, 2016).

However, the student's good behaviour and a practice of not asking questions may have been an expectation in the student's previous school experiences and does not necessarily mean that the student either understands the material or does not desire support.

Refugee students who arrive in Canada at the high school age face additional challenges to that of younger refugees. As young adults with access to education, refugee teens often have many adult expectations placed on them, such as being a source of income for their families (McWilliams & Bonet, 2016). The dual expectations of finding enough academic success in school to pursue a professional career, while also providing for their family, can be daunting. High school–aged refugees can often be considered the leaders of their family, particularly in situations when one or more of the parents are absent. Because the high school–age refugee has an opportunity to learn the local dominant language through school, the student's family often also expects this adolescent to work in addition to going to school. It is not uncommon for some of our students to work 40 hours per week while attending school full-time. This leaves little time for study, let alone sleep, which can compound physical and mental health issues associated with the pre-resettlement experience (Dryden-Peterson, 2016).

Additional to the "bread winner" expectations, students often become the families' cultural brokers. Their attendance is required by the family at doctors' appointments, immigration meetings, and school meetings for younger siblings to serve as both language and culture translator. These students are also sometimes the family chauffeur since they often have an easier time navigating the process of passing a written exam and acquiring a license than do their parents. All of these demands can result in students' absence from the classroom.

Many of the challenges explored here are often experienced by students who have, because of their age, only a limited number of eligible school years left in public education to develop their language to a level that would allow for successfully completing classes, gaining credit, and graduating. For teachers, many of these difficulties create obvious challenges in how to circumvent language and cultural barriers, address content knowledge and gaps in schooling, and still serve the needs of all their other students. Strategies to support refugee students will be explored at the conclusion of this chapter, but we reiterate here that a focus on getting to know the students' unique past experiences, their present situations, and their future goals is an essential first step in both supporting refugee students and in demonstrating care. It is important to note that students may not wish to share all of their past experiences with their teacher, as they may not want to revisit traumatic events. But having the students share what they are willing is a healthy first step.

CARE ETHICS CASE STUDY

This section on care ethics is grounded in Nel Noddings's (1984) work *Caring: A Feminine Approach to Ethics and Moral Education.* In it, we focus on how demonstrating care helps to establish relationships that allow beginning educators opportunities for gaining a deeper understanding of the unique needs of refugee students. Noddings (2012b) and others (see Held, 2006; Wilde, 2013) emphasize that we must both demonstrate and receive acknowledgement of care for a truly caring relationship to exist and, further, that care is relational at its core. Like care, Noddings argues, education is also fundamentally relational. As a result, it would make sense that care and education would have a natural connection, but in reality, the concept of care doesn't always take precedence in schools or teacher education programs (Wilde, 2013). Drawing on our experiences as both educators and researchers, we argue care ethics is an important component in supporting refugee students' success.

Case Study: One Student's Experience of Arrival

To demonstrate the critical need for Noddings's understanding of care ethics, this section details a case study of a former refugee student (who has since moved on to post-secondary education) and his experience in the high school setting. In investigating the experiences of one of my (Doug Checkley's) former students, I undertook a narrative exploration of his journey from a Nepal refugee camp, to a Canadian high school, to eventual enrollment in a Canadian university. We share an excerpt from his story here to demonstrate an individual refugee's experience of arriving in a Canadian high school and to illustrate the uniquely difficult experience he had in doing so. We follow this with an interview excerpt that expresses how this student sees care as the essential support for refugee students.

Hamal's First Days in Canadian Schools

For his first semester in a Canadian school, Hamal was enrolled in ESL (English as a Second Language) classes. His entire day was composed of classes that focused on language acquisition, reading comprehension, and a small amount of social studies curriculum. Being the only Nepalese student in the school was not without difficulty, and Hamal recalled one event that was quite painful.

Within his first few days of being at school, Hamal's class was to go on an off-campus field trip for an extended period of time. Unfortunately, since Hamal was still trying to navigate the busing system, he arrived late to his class only to find the class had left without him. When he arrived at his classroom to find a closed door and, upon opening it, the lights off, an initial panic set in. Hamal had no idea where his class had gone. Although the trip had been announced in class, he had not understood the significance of what was said since his English was still extremely limited. With his class gone, he had no guidance on the next steps; he did not know who he should talk to or where he should go. He only knew where to find his classroom after marking the route from the front door to his classroom on the first day. He could not, on his own, find the school office in the labyrinthine building he found himself in. Added to this was a real fear of discipline around being late for class, since this was deemed a serious infraction in his home school. As a result, he found himself *alone*—truly alone, as no one he knew within the school, or even Canada, could be easily found. He had no phone to contact family, and even if he had one, he would have been reluctant to use it for fear of letting his parents down.

Hamal had only met a couple of adults in the building—his ESL teacher and an administrator—but with the teacher gone and the office location unknown, there were few options for seeking support. At this point in his journey, his conversational English was also non-existent, so reaching out to a passing student or adult added additional fear: What if they could not understand him? What if it brought on punishment? Recognizing his limited options, Hamal sat down on the cold, hard, laminated floor outside the ESL classroom. There he waited for three hours, by himself, in a country literally on the opposite side of the world from his friends and home. From the fear rooted in being late, letting his parents down, and not being confident in conversing with strangers, he began to feel the tears well up. Many strangers, including the adults in the school, walked by but steered a wide berth around Hamal to avoid this unusual situation. Since Hamal was the first Nepalese refugee arrival, he reflected that they likely did not know how to help him any more than he knew how to ask for assistance. This was one of the most difficult experiences of Hamal's life—more difficult than life in a refugee camp. He had never felt so alone. In fact, in Nepal, he rarely had an opportunity to feel alone on account of the interconnected nature of the refugee camps. There was always a friend or family member to talk to and seek support from. It brought home to Hamal the need to have friends, connections, and support or positive relationships within school. There he waited until, eventually, his class returned. Quickly hiding his emotions, Hamal entered the class with the others and carried on the rest of the day as though all was well. He was relieved that it appeared he was not in trouble, but all the while, he kept silent about his painful experience.

"I Just Want My Teachers to Care about Me"

The above narrative was generated through one section of an in-depth interview that explored Hamal's experience from refugee camp to university. In concluding the interview, I posed this question to my former student: "What do you want teachers to know about your experience that may help other refugee students?" What follows is an excerpt from the transcript of his response:

> Everybody wants people to care about them, right? Not just teachers, but everybody. Obviously, you want to feel cared about, when you go to school, you want to feel that you're valued. If you go to [the] classroom and you have no friends, nobody to talk to, and your teacher doesn't care how you're doing, and nobody ask you nothing, obviously, you don't want to go to that class. Chances are you'll skip that class. So obviously, I think, I think teachers should care about their students, not just the ESL students, all their students, but it's just for the ESL students, you have to show them that you care, because they are from different backgrounds, right? *The way they show care back home can be different than the way you care here.* The culture, not just cultural, so many different things you have to consider, you might be caring, but at the same time, the students should know that you're caring. That's important I think, I just want my teachers to care about me, and to see how I'm doing, and to know why I'm doing what I'm doing. That is all I would want from my teacher. (Emphasis added)

In examining this section of the interview, we can clearly see the importance of care. Hamal's response also highlights the importance of cultural sensitivity when demonstrating care. In speaking about care, he described teachers offering help, knowing him, and understanding his goals. A teacher can help create a sense of comfort for their students by developing their relationship with their students and coming to know them (Due, Riggs, & Barclay, 2016). Hamal not only speaks to the importance of care, but also highlights that the teacher must make that care explicit: "You have to *show them* that you care." This means important work needs to be done to understand how to demonstrate care to refugee students, as Hamal indicated: "The way they show care back home can be different than the way you care here." Hamal's understanding supports Noddings's work in that the most important factor in his experience for supporting refugee students is the need for teachers to both care and understand how to demonstrate that care to their students. As this student wisely stated, this should be done for *all* students.

Care Ethics

To understand how to demonstrate care to refugee students, it is important to revisit the language of care ethics. Noddings (2012b) defines care ethics, first, as a relational ethic: a relation between the *carer* and the *cared-for*. These two actors, or roles, have responsibilities in maintaining the relation. Noddings states that it is essential that the carer, the person demonstrating care, is perceptive about the cared-for, the person to receive care. This understanding is necessary for the carer to recognize the **expressed needs** of the cared-for. To develop this understanding, through conversation and observation, the carer must be empathetic in listening to and observing the needs of the cared-for. Noddings applies a specific meaning to empathy in the ethic of care: "Empathy may be thought of as 'reading' of the other that engenders both feeling and understanding" (2012b, p. 55). Here, empathy is not projection, it is *feeling with* the cared-for. This places the emphasis on the extent to which teachers come to know their students: where they are coming from (their past experiences); where they are emotionally (physically and academically); and where they hope to go (their goals and aspirations).

Following this empathetic experience, it is then the responsibility of the carer to act upon the needs expressed by the cared-for, if possible. Noddings notes that not all needs can be met—ethically, physically, emotionally, or structurally—but it is the responsibility of the carer to do their best. The cared-for's responsibility, in contrast, is modest but crucial: "[They respond] in a way that shows that the caring has been received, recognized…. Without this response, there is no caring relation no matter how hard the carer has worked at it" (Noddings, 2012b, p. 53). With refugee students, this demonstration of reception can be non-verbal (e.g., positive body language) as well as verbal. Noddings emphasizes that without this relation, and the responsibilities being fulfilled, there is no care ethic being met. She contrasts this to *virtue caring*: the intention of care, without the reception, is not care.

Noddings (2012b) also makes a distinction between natural care and ethical care. Natural care occurs for teachers, parents, and spouses, when the care is easily given and readily accepted. Ethical care is present when the need is not easily met, and/or the response is not easily received. Included in ethical care is a need for authenticity. Noddings writes, "We have to show in our own behavior what it means to care…. Our caring must be genuine; the inevitable modeling is a by-product" (2012a, p. 431). Care for refugee students must be authentic, not formulated, and with the obstacles to their success explored above, teachers will not necessarily easily give it, nor will students necessarily readily accept it.

To assist teachers in the process of developing a care ethic, it is important to determine the available supports in the school, district, and community, a strategy explored in the concluding section.

To determine what care looks like for refugee students, **receptive listening** is key. Indeed, "Receptive listening is a powerful intellectual tool. But, from the perspective of care theory, it is more than that; it is the basic attitude that characterizes relations of care and trust" (Noddings, 2012c, p. 780). In following Noddings's care ethics, spending time listening to students' stories of experience and expressions of their needs, a teacher can develop trust and demonstrate care for their students.

Noddings (2005) highlights the importance of considering two types of student needs: expressed needs (needs originating from the student) and **inferred needs** (needs that teachers presuppose students to have). To outline the relationship between inferred and expressed needs, we offer an example. As an inferred need, a teacher could assume a student needs to record answers for an assessment in an audio, rather than written, format. The decision to employ this method may be grounded in the teacher's previous assessments of the student's work, in which the student demonstrated a greater aptitude for presenting their knowledge orally. This assumption is made by the *teacher* whose intent is to help their *student*. Alternatively, as an expressed need, a *student* could make a request to audio record their answers as a form of assessment, knowing that they are more comfortable speaking than writing in English. The same need is being addressed in both these examples, but they are originating from two different sources: the inferred need is from the teacher, while the expressed need is from the student.

It is important to highlight that Noddings (2005) does not valuate expressed needs over inferred needs. Inferred needs are often grounded in educational research and practical experience, therefore representing important needs. Rather, she demonstrates that there is often a tendency for teachers and researchers to rely primarily on inferred needs. As a result, by investigating the expressed needs, students' inferred needs are also strengthened. Most importantly, exploring expressed needs is critical for avoiding unmet needs that, unaddressed, might result in negatively impacting the students' learning experience. Beginning educators can deepen their understanding about how to best support refugee students' learning through exploring with the students their needs for optimal learning. As a result, over time, teachers will gain a wide variety of techniques that can be applied to future teaching situations.

With refugee students, it is also important that teachers inquire about their goals, both academic and non-academic, in the classroom. Noddings (2005) notes that teachers rarely ask students what their academic goals are, and what they are willing to contribute to achieve them, and in doing so, miss an opportunity to determine the student's expressed needs. With knowledge of those needs, the student and teacher together can create a success plan of expectations and needs to achieve the student's definition of success in the course. Success plans offer hope, and the hope to build their language skills, rather than frustration and hopelessness with curriculum and assessment that can often expand past their current abilities.

SUPPORTING REFUGEE STUDENTS WITH CARE

With over 17 million refugees worldwide (UNHCR, 2016), stemming from countries and cultures around the world, it is difficult to propose a singular method of supporting refugee students' academic success. Instead, this section offers strategies for supporting refugee students by establishing relationships and demonstrating care, which may create the foundation the students need to find a path for individual academic success. These suggestions are grounded both in research literature and in practical experience.

Student-Teacher Conferences

As Noddings (2005) outlines, it is essential in a caring relationship to establish trust through receptive listening—that is, asking open-ended questions and paraphrasing what the students share to ensure understanding. The process of receptive listening requires empathetic attention to refugee students as they explore any experiences they are willing to share. Teachers should explore with their students three key aspects: past experiences, current needs, and future goals and aspirations.

When exploring past experiences, even if the discussion is focused primarily on educational experiences, it is important to understand that these experiences can include deep trauma (McBrien, 2005). It is often not in the best interest of the students to ask them to recall all of their past experiences, instead letting them choose to share what they are willing. It is important to have available resources for the students, such as school counsellors or external support agencies, in case their shared experiences call for additional support. Additionally, if the student's language may cause difficulty in exploring this experience, seeking out a translator may be appropriate. This can be done with the assistance of immigrant services within the school and community, or within the student's own community. We suggest beginning this exploration by speaking with the students about what their educational experience was like before coming to Canada, including determining what the school looked like both in their home and during their pre-resettlement experiences.

The following are suggested questions teachers can use to help explore a student's previous educational experiences:

1. What language was school taught in?
2. What subjects were offered?
3. How often did you go to school in a week?
4. Were there times that you did not attend school?
5. How did you feel about school? What were you best at? What was the most difficult for you?
6. Outside of school, what topics/subjects did you like to learn about?

After teachers explore past educational experiences, a conversation about the student's current life can offer insight into what the student's responsibilities and needs are. This can help determine effective supports that can be offered to the student. Again, we offer some initial questions teachers can ask to focus the discussion on a student's current situation:

1. What do you enjoy most about this school?
2. Are you working? What responsibilities do you have outside of school?
3. What is the most difficult aspect of school for you right now?
4. Are there programs/clubs/activities you wish the school had?
5. Is there anything that you think I could do to better support you in this class?

Lastly, it is important to discuss what the student's current and future goals are. This will assist teachers in understanding what students want to accomplish through their education and what they are willing to contribute. Moreover, teachers can, as Noddings (2005) describes it, move a student's vague want into a felt need by establishing a success plan that the student and teacher can agree on to meet those needs. The success plan should include the agreed-upon responsibilities of both student and teacher. Some questions to assist in this process are as follows:

1. What are your goals in school, and what is your goal in this class?
2. What supports do you think will help you reach that goal?

3. What would you like to do after high school?
4. What do you need from me to support these goals?
5. What are you willing to do to reach these goals?

These initial meetings, and the success plans produced, establish a relationship and demonstrate that the teacher cares about what the student's needs are, and that the teacher is working to support the student. It is important to revisit these success plans through the course and reassess whether both parties are meeting their responsibilities, or if the goals need to be revisited. It is therefore important to establish during this initial meeting when subsequent meetings will take place. It is also important that the student and teacher both understand that there can be flexibility from both sides about the desired outcomes.

Understanding Available Supports

In the previous section, we mentioned that it is important to be connected not only to internal school counselling and wellness supports but also to external supports such as immigrant services. These supports, committed to helping refugee students in need, will help teachers navigate their way through situations in which teachers may not otherwise be comfortable or feel capable. Within the school or district, there may be additional support through lead teachers and specialists who can offer guidance to teachers working with refugee students. It is important that a teacher seeks out and determines what supports are available. As a former administrator (Doug Checkley) and a former counsellor (Sharon Pelech), we do suggest that one can start by approaching administrators and counsellors within the school to determine what supports are available. Scheduling an opportunity to work with specialists can deeply inform teachers' practices, as they will often understand the context of the local refugee populations.

Home Visits

An effective way of connecting with parents or guardians of refugee students is to offer to make home visits. Within refugee populations, there can be a reluctance from parents about coming to school to meet with teachers and school personnel. This reluctance can be brought on by past experiences with state persecution, poor experiences with a particular school, concerns about language barriers, work conflicts, and transportation issues (Georgis, Gokiert, Ford, & Ali, 2014). As a result, in order for teachers to have the opportunity to engage with parents, it is sometimes easier to visit them at home. Below are some essential considerations one must undertake before taking on a home visit:

1. Check with an administrator in the school for permission to inquire about a home visit; there may be a specific policy respecting home visits.
2. Always make sure that a home visit will be welcomed. Call and establish an appropriate time; communicate through the student if needed. Always check with the student about visiting the parents at home.
3. Never go alone—this is standard for any home visit for any student. Options for accompaniment can include an administrator, a counsellor, or possibly an immigrant services liaison.

Depending on the number of refugee students a teacher is working with, we do not necessarily suggest home visits for every student. However, if concerns about a student's engagement or attendance are arising, this connection can be helpful. It is important to come from a position of support, not discipline, in order to demonstrate care and help foster a positive parent-teacher relationship. Always discuss a home visit with a student first to establish if this may cause undue stress on the student or in their home. Once you have secured the student's agreement, a home visit can provide an excellent opportunity to communicate with refugee parents about how school operates in Canada, expectations of students, and the reality of struggles their child might face. Parents may have overwhelming expectations for their children to work 40 hours a week, support their families as cultural brokers and chauffeurs, and achieve academic success in order to become a doctor or lawyer. Home visits can allow for the management of those expectations and facilitate communication about realistic expectations. At the very least, home visits can provide teachers with the opportunity to offer a description of what an "average" student experiences in schools. Administrators, counsellors, and immigrant services liaisons can offer assistance in these discussions. Their experience in relevant matters means they may have the right level of sensitivity and cultural understanding for navigating these conversations. Home visits can demonstrate support for students and can help to establish trust and a sense of care.

Communicate Often and Purposefully with Students

As mentioned earlier, teachers may misperceive refugee students as either understanding the curriculum or, conversely, being unengaged because they are sitting quietly in the classroom and not asking questions. This behaviour may actually reflect their understanding of expectations in their previous schooling rather than indicate their comprehension of, or disengagement from, the current setting. It is important for teachers to be cognizant of the reality that school can look very different in other counties, and that the appropriate behaviour and expectations in Canadian schools can differ greatly from refugee students' past experiences.

It is also important to explore refugee students' understanding of concepts by checking in with them about their learning in a variety of ways. When doing so, have them demonstrate what they have learned rather than simply asking if they understand. The latter may simply receive an answer of "yes" to avoid embarrassment. Therefore, expectations must be made clear, and classroom skills, such as group work, must be taught. It is important to encourage refugee students to ask questions in class, engage in discussions and group work, and take part in hands-on learning activities. All of these pedagogical strategies may be novel to students, and therefore should be taught, encouraged, and reinforced.

Utilize Past Experience and Knowledge

It is important not to dismiss past knowledge that the refugee students bring to their classrooms (MacNevin, 2012). Instead, find ways to celebrate diversity and allow for students to talk about their past experiences, where comfortable, in class. For example, if looking at refugee issues in a social studies classroom, who better to shed insight on the lived reality of refugees than refugees themselves? This experience of sharing can serve not only as a powerful pedagogical tool but also as a means to connect refugee students to their classmates and, as a result, build empathy for the refugee population within a school. One only needs to listen to the current rhetoric on refugees in the politics of Canada and other countries to know that there is a lot of negativity presented about refugee populations.

In order to demonstrate care for refugee students, it is essential for teachers to make their classroom and school a welcoming and safe place. Celebrating the students' experiences and cultures within the classroom and school supports this. Start by discussing with the students what, if anything, they would be willing to share about themselves and their community—and in what form, to what degree, and where within the school would they like to do so. Examples we have experienced include classroom and professional development presentations on the refugee experience, potluck meals of cultural cuisine with the staff, performances of cultural dances in school dance performances, intramural soccer and badminton, and celebrating a religious holiday schoolwide. It is essential to let the students dictate what they are comfortable with, always understanding the traumas that can be associated with their past experiences. All of these strategies are aimed at bridging the gap between refugee and non-refugee students—often a challenge in schools.

Curriculum, Instruction, and Assessment

It is possible to demonstrate care for refugee students through curriculum focus, instructional practice, and assessment methods, even if these modes are less obvious conduits of care for educators. In meeting with students and determining their goals for the course, it is important to understand what the students are focused on. Do they hope to improve language, gain credit, or achieve a high academic standard? When students are high school age when they arrive in Canada, they may not have the educational background and skills to be successful in completing classes for credit. If they would rather focus on language or development of certain skills, modifying the curriculum to meet the students' current needs demonstrates care: the student is able to utilize the time spent in the classroom for growth. The need for modification of curriculum may not be readily apparent to the student or to the teacher, and therefore, after initial assessments occur, the goals for the course may need to be modified.

In instruction, it is important to remember that the pedagogical strategies employed in students' past educational experiences can greatly differ from the teacher's own practice in the Canadian school. Therefore, it is important to consider in what classroom and language skills the refugee students will require instruction and coaching. When lesson planning, it is important to bring in these considerations alongside other inclusive practices that are being employed on the students' behalf. Remembering that a language barrier is almost always a factor for refugee students, teachers can include hands-on experiential learning, which can reduce the translation of language a student needs to undertake to explore a concept. Where possible, if students can experience their learning without language, or with visuals alongside language, they can make better connections between their own language and the language of the subject and root their understanding in experience (Østergaard, 2015).

Encouragement of one-on-one opportunities for learning will also offer time for the teacher to assess the student's understanding, through the discussion of learning outcomes. Depending on the school, this can be within class time, or include before and after school times, lunch time, and/or independent learning times. Within one-on-one learning time, it is important for teachers to provide opportunities for students to demonstrate their learning in a variety of ways, and to continue to explore possible gaps in students' understandings in order to help them successfully meet their goals.

When assessing refugee students, teachers can offer a choice in modality, to provide opportunity for the students to find a means to best demonstrate their understanding. Utilizing scribes, readers, or technology where possible can assist refugee students in effectively communicating their understanding. Many refugee students will find it easier to communicate in spoken language than in written one. As a result, if the writing itself is not being assessed, allow the students to create a video file on a smartphone or tablet to assess the students' understanding of particular concepts. Again, these skills may need to be taught, but in doing so, the teacher offers the students their best opportunity to address the learning outcomes.

Learn about Their Culture and Language

By taking the time to learn about their students' culture and language, teachers can impact relationships within the classroom in two important ways. First, by being curious and learning about their students' cultures, teachers are demonstrating a deep sense of care about who the students are and what is important in their communities. Second, taking this time allows the teachers to model to their students how difficult the process of learning a new language and culture can be for anyone. When teachers struggle through pronunciation of the students' languages and seek their support to correctly use terms, the teachers are modelling that it is okay to fail and that it is common to seek support in learning a new culture and language. We are not calling for immersion in a language but an attempt to understand common words and phrases such as "hello," "thank you," "good job," and "I'm sorry."

When teachers understand students' cultural norms and occasionally draw on them in the classroom and in other exchanges, students often feel appreciative and more trusting of their teachers. These actions may even facilitate the students' academic success (McBrien, 2005). Some examples include becoming aware of and demonstrating different needs for physical space, mirroring body language, and following cultural norms for formal greetings. Additionally, when teachers reference popular culture from their students' homes, they help to establish relationships between teachers and their students: music, movies, and stories can be shared in a reciprocal learning experience where the teacher is modelling the experience of learning about a different culture. It is essential in undertaking this learning that the teacher and the student together determine appropriate times to discuss and use these learning opportunities. For example, students may not appreciate being greeted in their own language in front of the whole class, but they may appreciate it when they are interacting one-on-one.

All of the above strategies are focused on establishing trust, demonstrating care, and strengthening the relationships between refugee students and teachers. Most of these practices can be adapted to students in general, but here, the focus has been on supporting refugee students. It is important to note that all the strategies begin with talking with refugee students, which can be initially difficult for myriad reasons including language barriers and lack of trust. It is important for teachers to be resilient and to be committed to connecting with students, establishing their trust, listening to their needs, and respecting their comfort levels when employing strategies from one-on-one situations to school-wide involvement.

CONCLUSION

Refugee students face a variety of obstacles in transitioning to Canadian classrooms, which can include but are not limited to language barriers; trauma associated with displacement and living conditions in pre-resettlement situations; gaps in, limitations of, and absence from formal schooling for significant time periods; differences in pedagogical approaches; and cultural differences that need to be navigated to feel welcome and safe in Canadian schools. High school–aged students have additional expectations placed on them by families, schools, and themselves to serve as the cultural broker for their families; obtain work and support their families; and find success in school to pursue post-secondary education.

In order to support navigating these obstacles, we stress that educators need to develop trusting relationships with their refugee students through a continual demonstration of care. To initiate that demonstration of care, we support exploring students' past and current lives, and what their future aspirations are. This may require the assistance of translators or outside services like immigrant services. Beginning educators need to determine what supports for educators exist within their schools, districts, and communities in working with refugee populations and take advantage of those supports. Strategies such as home visits, focused communication, utilizing past experiences, modifying curriculum and assessment, and developing cultural awareness can be effective in demonstrating care and assuring acceptance of that care. Supporting refugee students is another challenging aspect of teaching, but with commitment to care, teachers can improve the experience for both the refugee students and for themselves.

QUESTIONS FOR CRITICAL THOUGHT

1. What challenges faced by refugee students that were explored in this chapter were surprising to you? How may this affect your approach to supporting refugee students?
2. What do you anticipate being the biggest challenge in demonstrating care for your refugee students and in receiving acceptance of that care? What can you do to mitigate those challenges?
3. What strategies are you aware of from other courses and experiences that are effective for demonstrating care? Do you anticipate those strategies could be used with refugee students?

GLOSSARY

Expressed needs: Needs that are stated in words or behaviour by the individual said to have the need.

Inferred needs: Needs that originate in someone other than the individual said to have the need.

Pre-resettlement experiences: Refugee experiences before permanent settlement in another country.

Receptive listening: Open and vulnerable attention to the experiences shared, where the listener feels with the speaker empathetically.

REFERENCES

Dryden-Peterson, S. (2016). Refugee education in countries of first asylum: Breaking open the black box of pre-resettlement experiences. *Theory & Research in Education*, 14(2), 131–148. https://doi.org/10.1177/1477878515622703.

Due, C., Riggs, D. W., & Barclay, K. (2016). Care for children with migrant or refugee backgrounds in the school context. *Children Australia*, 41(3), 190–200. https://doi.org/10.1017/cha.2016.24.

Georgis, R., Gokiert, R. J., Ford, D. M., & Ali, M. (2014). Creating inclusive parent engagement practices. *Multicultural Education*, 21(3/4), 23–27.

Government of Canada. (2015). *Facts and figures 2014—Immigration overview: Permanent residents: Canada – Permanent Residents by province or territory and urban area.* Retrieved from http://www.cic.gc.ca/english/resources/statistics/facts2014/permanent/11.asp.

Held, V. (2006). *The ethics of care.* New York: Oxford University Press.

MacNevin, J. (2012). Learning the way: Teaching and learning with and for youth from refugee backgrounds on Prince Edward Island. *Canadian Journal of Education/Revue canadienne de l'education,* 35(3), 48–63.

McBrien, J. L. (2005). Educational needs and barriers for refugee students in the United States: A review of the literature. *Review of Educational Research,* 75(3), 329–364. https://doi.org/10.3102/00346543075003329.

McWilliams, J. A., & Bonet, S. W. (2016). Continuums of precarity: Refugee youth transitions in American high schools. *International Journal of Lifelong Education,* 35(2), 153–170. https://doi.org/10.1080/02601370.2016.1164468.

Noddings, N. (2012a). *Philosophy of education* (3rd ed.). Boulder, CO: Westview Press.

Noddings, N. (2012b). The language of care ethics. *Knowledge Quest,* 40(5), 52–56.

Noddings, N. (2012c). The caring relation in teaching. *Oxford Review of Education,* 38(6), 771–781. https://doi.org/10.1080/03054985.2012.745047.

Noddings, N. (2005). Identifying and responding to needs in education. *Cambridge Journal of Education,* 35(2), 147–159. https://doi.org/10.1080/03057640500146757.

Noddings, N. (1984). *Caring: A feminine approach to ethics and moral education.* Berkeley: University of California Press.

Østergaard, E. (2015). How can science education foster students' rooting? *Cultural Studies of Science Education,* 10(2), 515–525. http://doi.org/10.1007/s11422-014-9604-1.

UNHCR (United Nations High Commissioner for Refugees). (2016). *UNHCR population statistics.* Retrieved from http://popstats.unhcr.org/en/overview#_ga=1.230067740.10 84630002.1477323046.

UNHCR (United Nations High Commissioner for Refugees). (2011). *Convention and protocol relating to the status of refugees.* Geneva, Switzerland: UNHCR. Retrieved from http://www.unhcr.org/protection/basic/3b66c2aa10/convention-protocol-relating-status-refugees.html.

Wilde, S. (2013). *Care in education: Teaching with understanding and compassion.* New York: Routledge.

CHAPTER 8

Treating English-Language Learners with Respect: Critical Praxis

Jeff Brown and Brett Reynolds

LEARNING OBJECTIVES

1. To evaluate the merits of showing respect or showing compassion towards English-language learners.
2. To describe specific ways that teachers can implement a respectful critical praxis in their own educational settings.

INTRODUCTION: THE SITUATION OF ENGLISH-LANGUAGE LEARNERS

Every year, thousands of **English-Language Learners (ELLs)**[1] attend Canadian post-secondary institutions in preparatory and mainstream programs. According to Decock, McCloy, Steffler, and Dicaire (2016), in 2015 there were over 34,000 international students in Ontario alone, making up 15 percent of the student body. About 71 percent of international students report their first language as a language other than English or French, along with 13 percent of domestic students, meaning that about 22 percent of Ontario college students are ELLs. From 2009 to 2015, the growth rate of these students far outpaced the growth rate of people who reported English as their first language. In 2015, ELLs accounted for a clear majority of students in college business, hospitality, and engineering/technology programs. The details will obviously vary from province to province, but throughout Canada, the numbers and the proportion of ELLs are growing.

Obviously, language proficiency poses a difficulty, even though the vast majority will have already met the English-language requirements of their respective colleges and universities. A typical requirement would be an IELTS (International English Language Testing System) score of 6.5, where an individual in band 6 "has generally effective command of the language despite some inaccuracies, inappropriate words and misunderstandings. Can use and understand fairly complex language particularly in familiar situations" (British Council, 2012). And yet, students often struggle with academic expectations, social life, and everyday interactions, along with culture shock, feelings of displacement, and pressures from their parents. They also often face negative or even hostile attitudes from their teachers. Ferris, Brown, Liu, and Stine describe an interview in which a student reports that "a teacher said that, on the first day of class, she encourages second language (L2) writers to drop her course by writing in bold letters: 'This is not an ESL class' at the top of her syllabus. She added that if such students 'insist on staying' in the class, then they receive the same instruction as the monolingual English speakers and are held to the same standards" (2011, p. 220).[2]

It is difficult to imagine another scenario in which it would be deemed acceptable to single out a specific group of students in this manner. Munro, Derwing, and Sato (2006) describe the misunderstandings and stereotyping that can be associated with a non-Canadian accent. Cheng and Fox (2008) report ELLs' fears of being misunderstood and mocked by peers. Our own professional experience indicates that these sorts of issues and attitudes are hardly exceptional. Though many ELLs succeed and even excel in their academic programs, it is obviously a very difficult situation to be in.

COMPASSION VS. RESPECT

Compassion: Its Meaning and Use

Given these difficulties, a teacher might be surprised that we do not advocate compassion for ELLs. We do not make the unreasonable suggestion that teachers withhold compassion from their ELLs. Indeed, there will of course be times when compassion is appropriate. But our position is that compassion should not be our default attitude towards ELLs. The default attitude, rather, should be **respect**. Before examining the meaning of *respect*, we must clarify what we take *compassion* to mean.

We adopt the plain meaning of *compassion* here: a feeling of "sorrow or concern for the suffering of another person, coupled with the desire to alleviate that suffering" (Stellar & Keltner, 2014, p. 330). We did not arrive at this definition because of any lack of complexity regarding how it should be best defined. Complications with traditional definitions of the term began several centuries ago. For example, Butler (1726) observed that compassion can give rise to a feeling of one's own good fortune and superiority relative to others. He adds, however, that this is a mere by-product of compassion, which he claims is broadly understood to be "an Affection the Object of which is Another in Distress" (p. 81, note). Echoing this, the *Oxford English Dictionary* (OED) notes that compassion "is shown towards a person in distress by one who is free from it, who is, in this respect, his superior" (compassion, n.d.). It is this aspect of compassion that we find troubling. If teachers adopt a disposition of compassion towards ELLs, do they position themselves as their students' superiors? We will see that it is precisely such a positioning that can impede the respect that is a necessary condition of the ethical treatment of ELLs.

In terms of a distinction between *compassion* and *respect* as practical terms, corpus linguistics can suggest an answer. Under Firth's dictum that "you shall know a word by the company it keeps" (1957, p. 11), a search of the *Corpus of Contemporary American English* (COCA) (Davies, 2008) for noun or adjective collocates occurring within four words to the right of the string *compassion for* returns the following results in descending frequency order: *people, others, victims, poor, animals,* and *suffering.* While *people* and *others* are neutral with respect to power relationships, the other words support the idea that the compassionate are typically superior to the object of their compassion, as people usually see themselves as more powerful than victims, the poor, animals, and those who are suffering. More evidence comes from the following typical examples taken from the COCA:

1. *The love, kindness and <u>compassion</u> that we have received in our time of need.*
2. *The country's well-being can be maintained while simultaneously showing <u>compassion</u> and respect for a disabled leader.*
3. *Each of us is experiencing an intense feeling of <u>compassion</u> for the victims of the attacks.*
4. *We have to do a much better job of showing our <u>compassion</u> for the poor.*
5. *<u>Compassion</u> for animals still leads many to vegetarianism.* (Davies, 2008)

Although the use of the word *compassion* tends strongly in the direction of positioning the compassionate above the object of compassion, it is not always so. The following examples in the COCA imply no power difference:

6. *We believe Judaism is about <u>compassion</u> and justice for all people.*
7. *Listen to each other with respect, love, <u>compassion</u> and a true desire to bring our energies and souls together.* (Davies, 2008)

Interestingly, examples six and seven link compassion to words such as *justice* and *respect*, which demonstrates compassion is not excluded from these concepts. Instead, they need to be invoked to tap into that aspect of compassion. The other corpus examples cited make it clear that compassion generally brings with it a perceived power imbalance or position of privilege on the part of the person expressing the compassion.

Respect: Its Meaning and Use

In contrast to *compassion*, which has only one non-obsolete sense in the *Oxford English Dictionary*, *respect* has four numbered common senses (and some less common ones). We are interested in the definition that reads a "deferential regard or esteem felt or shown towards a person, thing, or quality" (respect, n.d.), and we are, of course, concerned with respect towards a person. Even understood in this particular sense, respect remains a complex notion, and theorists "have variously identified [respect] as a mode of behavior, a form of treatment, a kind of valuing, a type of attention, a motive, an attitude, a feeling, a tribute, a principle, a duty, an entitlement, a moral virtue, [and] an epistemic virtue" (Dillon, 2016). While all of these are relevant to a certain extent, we will focus on respect as an attitude or feeling, which we take to be most commensurate with compassion.

Kövecses (1990) investigates various emotion concepts through the lens of cognitive linguistics, considering the metaphors that underlie them. He finds that "a large part of our conception of respect is based on the metaphorical notion of a person's having a certain worth, or value." Moreover, "the notion of respect is intimately linked to that of power—either in its metaphorical or non-metaphorical forms" (p. 109). So, like compassion, respect has power as part of its meaning, but in this case, it is the object of the feeling who is empowered, not the person feeling respect. The evidence from the COCA anticipates a core element of the pedagogical stance that is most constructive and appropriate regarding ELLs—critical **praxis**. Empowering learnings, we will see, is central to the project of a critical praxis in education.

Echoing our corpus analysis of *compassion*, we decided to investigate the most common fillers for the frames *respect for* and *compassion for*, both followed by a noun. Table 8.1 lists the nouns that appear relatively more frequently[3] within four words to the right of *for*. Those appearing in the first column with *respect* are largely abstract nouns, reflecting the fact that one can have respect for an abstraction but only have compassion for a living thing. Those on the right with W1 and W2 ratios greater than 0.5 are typically powerless, or at least lacking in power: the suffering, victims, children, and animals. On the other hand, the word *beings* doesn't clearly support this pattern, and it might be surprising that *man* is more common with compassion than *women* until you realize that "man" is being used in the more general sense of "person." Overall, this collocational analysis provides suggestive evidence that typical usage of the terms *compassion for* and *respect for* is in line with being compassionate to those lacking power and respectful towards those who are empowered, respectively.

Table 8.1: Nouns Collocating Comparatively Strongly with *Respect for* and *Compassion for* in the COCA

Collocate	W1	W2	W1/W2	Collocate	W2	W1	W2/W1
rights	293	1	293	suffering	11	1	11.0
law	143	0	∞	victims	31	12	2.6
authority	106	0	∞	beings	11	9	1.2
dignity	82	0	∞	children	14	15	0.9
elders	62	0	∞	animals	15	19	0.8
rule	62	0	∞	man	17	35	0.5
diversity	60	0	∞	others	49	141	0.3
sovereignty	56	0	∞	people	64	193	0.3
tradition	48	0	∞	family	10	54	0.2
autonomy	46	0	∞	women	10	120	0.1

Note: W1 and W2 are the search terms *respect for* and *compassion for*, respectively. The values are the frequency of the collocate appearing within four words to the right of the search term.

Source: Davies, 2008.

Compassion vs. Respect: Ethical Implications

Power will not *necessarily* engender respect, but by respecting people, we believe that we imbue them with a degree of power they would not otherwise have, at least in relation to the subject and perhaps beyond. As Dillon remarks, "respect also aims to value its object appropriately, so it contrasts with degradation and discounting" (2016). Without the respect that can empower people, there can be no actual ethical relationship since one of the players will be divested of the power of agency. In this sense, it is the ethical duty of teachers to adopt an attitude of respect towards ELLs.

Kant's idea of a moral imperative is helpful here. As Dillon (2016), invoking the categorical imperative, explains:

> This duty of recognition respect owed to others requires two things: first, that we adopt as a regulating policy a commitment to control our own desire to think well of ourselves (this desire being the main cause of disrespect), and, second, that we refrain from treating others in the following ways: treating them merely as means (valuing them as less than ends in themselves), showing contempt for them (denying that they have any worth), treating them arrogantly (demanding that they value us more highly than they value themselves), defaming them by publicly exposing their faults, and ridiculing or mocking them.

Following this out, we argue that teachers have a duty to ELLs (and indeed to all students). The second requirement in the passage quoted above expresses the Kantian duty to recognize others as ends in themselves (to acknowledge their autonomy) rather than as means to achieving our own ends. This duty of recognition stems from the mutual respect that is at the core of **ethics**. Hence, in contrasting respect with compassion we are actively advocating for the ethical treatment of ELLs. The issue of respect is in fact an *ethical* issue. In a discussion on this topic, Tardy and Whittig (2017) identify respect as a central requirement of the ethical treatment of ELLs (and, specifically, second-language writing students). In so doing, they draw upon the work of Silva (1997), who "based his use of the *ethics* on the notion of respect" (Tardy & Whittig, 2017, p. 921). Pennycook elaborates on this by distinguishing three basic ethical principles: the principle of equal treatment, the principle of respect for persons, and the principle of benefit maximization (2001, p. 136). This aligns with Dillon's (2016) characterization of respect as it pertains to ethics and the autonomy of individuals:

Thus, we respect others as persons (negatively) by doing nothing to impair or destroy their capacity for autonomy, by not interfering with their autonomous decisions and their pursuit of the (morally acceptable) ends they value, and by not coercing or deceiving them or treating them paternalistically.

We do not propose a false dilemma that suggests one must choose between compassion and respect. The two can coexist and by no means do these exhaust the range of attitudes a teacher can have towards ELLs. Empathy, accommodation, and tolerance, for instance, are concepts that are often discussed in educational settings. Indeed, Simon's (1992) notion of "compassionate justice" might be applicable here. What we *are* arguing is that, in the context of education focused on ethics, respect is relatively more important and is a better option on an ongoing basis because it is a necessary condition for the ethical treatment of second-language students.

At this point, we should address a possible concern that we are conflating *compassion* and *pity*. Barad (2007) points to Aquinas and the Dalai Lama as being among those who clearly distinguish between compassion and pity. We take the point. To be sure, the terms have distinct meaning, and we are not confusing the two. As we have attempted to show, the plain meaning of compassion tends to imply a power difference, and though it would be naive to suggest that avoiding compassion will erase the power difference, we believe that cultivating respect may. If teachers are to show compassion towards ELLs because they are ELLs, then the implied power differential is an aspect that we find troubling.

Again, this is not to say that teachers should never be compassionate towards their students, ELL or otherwise. There are undoubtedly times when any student has suffered a misfortune, acute or chronic, and compassion is the appropriate response from teachers. The difference between such situations and those to which we object is that ELLs may become the object of compassion simply because of their relatively unalterable position in Canadian society, practically speaking. This applies to students in English-language courses (i.e., ELL), as well as to ELLs—students whose first language is not English and who may be struggling with language-related issues—in mainstream college courses (i.e., content courses that presume English-language proficiency).

An example of a case where compassion towards ELLs may be warranted is discussed in Carson and Johnston (2000). They suggest compassion on behalf of university professors towards their students when it comes to cultural diversity awareness training in a teacher education program in Alberta. Having found that there was a good deal of resistance to the suggestion that the majority culture oppressed minority groups, they observe that "leaving [majority] students to founder in a sea of white guilt or self-righteous anger leads to silence and an entrenched resistance to difficult knowledge. Such responses are neither helpful nor pedagogical" (p. 81). They go on to say that "racism has visited suffering upon both its victims and upon those who must now bear the responsibility for the 'sins of the past'" (p. 81) and that compassion on the part of the professor is an appropriate response. Note that the compassion suggested here is in response to some lessons that proved particularly painful for many involved. In particular, they do not appear to be suggesting a general ongoing attitude of compassion for minority students.

In sum, an indiscriminate attitude of compassion by teachers towards ELLs is troubling because it suggests the teacher is in a superior position. By contrast, a generally respectful stance towards ELLs empowers them. This empowerment, we will show, is key to implementing a critical praxis.

CRITICAL PRAXIS

Can the respect that underpins the ethical treatment of second-language students be consciously developed? It can if critical praxis is the prevailing pedagogical approach. Paulo Freire, a seminal figure in this view of education, characterizes praxis as a fundamentally dialogic construct in which students and teachers "become jointly responsible for a process in which all grow" (2005, p. 80). While we should be wary of a direct application of Freire's ideas to other educational contexts, this notion of *joint responsibility* is, nonetheless, a key distinguishing feature of respect (as contrasted with compassion). This joint responsibility implicates teachers and students in an ethical relationship—a relationship of which respect is a foundational element. As Simon notes, "Ethics are not acted out in the spirit of human isolation but rather mirror the responsibilities of relationship" (1992, p. 26). To engage in praxis involves establishing a dialogue with learners, a dialectic in which knowledge is co-constructed and developed as fundamentally empowering. *Praxis* can be defined as the "continuous reflexive integration of thought, desire and action" (Pennycook, 2001, p. 3; cf. Simon, 1992, p. 49). It is "critical" in the sense of being involved in a critique of society or any systemic power structure. What critical praxis critiques are assumptions and received conventions that can obscure—gloss over, as it were—social inequalities and injustices that, because our classrooms are microcosms of the larger world, can in turn become pedagogical or educational injustices. The term *praxis* originates with the ancient Greeks. In Aristotle, it designates a type of "practical wisdom," touching upon the "sphere of thought and action that comprises the ethical and political life" (Schrag, 1995, p. 638) of human activity. Praxis—the thought and action tied to the ethical—requires that we be critical and obliges us to confront injustices in our educational system and in our classrooms.

An empowering response to these injustices is the establishment of a class-room space in which students subjected to them—in this case, ELLs—are treated as autonomous individuals who can in turn respond and co-create an effective learning environment. Critical praxis, ultimately, seeks to free us from the forces that disempower us. The dialectic of praxis is inherently critical in that it constantly problematizes what is given, questions received assumptions, and places the *ethical*—i.e., a mutually respectful relationship of responsibility—at the heart of pedagogy. For this reason, critical praxis is "an ongoing project and certainly not a prescriptive set of practices" (Simon, 1992, p. xvi). It cannot be a codified method, since there will always be tensions and practical realities in-volved that cannot be ignored and that will have to be navigated. For example, an educator who attempts to engage in critical praxis must still acknowledge that they are part of an institutional structure that places them in a position of authority; they still have to assign individual grades and make decisions that will have an impact on their students. Praxis demands that the critical practitioner confront this tension rather than simply accept it as "how things are." For this reason, critical praxis is also transformative, "aiming not just to describe but also to change" (Pennycook, 2001, p. 162). There is no simple formula for such change; it is something that has to be constantly negotiated.

The change we see critical praxis bringing about for ELLs requires that they are treated with genuine respect. Now, most would agree that ELLs have a good deal to be respected for. Learning a second language to the level required to enter a tertiary educational institution in Canada is a complex and admirable feat. Pulling up stakes and moving to another country knowing you're going to be in a linguistic minority is also a daunting proposition that these students have faced down and overcome. To be sure, respect in these matters is warranted and due (presumably, a teacher inclined to declare "this is not an ESL class" at the beginning of a course still has a basic appreciation for what second-language learners have accomplished). However, the respect we advocate for ELLs must run deeper than respect for grasping a second language; it must inform our peda-gogical approaches and our classroom practices in a more profound manner than it currently does. In the remaining sections, we suggest some ways in which this might be done.

The Strengths of Respect for an ELL Praxis

One of the merits of respecting students is that such an approach stands a better chance of engendering mutual respect, while compassion is most likely to engender gratitude. This returns us to the ideas of co-responsibility and ethics. To be co-responsible, students must be recognized as ethical agents, able to participate in the dialectic of learning. Respect—as opposed to compassion—is consistent with this recognition of student *agency*. Agency is, admittedly, a contested notion, yet it is still irrevocably linked to autonomy and the "socioculturally mediated ability to act" (Ahearn, 2012, p. 278). The idea that the ability to act is mediated by sociocultural factors is crucial to keep in mind. We have reviewed the sociocultural (and economic and political) factors that impact ELLs and, to a certain extent, limit their ability to act. But an attitude of respect recognizes them as individuals who can still actively engage in the learning process, whereas compassion situates them as passive subjects. Again, this brings us to ethics and the role of ELLs as ethical agents, deserving of and responsible for their part in education based on critical praxis.

Compassion, being the urge to alleviate suffering, directs the teacher to short-term thinking. It is antithetical to the goals of compassion to push a suffering student to work harder, to spend hours practicing in ways that require difficult levels of mental effort, are often boring, and can result in errors that are potentially embarrassing. Yet this kind of deliberate practice (Ericsson & Lehmann, 1996; van Gog, Ericsson, Rikers, & Paas, 2005) is exactly what teachers should be pushing their students to do in order to have them most swiftly move beyond their current difficulties and rise to a level of English-language proficiency that will facilitate their educational, work, and social goals.[4] The respectful teacher is confident (not over-confident) in the abilities of their students and in their capacity to overcome their situation (with appropriate supports), and is willing to urge them to short-term unpleasant practice for their long-term benefit.

Along these lines, part of the job of a teacher is to assess and to hold students accountable to their responsibility for meeting learning outcomes. A compassionate teacher must evaluate the plight of their students, but this is distinct from assessing their learning. There are cases in which a student fails to achieve learning outcomes, and a compassionate teacher should face a good deal of cognitive turmoil in such cases. Informing a student that, despite the time, effort, and money invested in a course, they have been unsuccessful in meeting learning outcomes will almost certainly add to the student's suffering. Not only does the respectful teacher avoid this cognitive turmoil, but they also retain a respectful stance towards ELLs by not lowering goals and by maintaining rigorous learning outcomes and standards. This is consistent with treating ELLs as autonomous individuals: "We also respect them (positively) by protecting them from threats to their autonomy (which may require intervention when someone's current decisions seem to put their own autonomy at risk)" (Dillon, 2016). But respecting them also means requiring them to meet their courses' learning outcomes in order to pass and holding them accountable to standards of academic honesty "by promoting autonomy and the conditions for it (for example, by allowing and encouraging individuals to make their own decisions, take responsibility for their actions, and control their own lives)" (Dillon, 2016). Critical praxis, informed by respect rather than compassion, underpins this delicate balance.

IMPLEMENTING RESPECT

Universal Design for Learning

Most college instructors are not, nor should they be expected to be, language teachers. After all, college instructors are assigned courses based on content expertise, meaning that the focus of their course is on the content, not on the language being spoken and heard. Yet it is clear that many learners in Canadian post-secondary courses are from an ELL background and struggle or even fall behind because of language-related difficulties. The appropriate response to this situation is one of respect, and such a response can profitably be informed by the principles of the **Universal Design for Learning (UDL)**. Given the role of respect in ethics, UDL is thus the most ethical pedagogical approach to apply to this issue of diversity—including linguistic diversity—in the classroom. As Rose and Meyer recognize, "cultural, educational, and legal changes have significantly altered the mix of students in regular education classrooms" (2002, p. 5). More specifically, "today's typical classroom might include students whose first language is not English" (p. 5), and as noted above, some college programs enroll predominantly ELLs (Decock, McCloy, Steffler, & Dicaire, 2016). Therefore, the most promising pedagogical approach is one that respects this diversity without stigmatizing it. This returns us to the position of the teacher in Ferris, Brown, Liu, and Stine (2011) who maintained that "ESL students" who "insist[ed]" on staying in that teacher's class would be held to the same standards and given the same instruction. The point is precisely that such instruction, in any case, should adhere to ethical standards of respect. Issuing a warning based on stereotypes is disrespectful, but universal application of standards is not. Certainly, "the challenge posed by greater diversity and greater accountability is to enable students with divergent needs, skills, and interests to attain the same high standards" (p. 6). No educators want to abandon appropriate standards; yet such standards can be adhered to if the situation of diverse learners is recognized, treated respectfully, and dealt with in a pedagogically responsible manner.

UDL has its origin in the architectural movement known as *universal design,* the guiding principle of which is simply to design structures so that they are accessible for all. Extending this principle to education and curriculum design implies that curriculum should, from the start, be designed in such a way that it accommodates all learners and respects the legitimacy of the challenges facing all learners. The framework of UDL is based on three fundamental principles: multiple means of representation, multiple means of expression, and multiple means of engagement (Rose & Meyer, 2002). In the present context, perhaps the most relevant of these principles is the first, which "recommends that the teacher provide multiple representations of the same information" (p. 75). This is particularly crucial in contexts where content is the focus but language might be an issue (i.e., outside of the ELL-specific classroom). Presenting material in a variety of ways so that issues related to language are included means respecting these as learning issues and not ELL issues. It reflects the realization that "learning is multifaceted and that barriers in the curriculum can arise in a number of places" (Rose & Meyer, 2002, p. 74).

Bearing this first principle of UDL in mind, instructors might, for example, consider how they work with textbooks in their courses. For example, teachers can create outlines for individual chapters, which can help all students—and, in particular, ELLs—follow lectures and see the logical connections between main ideas. Reviewing key vocabulary terms at the beginning or end of each class is another way of consolidating students' understanding of the material. A glossary is an effective way to ensure that ELLs can focus on the necessary vocabulary, while non-ELLs will benefit from using the glossary as a review and/or discussion activity. As an alternative, all students can work together in class to create their own glossary. If the course is supported by an online learning management system (such as Blackboard or Desire2Learn), this can be used in a way that will support both ELLs and students without second-language issues. Group activities for reading comprehension can also support active, student-centred learning that increase engagement on the part of all students while at the same time, providing additional scaffolding for students struggling with language. In keeping with the first principle of UDL, these suggestions promote multiple means of presenting material, and this benefits all learners.

Our goal is here to simply indicate how UDL is the most effective way for ensuring that ELLs (and, indeed, all students) are respected in a curriculum. For this reason, we have restricted ourselves to some suggestions regarding the first principle of multiple means of representation. However, we encourage readers to consider how these same concerns might be accounted for by the other two principles of UDL and how this might enrich learning environments not only for ELLs but for all learners.

A Respectful Approach to Textual Borrowing

We now turn our attention to a specific issue to see how the respectful approach to ELLs we argue for might apply to teaching. In the post-secondary educational (ELL and non-ELL) context, the issue of plagiarism is increasingly receiving a more nuanced treatment, one that recognizes the myriad factors that are at play when students commit the academic offence of plagiarism (Flowerdew & Li, 2007; Howard & Robillard, 2008; Pecorari, 2008; Pennycook, 1996, 2016; Petrić, 2004). To be sure, there are acts of textual borrowing that are straightforwardly dishonest—for example, buying or copying-and-pasting an entire text and submitting it as one's own. But often, the situation is much more complex than that, and these complexities are particularly acute in the case of second-language students. Rather than outright copying, ELLs often engage in language reuse (Flowerdew & Li, 2007) or the "borrowing" of other authors' words (Pennycook, 1996). Problems involved with language reuse and the borrowing of words further suggest the importance of distinguishing between "intentional" and "unintentional" (Petrić, 2004) plagiarism. But teachers, often looking down upon their students, fail to acknowledge how central textual borrowing is to everything we do creatively and academically. As Lethem (2007) explains,

> Any text is woven entirely with citations, references, echoes, cultural languages, which cut across it through and through in a vast stereophony. The citations that go to make up a text are anonymous, untraceable, and yet already read; they are quotations without inverted commas. The kernel, the soul—let us go further and say the substance, the bulk, the actual and valuable material of all human utterances—is plagiarism. (p. 68)

Surely, the distinction between intentional plagiarism (copying entire swaths of existing text and calling it one's own) and unintentional plagiarism (language reuse often exacerbated by ELL-specific issues) matters, and to refer to all instances of language reuse as "plagiarism" is not only unfair but inaccurate. Hence, we find it much more constructive to adopt the term *textual borrowing* to refer to the latter cluster of issues, and reserve *plagiarism* for that which is intended to deceive.

A respectful (and constructive) approach to textual borrowing by ELL writers is the opposite of a response to plagiarism. It means adopting a pedagogical approach to this (and related) issues, rather than a punitive approach. ELLs-specific issues have "led researchers to call for extensive pedagogical support for L2 writers rather than punishment" (Pecorari & Petrić, 2014, p. 275). This applies to both the ELL classroom and to mainstream college courses with ELLs in them. Such pedagogical support draws upon a respectful acknowledgement of the challenges facing ELLs, without absolving them of their responsibilities. Most importantly, this approach is consistent with a broader UDL perspective since all students stand to benefit from this more inclusive approach to the issue. A pedagogical approach acknowledges reasons why L2 students borrow text and treats these as an intrinsic part of writing development. It utilizes these as resources in writing instruction and incorporates them into the structure of the course. In this manner, the course supports ELL writing development. A respectful UDL perspective underpins this approach and informs a learner-centred classroom culture based on dialogue. For teachers who wish to support this practice, it is essential that they create both summative and formative assignments and assessments. This respectful pedagogical approach to textual borrowing contrasts with a punitive approach, which limits itself to punishing instances of perceived plagiarism and utilizes these for academic prohibition. Such an approach merely focuses on making it difficult for students to commit plagiarism, warning about the evils of plagiarism and catching academic offences but making no attempt to alter the classroom culture.

If we want to teach, and not just punish, we need to recognize that textual borrowing as a resource utilized by the L2 learner is a "by-product of the student's struggle, not yet won, to find her own authorial voice" (Pecorari & Petrić, 2014, p. 273) and that its misapplication is often the result of unintentional factors (e.g., cultural background, academic literacy, source documentation). The use of sources—and the often-murky distinction between what is a specialized source and what is considered general knowledge—is particularly problematic. Indeed, this highlights the issue of what even constitutes an "original" idea:

For substantially all ideas are secondhand, consciously and unconsciously drawn from a million outside sources, and daily used by the garnerer with a pride and satisfaction born of the superstition that he originated them; whereas there is not a rag of originality about them anywhere except the little discoloration they get from his [or her] mental and moral caliber and his temperament, and which is revealed in characteristics of phrasing. (Lethem, 2007, p. 68)

A respectful pedagogical approach to writing involves explaining citation and reference, not as a way to show where you got your ideas—with the underlying implication that the teacher doubts the students' capacity to say anything original that is also interesting—but as putting your ideas in the context of others' and providing a road map for your readers, should they wish to learn more about what you've said. It's about attributing the right ideas to the right sources, not in order to give them "credit" or display the breadth of your erudition, but to make sure that the various viewpoints and voices don't get muddled up and mixed together. Quotation isn't a prophylactic against accusations of word theft. It's a tool used to show the precise wording of the original for the purposes of analysis or even criticism.

If we do not respect our students as authors, they will not regard themselves as such. Moreover, they will see their writing as an act of toil without authorly purpose, as no more than a display of compliance and evidence of some kind of competence, submitted to us for review. From this perspective, the purpose of citation, quotation, and reference is adherence to rules. Its application is bureaucratic, and it amounts to little more than custom. A pedagogical approach to writing seeks to "empower students to develop ownership of their writing" (Lee, 2016, p. 262). The development of such ownership is a concrete example of the learner empowerment sought by critical praxis based upon respect for the challenges faced by ELLs.

It's important to point out that non-ELLs will also benefit from a constructive approach to writing that includes a broader awareness of the factors involved in writing development and the use of sources—one that does not merely focus on labelling them academic criminals after they commit transgressions in their textual borrowings. Moreover, such an approach does not stigmatize ELLs, but ensures that the specific issues they face are acknowledged and accounted for in our pedagogical practices. Once again, this brings to bear some of the key insights of UDL.

CONCLUSION

Concerns and Reservations

As indicated earlier, we understand that there may be some concerns and reservations about our position. To address those concerns, first, we reiterate that we do not rule out compassion and fully believe that it is appropriate in particular situations. We argue only against compassion as a *default* stance towards ELLs. Second, we do not wish to be seen as making the argument that respect means removing all safety nets, leaving people entirely to their own devices, and refraining entirely from trying to influence their choices or help them avoid mistakes. Fortunately, most post-secondary institutions have resources and supports for struggling students (e.g., counselling services, accommodations systems); these resources are crucial, and the responsible educator must be aware of and utilize them when appropriate. Nor do we believe that ELLs are on a level playing field with non-ELLs. We have an acute awareness of the sociopolitical factors affecting ELLs and proceed from the basis that they face systemic inequalities and obstacles.

Some readers might be concerned that we have cited no comparative studies in the course of outlining our position. The reason for this is that there is, at present, a lack of a research base on the effect of teacher compassion or respect on student success. The bulk of research on compassion in teaching seems to take compassion as the dependent variable (e.g., Taylor et al., 2016). We find very little research that considers the effects of a teacher's level of compassion on students. One might hypothesize that having a compassionate college teacher results in higher grades or higher course completion rates. Effects on the teachers themselves, including their level of engagement, stress, or satisfaction, would be interesting as dependent variables with teacher compassion as the independent variable. We have turned up very little research touching on these questions (but see Eldor & Shoshani, 2016), and what exists is quite limited in its generalizability. Much the same can be said about respect as a dependent variable (but see Knesting, 2008; Stronge, Ward, Tucker, & Hindman, 2007). In the end, there simply isn't that much out there on this issue, but as we suggest in closing, perhaps this is not surprising.

Final Thoughts

The lack of empirical research on this subject may be a reflection of how difficult it is to quantify and define the variables of *compassion* and *respect*. In fact, we suggest that understanding the terms in the manner we outline in the initial sections of this chapter would be an effective starting point. How a study might then be designed and conducted—and whether it would even be ethical to undertake such a study—are other questions entirely. Given the lack of research base, our arguments are largely grounded in our considered judgment, our extrapolation from the indirect evidence, our sound pedagogical practices, and our combined personal experience. Our central contention is that respect rather than compassion is the appropriate response to the challenges facing ELLs in the Canadian post-secondary context. We feel we have presented compelling arguments and welcome further discussion of these issues. Indeed, if it initiates a more extended conversation on this topic among educators and educators-in-training, then our discussion here has served its purpose.

QUESTIONS FOR CRITICAL THOUGHT

1. Do you agree with the authors' central argument that respect rather than compassion is the appropriate response to the situation faced by English-language learners? Why or why not?
2. The authors discuss the first UDL principle of multiple means of representation with respect to English-language learners. How might the other two main principles of UDL be applied with an eye towards respectful support of English-language learners?
3. Do post-secondary teachers have ethical duties towards their students beyond meeting the learning outcomes of a course? Discuss.

GLOSSARY

English-Language Learners (ELLs): English-Language Learners are those learning English who have a dominant language other than English and have the goal of improving their communicative competence in English. ELL classes are those classes whose primary goal is to support ELLs in doing so. Some writers use ESL or ESOL (English as a second or other language), EFL (English as a foreign language), or EAL (English as an additional language).

Ethics: The branch of philosophy that is mainly concerned with the concepts of right and wrong (and the conduct, duties, and responsibilities related to these concepts). People's ethics consist of the moral principles they use to decide what is right and wrong and what they do based on those decisions.

Praxis: Refers to the doing of things, usually in a specific domain. Thus, teacher praxis refers to what teachers do as teachers in their interactions with their students. Praxis is best understood in contrast to theorizing and creating. A critical praxis is one which aims to effect a change in the structure of society by confronting injustice and power imbalance.

Respect: An attitude towards a person based on the acknowledgement of that person's value or worth as a moral agent. Such an attitude affords the object of respect a certain degree of power (in this regard, respect can be contrasted with compassion).

Universal Design for Learning (UDL): An approach to education—inspired by the architecture movement known as *universal design*—that proceeds from the principle that curricula should be designed from the outset to be accessible to all learners. The UDL framework is based on the principles of multiple means of (1) representation, (2) expression, and (3) engagement.

NOTES

1. We understand the issues with the ELL term and considered using terms like "English as a Second Language", "non-native speakers of English," "limited English proficiency," and other phrasings, but we found each of them to be problematic. We beg the reader's indulgence and understanding that a label is not a working definition. We intend the term to cover all students who face barriers to post-secondary studies caused by their English-language abilities, stemming from the timing and extent of their English learning but not from any disability.

2. The problem here, from our point of view, is the implicit, hostile encouragement of ELLs to leave, and the failure to hold everyone to the same set of standards. A likely additional problem would be the conflation of being inflexible on learning outcomes with being inflexible on teaching and assessment practices.

3. These are not the nouns that appear most frequently in their respective frames but those for which the ratio of the frequency in one frame relative to the other is highest. Note, for instance, that *people* is actually the second-most frequent collocate with *respect for,* but it is also the most common collocate for *compassion for.* The ratio-based rankings go some ways to compensate for the fact that some nouns (e.g., *people*) are simply much more frequent in all contexts. For expository convenience, we have chosen to rank real-number ratios above ∞.

4. We do not mean to assert that all useful practice is unpleasant. The point is that without the kind of effortful, deliberate practice that pushes beyond levels of comfort, students are unlikely to progress at an optimal rate in their programs of study.

REFERENCES

Ahearn, L. M. (2012). *Living language: An introduction to linguistic anthropology*. West Sussex, UK: Wiley-Blackwell.

Barad, J. (2007). The understanding and experience of compassion: Aquinas and the Dalai Lama. *Buddhist-Christian Studies*, 27, 11–29.

British Council. (2012). *IELTS guide for teachers*. Retrieved from https://www.britishcouncil.it/sites/default/files/ielts_guide_for_teachers_italy.pdf.

Butler, J. (1726). *Fifteen sermons preached at the Rolls Chapel*. London: W. Botham, for James and John Knapton.

Carson, T., & Johnston, I. (2000). The difficulty with difference in teacher education: Toward a pedagogy of compassion. *Alberta Journal of Educational Research*, 46(1), 75–83.

Cheng, L., & Fox, J. (2008). Towards a better understanding of academic acculturation: Second language students in Canadian universities. *Canadian Modern Language Review*, 65(2), 307–333. https://doi.org/10.3138/cmlr.65.2.307.

compassion [n. 2]. (n.d.). In *Oxford English Dictionary*. Retrieved from http://www.oed.com/view/Entry/37475.

Davies, M. (2008). *The corpus of contemporary American English: 560 million words, 1990–present*. Retrieved from http://www.english-corpora.org/coca/.

Decock, H., McCloy, U., Steffler, M., & Dicaire, J. (2016). *International students at Ontario colleges: A profile*. Ottawa: Canadian Bureau for International Education.

Dillon, R. S. (2016). Respect. *Stanford encyclopedia of philosophy*. Retrieved from http://plato.stanford.edu/archives/win2016/entries/respect.

Eldor, L., & Shoshani, A. (2016). Caring relationships in school staff: Exploring the link between compassion and teacher work engagement. *Teaching and Teacher Education*, 59, 126–136. https://doi.org/10.1016/j.tate.2016.06.001.

Ericsson, K. A., & Lehmann, A. C. (1996). Expert and exceptional performance: Evidence of maximal adaptation to task constraints. *Annual Review of Psychology*, 47(1), 273–305. https://doi.org/10.1146/annurev.psych.47.1.273.

Ferris, D., Brown, J., Liu, H. (Sean), & Stine, M. E. A. (2011). Responding to L2 students in college writing classes: Teacher perspectives. *TESOL Quarterly*, 45(2), 207–234. https://doi.org/10.5054/tq.2011.247706.

Firth, J. R. (1957). *Papers in linguistics, 1934–1951*. Oxford: Oxford University Press.

Flowerdew, J., & Li, Y. (2007). Language re-use among Chinese apprentice scientists writing for publication. *Applied Linguistics*, 28(3), 440–465.

Freire, P. (2005). *Pedagogy of the oppressed* (M. B. Ramos, Trans.). New York: Continuum.

Howard, R. M., & Robillard, A. E. (Eds.). (2008). *Pluralizing plagiarism: Identities, contexts, pedagogies*. Portsmouth, NH: Boynton/Cook Publishers.

Knesting, K. (2008). Students at risk for school dropout: Supporting their persistence. *Preventing School Failure: Alternative Education for Children and Youth*, 52(4), 3–10. https://doi.org/10.3200/PSFL.52.4.3-10.

Kövecses, Z. (1990). *Emotion concepts*. New York: Springer-Verlag. https://doi.org/10.1007/978-1-4612-3312-1_7.

Lee, I. (2016). Putting students at the centre of classroom L2 writing assessment. *The Canadian Modern Language Review*, 72(2), 258–280.

Lethem, J. (2007, February). The ecstasy of influence: A plagiarism. *Harper's Magazine*, 59–71. Retrieved from https://harpers.org/archive/2007/02/the-ecstasy-of-influence.

Munro, M. J., Derwing, T. M., & Sato, K. (2006). Salient accents, covert attitudes: Consciousness-raising for pre-service second language teachers. *Prospect*, 21(1), 67–79.

Pecorari, D. (2008). *Academic writing and plagiarism: A linguistic analysis*. London: Continuum.

Pecorari, D., & Petrić, B. (2014). Plagiarism in second-language writing. *Language Teaching*, 47(3), 269–302. https://doi.org/10.1017/S0261444814000056.

Pennycook, A. (2016). Reflecting on borrowed words. *TESOL Quarterly*, 50(2), 480–482. https://doi.org/10.1002/tesq.294.

Pennycook, A. (2001). *Critical applied linguistics: A critical introduction*. Mahwah, NJ: Lawrence Erlbaum.

Pennycook, A. (1996). Borrowing others' words: Text, ownership, memory, and plagiarism. *TESOL Quarterly*, 30(2), 201–230. https://doi.org/10.2307/3588141.

Petrić, B. (2004). A pedagogical perspective on plagiarism. *NovELTy*, 11, 4–18.

respect [n. (and int.)]. (n.d.). In *Oxford English Dictionary*. Retrieved from https://www.lexico.com/en/definition/respect.

Rose, D. H., & Meyer, A. (2002). *Teaching every student in the digital age: Universal design for learning*. Alexandria, VA: Association for Supervision and Curriculum Development.

Schrag, C. O. (1995). Praxis. In R. Audi (Ed.), *The Cambridge dictionary of philosophy* (pp. 638–639). Cambridge, UK: Cambridge University Press.

Silva, T. (1997). On the ethical treatment of ESL writers. *TESOL Quarterly*, 31(2), 359–363.

Simon, R. (1992). *Teaching against the grain: Essays towards a pedagogy of possibility*. London: Bergin & Garvey.

Stellar, J. E., & Keltner, D. (2014). Compassion. In M. M. Tugade, M. N. Shiota, & L. D. Kirby (Eds.), *Handbook of positive emotion* (pp. 329–341). Retrieved from http://socrates.berkeley.edu/~keltner/publications/StellarKeltner2014.pdf.

Stronge, J. H., Ward, T. J., Tucker, P. D., & Hindman, J. L. (2007). What is the relationship between teacher quality and student achievement? An exploratory study.

Journal of Personnel Evaluation in Education, 20(3–4), 165–184. https://doi.org/10.1007/s11092-008-9053-z.

Tardy, C. M., & Whittig, E. (2017). On the ethical treatment of EAL writers: An update. *TESOL Quarterly*, 51(4), 920–930. https://doi.org/10.1002/tesq.405.

Taylor, C., Harrison, J., Haimovitz, K., Oberle, E., Thomson, K., Schonert-Reichl, K., & Roeser, R. W. (2016). Examining ways that a mindfulness-based intervention reduces stress in public school teachers: A mixed-methods study. *Mindfulness*, 7(1), 115–129. https://doi.org/10.1007/s12671-015-0425-4.

van Gog, T., Ericsson, K. A., Rikers, R. M. J. P., & Paas, F. (2005). Instructional design for advanced learners: Establishing connections between the theoretical frameworks of cognitive load and deliberate practice. *Educational Technology Research and Development*, 53(3), 73–81. https://doi.org/10.1007/BF02504799.

CHAPTER 9

Help, I'm Being Yelled at by a Parent! Overcoming Interpersonal Challenges with Compassionate Assertiveness

Dawn McBride and Alyson Worrall

LEARNING OBJECTIVES

1. To understand the elements of compassionate assertiveness.
2. To understand one's automatic responses when under stress and the role of emotional self-regulation.
3. To learn specific skills to resolve conflict with compassion and empathic understanding.

INTRODUCTION

> *Parent:* Unbelievable. You gave my son all this homework!
> *Teacher:* But you do not understand; it is required that I ...
> *Parent:* You are far too young to be teaching him!
> *Teacher:* Excuse me, I have a four-year teaching degree, plus I have ...
> *Parent:* Because you don't know how to teach, you compensate by giving way too much homework! I am going to talk to the principal about this!
> *Teacher:* [Frozen]

Does this scenario look or sound familiar? Of course it does! Teachers frequently encounter parents who seem intimidating, and it can be a very stressful part of the job (Addi-Raccah & Grinshtain, 2017; Butt & Zahid, 2015; Dor & Rucker-Naidu, 2012; Gwernan-Jones et al., 2015; Simbula & Gugliemi, 2010). We have discovered that many teachers, especially new ones, are not taught how to handle exchanges with these intense parents in such a way for there to be effective resolutions to the issues they raise. We remember many encounters with parents where we were left shaken by the experience of not being liked or seen as good enough by the parent. Many teachers, including both of us, were not trained how to deal with conflicts outside of the classroom. This gap is evidenced by the paucity of literature uncovered during a search for articles addressing this topic.

In most teacher training programs, time is spent teaching students methods for classroom management and leadership, but little, if any, time seems to be spent helping future teachers learn how to manage verbal conflicts with adults with whom they will interact in the course of their professional careers (e.g., parents, colleagues, administrators). For example, our syllabi survey of the published calendars of universities across Canada offering teacher education degrees revealed few that had a specific course in interpersonal communication skills. Of those institutions that did have such courses, the focus appeared to be on the skills necessary for managing a group of students. Furthermore, our search of the literature, using key words such as "assertiveness" and "**conflict resolution**" among others, garnered few scholarly, education-related resources addressing such issues. Of those that were found, the focus was on providing conflict management skills to administrators or changing a school's environment (Austin & Harkins, 2008; Ghamrawi, 2013; Mansfield, Beltman, Broadley, & Weatherby-Fell, 2016; Trinder et al., 2010). Likewise, our extensive journal database search revealed few resources for preparing advanced education students to work with parents who presented their concerns in a critical, sometimes verbally aggressive manner.

To address this long-standing gap in helping teachers—particularly new educators—we developed a very specific communication plan for teachers to use when confronted by highly activated adults (McBride, 2015). We have refined our plan over the years to ensure teachers learn the art of engaging with what we call "grumpy parents" in a manner that is caring and deeply respectful. We have come to term this plan **compassionate assertiveness**. Our character-education approach fosters attunement, **empathy** awareness, **emotional regulation**, and problem-solving skills. We have received excellent support for our approach, as our pre- and post-survey data from our assertiveness training workshops revealed numerous beneficial self-reported changes. Compassionate assertiveness is designed to help teachers build a caring connection with intense parents, a process that is vitally important because the child, about whom both the parent and the teacher care, benefits when the teacher and parent have a productive relationship.

HOW TO BE COMPASSIONATELY ASSERTIVE IN SEVEN (EASY!) STEPS

Your Thinking Brain Gets Hijacked

Let's return to the scenario at the start of the chapter, where a highly critical parent is frustrated with you because the parent believes you, the new teacher, are assigning too much homework. During this stressful encounter, there is a structure deep within your brain, known as the amygdala, that has immense power to shut down your ability to think and engage in logical reasoning—the task of the prefrontal cortex (Van der Kolk, 2014). This part is on high alert for any physiological signals that you are tense, such as holding your breath, an accelerating heart rate, your shoulders moving upward, and your arms crossing in defense (Levine, 2015). At lightning speed, your emotions—usually fear, panic, feelings of being overwhelmed, and helplessness—start spinning out of control. The amygdala shuts down your thinking brain (it hijacks the executive thinking function of the prefrontal cortex) and activates the survival alarm system of the sympathetic nervous system (Goleman, 1995; Kim, Dager, & Lyoo, 2012; Ressler, 2010). Suddenly, a rush of cortisol and adrenaline stress hormones flood your system, and the survival alarm reactions are evoked. Commonly known as the 3Fs, these responses are fight back, flee far (escape), or freeze (Pernicano, 2014).

For example, when your amygdala hijacks your thinking brain, you are no longer considering a win-win solution. Instead, you are focused on how you are going to withstand or escape the situation. For instance, you might find yourself fighting with the parent by getting louder than the parent to make your point, and you might even perceive the parent to be such a threat that you believe you need to report the incident to prevent them from being allowed in the school unescorted. Alternatively, if your instinct is to flee in a stressful situation, then you might lie by making up an excuse that you have another meeting to get to in order to end the conversation with the parent, or you may avoid meeting parents as much as possible. The freeze response might entail becoming very still, breaking all eye contact and social engagement with the parent, and trying to ignore what the parent is saying or doing. You might also start feeling as though you are in a bit of a daze or as if you are floating away from the scene of conflict.

When the alarm system is activated and the 3Fs are engaged, the conversation becomes very narrow and self-centred, and the only focus is on survival—not a resolution that is fair and compassionate for both parties. It is important to recognize that when the amygdalae of both parties are hijacking their thinking brains, this activated energy, which we like to call "red energy," fuels each other's alarm reactions. The parent's intense stress reaction triggers the teacher's stress reaction, whose stress reaction triggers the parent's, and so on. It becomes an escalating cycle, and any resolution of the situation is far from respectful, compassionate, and productive.

Over time, with repeated unsuccessful encounters with highly activated individuals—such as between the teacher and the intense parent—anxiety symptoms may emerge, along with a dreaded sense that these encounters are becoming traumatic since "trauma, by definition, is unbearable and intolerable" feelings (Van der Kolk, 2014, p. 1). Thus, both the parent and teacher may emotionally suffer when they get caught in red energy.

Compassionately Engage a Hijacked Brain

We believe it is ethically and morally imperative for teachers to embrace the notion that it is their job, as educators and professionals, to find ways to maintain their composure (i.e., gain control of their amygdalae and starve their red energy) so they can, with skill and patience, compassionately engage an irate parent. In other words, it is your job to take the high road. Your job is to convey to "red" parents that you are creating space for them to feel listened to and heard. And once they feel heard, and not before, you will shift the conversation to solving the problem that is upsetting the parent.

By engaging in self-regulating behaviour while you are encountering a stressor (e.g., an irate parent), you can activate what we call your "blue energy," also known as your parasympathetic nervous system. You can achieve this by taking breaths, not bracing, and telling yourself you can handle this situation with grace and care. Once your blue energy is starting to drown out your red energy, you will have access to higher order executive functioning, which means it will be easier to think. It will not feel as challenging to recall the steps to take when you are confronted by a challenging, difficult adult. Sound impossible? It's not!

Overview

For nearly a decade, we have been helping new and experienced teachers develop blue energy resources to build their emotional strength and confidence so as to

effectively block their amygdalae from taking over in a "red" con.
Shifting into blue energy is Step 1 of seven steps designed to help teach
nicate with people who are verbally aggressive and caught in their own

We like to use colours as metaphors that represent conflict and ch.
ergy, as this removes negative labels when describing challenging, inti ...uating
folks. It also allows you to visualize a stressed-out parent as simply a parent with
too much red energy, and it is your job not to catch their red energy. Instead, you
are constantly going to be offering your calming, blue energy to the parent to
help them drain their red energy (Steps 2 and 3). The idea of red and blue energies comes from somatic-experiencing literature (Levine & Kline, 2008).

In the following section, we describe in detail the seven steps in our compassionate communication model. For each step, we explain its purpose and
function.

The Seven Steps of Compassionate Communication

Step 1: Disarm

You, the Teacher: Stand to meet parent, take a breath, drop your shoulders, and offer an appropriate gesture of greeting that takes into account cultural norms.

When you are confronted by a person mired in red energy, you, as previously
mentioned, will likely have an urge to use one or more of the 3Fs to protect yourself. However, you are not in danger of death when someone is yelling at you.
Yes, it is very uncomfortable and upsetting, but it is not the same as a lion charg-
ing at you. Unfortunately, the amygdala is not aware that the parent yelling is not
a lion; your alarm system gets triggered and your sympathetic nervous system is
in high arousal (red energy is flooding your body). You need to disarm yourself
and deactivate this automatic response, to shift into blue energy as quickly as possible. One way is to take some deep belly breaths. It may sound simple; however,
it is highly effective because the brain gets the message that there can't be danger
if belly breathing is happening. Another tip is to try to drop your shoulders,
moving them away from your ears. You will likely have raised your shoulders
unconsciously as your brain sends survival signals to protect the vital blood vessels in your neck. Dropping your shoulders counters this response and signals
that you aren't in danger. We also suggest you keep your arms away from your
chest, as crossing your arms could be interpreted as an attack signal by the brain

of the parent. In addition, consider some supportive self-talk as a way to tell your brain/nervous system that you are okay—you will not die just because someone is yelling at you. Here are some of our self-talk favourites:

- I am safe.
- I am safe. The person is just venting with words.
- This might be scary, but I can handle it. I have handled worse.
- It is part of my job to stay calm ... to listen.
- I am going to take the high road.
- Right now, I need to listen, not fix.
- I need to make sure my face shows that I am curious/interested.

Step 2: Warmly greet the parent. Don't give up!

You, the Teacher: Hello, I am glad you came in. I'm pleased to meet you. Would you like to sit down?

Disarming yourself and greeting the parent are two steps in our compassionate communication process, but they are likely to occur simultaneously. Having regained control of your amygdala and engaged your own blue energy, your next job is to gently help the parent to do the same. Do not expect the parent will instantly move into blue energy. As you read previously, when someone is stuck in red energy, the thinking portion of the brain is not online. It's up to you to send signals to the upset parent's nervous system that you are not a threat and that the parent is not in danger. They may remain in one or more of the 3Fs, and that is okay, as you can still convey you are a professional who is compassionate, interested in what the parent has to say, and not a threat. Keep finding your blue, as eventually your mirror neurons may influence the parent's deactivation (Goleman & Boyatzis, 2008; Rothschild, 2006). When the parent's nervous system gets these messages, it will begin to slowly turn down its own alarm system. Remember, you are building a relationship between the two of you, and this will take time. By sincerely offering the warm greeting—"Hello, I'm pleased to meet you. Would you like to sit down?"—while you take some easy breaths and relax your shoulders, it is as if you are communicating directly to the parent's amygdala that you are not a threat, and you are going to create space for the parent to feel respect and care.

These early signals that you are not a threat may not be received initially, so you might have to repeat the process, especially if the parent responds negatively to the first greeting. For example, if the parent were to respond to your initial greeting with, "I'm not pleased to meet you. I had to wait a long time to speak with you while you were on the phone," you simply remind yourself that it can take a while for the amygdala to get the message that you are not a threat. In the meantime, keep sending non-threatening messages by continuing to breathe and staying calm.

It can be a wonderful gesture of care and support to offer some acknowledgement of the parent's negative response to your greeting, such as, "You're right. It can be very frustrating to wait, particularly if you have something urgent to talk to me about. I want to hear your concerns about your child. Would you like a coffee while we sit and talk?"

Step 3: Listen with empathy and learn (This step may take a long time!)

You, the Teacher: I'm glad we have this opportunity to talk about your child. What would you like to tell me?

Step 3 can be difficult to master when first learning our compassionate assertiveness method. You have worked hard to get where you are and having someone in red energy attack any aspect of your professionalism can cause you to defend yourself, as illustrated in the scenario that started this chapter. However, you need to avoid this response and provide space for the parent to express their concerns, in whatever way these are delivered! Remaining in blue energy, focusing on listening to what the parent is telling you, and validating the parent's concerns, whether you agree or not, are aspects of what we deem **compassionate listening**.

If you can hold the belief that both of you want what is the best for the student, then it will be much easier for you to open up space for the parent to tell you their concerns. Here are some ways to help the parent understand you are not a threat and that you are open to hearing what the parent wants to tell you:

- I want to help. Please tell me what you are concerned about.
- I am interested; tell me what you would like me to know.
- I have the time to listen to your concerns. Where do you want to start?
- Sounds like you have something important to tell me.
- Please tell me how I can help you.

This step is like handling an over-inflated red balloon that is about to pop. Your job is to let the air out of this balloon gently—to let it deflate slowly. In our view, when you provide space for parents to air their concerns, without interrupting or retreating into a defensive stance or jumping to problem-solving, you are deflating this imaginary red balloon in readiness for Step 4.

The most common way to show you are listening to the parent (the aim of this step) is to use your body (e.g., nodding your head slowly, leaning into the conversation rather than pulling away). It also helps to offer an appreciation for sharing a concern, such as "I appreciate your telling me this" or "It is very helpful for me to hear your perspective." You can listen and validate parents' concerns without agreeing with them. If culturally appropriate, it is a very good idea to maintain gentle eye contact, as this tends to show you are listening and will continue to do so. This step may take less than a minute, or it may take much longer.

Be warned: the parent may have a laundry list of concerns. This is not a problem, as this step is about inviting air from the red balloon to release. In our experience, it is hard for someone to stay in red energy when the listener is in blue energy and remains calm and interested while allowing space for the laundry list to unfold. Below are some ways to invite the parent to continue telling you what they think is important for you to know. Perhaps use one or two of these questions each time the parent finishes making a point (e.g., during a period of silence):

- What else would you like me know about _____?
- What else? (said in a warm, sincere manner)
- Anything else you would like to tell me about _____?
- Do you have any other concerns?
- Is there anything else you would like to me know?

Empathy—Seeing the Parent's Perspective

To successfully transition out of this step, you need to put yourself into the shoes of the parent to compassionately and empathically connect to them. Your job is to ignore the parent's red-energy delivery and listen for the core message. To do this, consider that the parent may make some point, even a small one, that could help you to have more success with the student or to refine your skills as a teacher. No one is perfect, and we always have something to learn. Perhaps the parent is actually afraid when talking to people who have some authority, so they use fight energy (from the 3Fs) as a way to feel safe. Holding compassion for the parent while they learn there is nothing to fear will be key here. Also, given the parent knows the child better than you do, the fight energy might be that of a mother bear trying to protect her cub. The parent may be trying to offer you some valuable tips on how to help the child thrive in the classroom. For example, one of us recalls a parent saying that the homework assignments seemed very disjointed with little rationale or purpose. As a result of finding some truth in this parent's red-energy speech, it was decided to send short notes home to parents, explaining the goals and objectives of the homework and delineating how the homework linked to the entire unit of the study.

Step 4: Repeat back

You, the Teacher: (In a warm and non-judgmental tone, and with genuine curiosity) Let me be sure I understand your concern. You're worried about the amount of time your child is taking to complete the homework I assign. Is that correct?

Summarize

When you decide to start Step 4, it is because the parent has exhausted their laundry list of complaints, and you are ready to convey to the parent a summary of what you heard. Even if the concerns do not seem all that serious to you, it is a very serious matter from the parent's perspective. It is vital you show the parent that you are able to appreciate this perspective. People will start to calm down when they believe that they are being taken seriously and have been heard. When this happens, you may also learn more about the underlying fears, motivations, and concerns of the parent.

In this step, it is important that you continue to send both verbal and non-verbal signals to the parent that you are engaged and interested in the information you are receiving. While this is often called active listening, we prefer to think of it as compassionate listening, as your focus is not on your internal dialogue and a need to put yourself first. Rather, you are focused on truly hearing what the person in front of you has to say. This is not a time to talk about your experiences and how what the parent is saying is like something that happened to you. The parent's story concerning the child is unique, and the parent deserves to have your complete attention. When engaging in compassionate listening:

- Avoid crossing your arms. This can activate the parent's alarm systems, and yours!

- Keep your frontal area open. If you cover up (arms or legs crossed), then you might be sending a mixed message, such as, "I really do not want to hear what you are saying."
- Face the speaker with warmth, as much as culture and the person permit, and, if you want, tilt your head to convey interest.
- Maintain an upright body position. Avoid slouching, as this could imply a lack of interest on your part, which could easily activate the other person's alarm system.
- Try to keep your palms open, relaxed, and slightly on an angle.
- Gently lean towards the person, especially if they become emotional. Avoid the impulse to pull away.
- Make slow movements, as sudden moves can trigger the speaker's alarm system.
- Be aware of what your eyebrows are doing. Think calming words and see soothing images to keep yourself from sending mixed messages with your facial features.

In addition to the non-verbal cues listed above, compassionate listening requires you to use summary statements that indicate you are receiving the information without judgment. You want the parent to know that what is being said is important to you, as are they. Ask if the parent is comfortable with your making notes as they talk. Making sure that you completely understand the parent's concerns is part of this. Some of the summary statements you can use to do this, in addition to the one in the box, are the following:

- I want to make sure that I am getting where you are coming from. So, _____.
- Just to be clear, as I understand it, the situation so far is _____.
- You are raising two main concerns: (1) _____ and (2) _____.
- If I am following you correctly, you are telling me that _____.
- Am I getting this right? Please feel free to correct me.
- Let me make sure I am hearing you correctly. Please correct me if I am off the mark. You said _____.
- I am sorry. There are so many points here; can I just take you back to where you said _____?

After you attempt to summarize what you think were the main issues the parent wanted you to hear, do not assume you can proceed to the next step (resolving the conflicts). It is common, after a parent in red energy starts to feel heard, that they will want to continue to unload their concerns about the student, you, or the school. Be prepared to be patient and listen. Imagine again the image of an over-inflated red balloon. If you move too quickly to problem-solving mode, it will be like putting a pin into that balloon. The explosion will be loud and leave a mess of balloon pieces everywhere. However, if you show the parent you are still listening and avoid problem-solving, it is like slowly allowing the air to escape from the balloon.

Zingers

A significant challenge when the balloon is deflating is the parent aiming a zinger directly at you. We define *zingers* as those moments when someone makes a sharp, mean, or hypercritical comment about you. Examples might be "You are too young to be teaching my child!" or "No offence, but my son must get into a good college, and you don't seem smart enough to be teaching this advanced mathematics class."

Zingers can be tough to cope with, as your amygdala gets triggered and signals you to respond to the hurtful comment by using one of the 3Fs: respond in kind (fight), shut down the conversation (flight), or go numb (freeze). It may sound impossible to stay calm during a zinger, but you can by using logic—your prefrontal cortex. You must convince your nervous system you are not in danger, even though the comment may have stung a bit. Staying in control of your amygdala, and thereby your blue energy, is critical.

One strategy to lower the impact of the zinger is to tell yourself that your self-esteem is not dependent on this parent liking you; your self-esteem comes from acting in ways that showcase your taking the high road. We also encourage you to engage your compassion and let the red comments fade away, as we all say things in the heat of the moment that we later regret. The parent, who is unloading a pile of complaints on you, is not thinking clearly (their amygdala is keeping them in fight mode). Maintaining empathy for this parent is part of compassionate communication. However, sometimes, you may want to respond to a zinger. We have had success in helping teachers deal with zingers by having them use an assertiveness technique called "fogging" (Smith, 1975).

Fogging is just what it sounds like. It is very difficult for a person to maintain an attack if it feels as though they are punching fog. It tends to take the wind out of the sails of the person who is on the attack. Your job is to find a grain of truth in whatever verbal attack is directed at you and deflect the comment. Remember, you're not perfect; something might be true in the statement even if you don't think so. Fogging works because it shows the person you listened to them and that you are not going to overreact or get defensive. Both of us have had the experience of using the fogging technique, with softness and care in our voice, and having the parent respond with a stunned look because they expected us to attack in response to a zinger. Instead, we demonstrated that we would not return a zinger, as we were staying in blue energy and had compassion and understanding for the parent. In most cases, the parent later apologized!

Some examples of fogging techniques are the following:

- *Parent:* You are far too young to teach my kid!
- *Teacher:* Yes, I am young.
- *Parent:* My daughter says you talk way too fast!
- *Teacher:* Yes, sometimes I do talk fast.

Other fogging returns to a zinger that we have seen used with success include:

- You could be right. There are things I could improve.
- That's a point I need to think more about.
- You may be right. Sometimes I am not as organized as I would like to be.
- Yeah, I agree, that part is true.

Step 5: Ask

You, the Teacher: Is this a good time to start looking at some solutions?

Having successfully laid the groundwork in the previous steps, you take this step to focus on how you and the parent can best help the child. You may not get to share your point of view. If you have rushed any of the previous steps, then you may find yourself back at one of them. However, if the parent is feeling heard, understood, and respected, they are likely to shift into some blue energy, and the chances of successfully negotiating an action plan with the parent to address the concerns expressed are greatly increased.

After the parent accepts your invitation to move into problem-solving mode, continue the invitation by asking which problem the parent would like to focus on first. Then, follow up by asking whether the parent has any ideas on how to resolve the situation. Sometimes, having listened with compassion to what the parent had to say will be all that was needed. There may be no problem to solve.

The parent will be satisfied that you now know everything they wanted to tell you and will trust you to use the information wisely. When this happens, you can move swiftly to Step 6.

It is always good if the parent generates some suggestions, as the ultimate solution will likely be more acceptable if some of what the parent asked for is incorporated into the answer. Warning: The parent may present solutions that are impossible to implement! Do not judge the solutions offered, as your focus is on maintaining the relationship that you have established and continuing to show that you are hearing what the parent has to say. Once the parent has finished offering possible solutions, warmly thank them for the ideas. It is also a nice gesture if you share how glad you are that both of you are focused on helping the child. At this point, you can ask if you may share your thoughts on the matter. Again, if you have taken the time to establish a good relationship, a parent will rarely say no.

If the parent invites you to share your ideas, then do so. Keep your ideas short and to the point. Between your ideas and the parent's ideas, try to get at least three options on the table that each of you can discuss. We like to suggest using a pro/con table. Eventually, the task is to negotiate a solution that is workable. During the negotiations, you can invite ongoing cooperation and offer positive comments about being able to work together on a solution.

Below is a list of statements that work well when interwoven in this step, when it is relevant to do so:

- What ideas do you have on _____?
- How can we solve this problem together?
- What can we do to get around this problem?
- What ideas do you have on how we can avoid this type of situation again?
- I am curious: What thoughts have you given to how we can make sure that this does not happen again?
- What if we _____?
- I really look forward to finding a solution with your help/input.
- Great idea. What other ideas are there?
- Do we think we could come up with five brainstorm ideas? Sure, we can!
- Thank you for sticking around so we could find a resolution.
- I appreciate that we are talking about solutions now. Thank you.
- You are really focused on moving out of the problem and into a solution—nice!

This step may be very easy to complete, or it may take significant time to work out a solution. When time is an issue, as it often is during a parent-teacher interview schedule, you might want to propose a second meeting at a mutually convenient time where you can offer the parent more time to come to a satisfactory solution that benefits the child. It is a good idea to have written down the action plan so that you are sure to implement what the parent agreed to. This will be helpful for moving towards Step 6.

Step 6 : End on a good note

You, the Teacher: (Warmly and with a culturally appropriate gesture of appreciation) Thank you for taking the time to meet with me. I know how much you care about your child. I'm glad we worked together to find a solution that will help resolve your concern.

Think of this step as being similar to thanking the people who invited you to a party. You'd like to be remembered as a thoughtful guest. You'd also like to be invited back! With the parent, you'd like to be remembered as a caring and respectful professional who took the time to listen and really understand them. You'd also like to be able to maintain good communications with the parent in the future. If the parent leaves with the impression that you are someone who genuinely listens and understands, then you are more likely to be able to work effectively with the parent.

Step 7: Follow up

You, the Teacher: (Phone call at a time that is convenient to the parent, or an email within a reasonable time after implementing the solution) Hi, I'm just checking in to see if you are noticing any positive changes since we talked.

The most frustrating thing for a parent is to leave the meeting you have had with expectations of action and then have nothing happen or not know what is happening. A simple phone call or email from you, updating the parent on what you are doing and asking what differences the parent is noticing, will go a long way towards cementing the good working relationship with the parent that you worked so hard to achieve.

DOES THIS APPROACH WORK?

We have presented this approach to many groups of new and experienced teachers, and the feedback has been overwhelmingly positive. We have statistical evidence from our formal research with student teachers that supports the efficacy of our version of compassionate communication. Specifically, the data showed significant increases in the student teachers' self-reported ability and confidence to handle an encounter with someone who is locked in red energy. In addition, our seven-step communication plan appeared to address the needs of the student teachers in a very practical, compassionate, and immediate manner, as evidenced by their extremely high satisfaction scores for the training they received on our model. Experienced teachers also found this approach useful as it organized aspects of what they had been doing in their interactions with what they deemed to be difficult parents. In addition to training student teachers in this approach, we also provided them with practical tips gleaned from our experiences when working with people stuck in red energy. We were able to distill these into five points that mesh with compassionate communication, which you will find in the Appendix.

CONCLUSION

Many new teachers arrive in the classroom well prepared to manage their daily interactions with their students. Indeed, the focus in teacher training is on this type of interpersonal conflict. However, when faced with a critical adult, often a parent of one of their students, new teachers may find themselves looking over their shoulders for the adult in the room who will handle the intimidating parent. It may come as a shock to them that they are now the person that must handle the conflict, since they no longer are in the somewhat artificial reality of their practicum placement. Our approach, backed by research, has the potential to help beginning teachers negotiate the unfamiliar terrain of adult conflict. The gaps that currently exist in teacher research and in syllabi of teacher education programs can be addressed by further study of this approach and by offering assertiveness training as a regular part of teacher training.

We end the chapter by inviting you to think of how you would respond with empathy and compassion to a parent who starts the conversation with you by saying, from the deepest of red energy, "How dare you …" Imagine what you can do and say now so that the conversation will end with both of you having respect for and understanding of each other.

QUESTIONS FOR CRITICAL THOUGHT

1. As you consider the seven steps, which step stands out as the most important to you? Which step do you anticipate you will need to practice in order to gain confidence that it will work?
2. How do you see these steps working when you are dealing with students? Or when you are in conflict with a school administrator?
3. We would like you to recall a time you were in a red-energy conversation with someone. As you consider this scene, let's focus on the positives: (a) What did you say or do that helped to starve your red? and (b) What did you say or do in this conversation that reflected finding some blue? We invite you to consider how you might already have some tools and strategies to stop your amygdala from hijacking your thinking brain. Consider how your own tools could be used the next time you feel red energy.

GLOSSARY

Compassionate assertiveness: A process of resolving differences in such a way that all parties involved are treated with respect and dignity, without any one party either dominating or adopting a purely submissive role.

Compassionate listening: A way of taking in information from another person while setting aside one's own need to be seen as important or as an expert, keeping the focus on the other person and not one's own experiences.

Conflict resolution: The process of negotiating a best-case, not necessarily ideal, solution to a confrontation in which the parties involved do not become locked into win-lose thinking.

Emotional regulation: The process used by an individual to slow down the primitive alarm reactions of the brain and re-engage the thinking portion of the brain, which will allow the individual to react to a situation or person with compassion and understanding.

Empathy: The ability to appreciate the perspective of others and react with understanding.

REFERENCES

Addi-Raccah, A., & Grinshtain, Y. (2017). Forms of capital and teachers' views of collaboration and threat relations with parents in Israeli schools. *Education and Urban Society*, 49(6), 616–640. https://doi:10.1177/0013124516644052.

Austin, M. S., & Harkins, D. A. (2008). Shifting spaces and emerging voices: Participation, support, and conflict in one school administrative team. *Early Education Development*, 19(6), 907–940.

Butt, A., & Zahid, Z. M. (2015). Effect of assertiveness skills on job burnout. *International Letters of Social and Humanistic Sciences*, 63, 218–224. https://doi.org/10.18052/www.scipress.com/ILSHS.63.218.

Dor, A., & Rucker-Naidu, B. (2012). Teachers' attitudes toward parents' involvement in school: Comparing teachers in the USA and Israel. *Issues in Educational Research*, 22, 246–262.

Ghamrawi, N. (2013). Teachers helping teachers: A professional development model that promotes teacher leadership. *International Education Studies*, 6(4), 171–182. Retrieved from https://files.eric.ed.gov/fulltext/EJ1067641.pdf.

Goleman, D. (1995). *Emotional intelligence: Why it can matter more than IQ.* New York: Bantam Books.

Goleman, D., & Boyatzis, R. (2008). Social intelligence and the biology of leadership. *Harvard Business Review*, 86(9), 74–81.

Gwernan-Jones, R., Moore, D. A., Garside, R., Richardson, M., Thompson-Coon, J., Rogers, M., & Ford, T. (2015). ADHD, parent perspectives and parent–teacher relationships: Grounds for conflict. *British Journal of Special Education*, 42(3), 279–300. https://doi.org/10.1111/1467-8578.12087.

Kim, J. E., Dager, S. R., & Lyoo, I. K. (2012). The role of the amygdala in the pathophysiology of panic disorder: Evidence from neuroimaging studies. *Biology of Mood and Anxiety Disorders*, 2(1). https://doi.org/10.1186/2045-5380-2-20.

Levine, P. A. (2015). *Trauma and memory: Brain and body in a search for the living past: A practical guide for understanding and working with traumatic memory.* Berkeley, CA: North Atlantic Books.

Levine, P., & Kline, M. (2008). *Trauma-proofing your kids.* Berkeley, CA: North Atlantic Books.

Mansfield, C. F., Beltman, S., Broadley, T., & Weatherby-Fell, N. (2016). Building resilience in teacher education: An evidenced informed framework. *Teaching and Teacher Education*, 54, 77–87. https://doi.org/10.1016/j.tate.2015.11.016.

McBride, D. (2015). When harshly criticized or verbally attacked: A six-step communication plan for teachers. *The Alberta Counsellor*, 34(1), 29–36.

Pernicano, P. (2014). *Using trauma-focused therapy stories: Interventions for therapists, children, and their caregivers.* New York: Routledge.

Ressler, K. J. (2010). Amygdala activity, fear, and anxiety: Modulation by stress. *Biological Psychiatry*, 67(12), 1117–1119. https://doi.org/10.1016/j.biopsych.2010.04.027.

Rothschild, B. (2006). *Help for the helper: The psychophysiology of compassion fatigue and vicarious trauma.* New York: W. W. Norton.

Simbula, S., & Gugliemi, D. (2010). Depersonalization or cynicism, efficacy or inefficacy: What are the dimensions of teacher burnout? *European Journal of Psychology of Education*, 25(3), 301–314. https://doi.org/10.1007/s10212-010-0017-6.

Smith, M. (1975). *When I say no, I feel guilty: How to cope, using the skills of systematic assertive therapy*. New York: Bantam Books.

Trinder, M., Wertheim, E. H., Freeman, E., Sanson, A., Richardson, S., & Hunt, S. (2010). Comparison of the effectiveness of two forms of the Enhancing Relationships in School Communities Project for promoting cooperative conflict resolution education in Australian primary schools. *Journal of Peace Education*, 7(1), 85–105. https://doi.org/10.1080/17400201003640228.

Van der Kolk, B. A. (2014). *The body keeps the score: Brain, mind, and body in the healing of trauma*. New York: Viking.

APPENDIX

Our Compassionate Communication Approach: Five More Tips

1. Stay Grounded

This is both a physical and a psychological concept, and it underlies Steps 1, 2, and 3. It can be helpful to remember that verbal attacks are rarely personal and have more to do with the person delivering them than the person receiving them. It is like waiting for a storm to pass. Very few people will continue to storm at you when it becomes obvious that you will not be rattled. You may be the first person who is really making the effort to connect with them with empathy and understand how much they care about the focus of their concerns.

2. If You're Wrong, Admit It!

Parents often arrive expecting to be stonewalled and ignored. As has been noted previously, nobody is perfect. When the parent's concern is about something you know may not have helped the child and that you could have done differently, offer an immediate, open, and honest apology. It is not what the parent expects. It sends the message that you accept your flaws and will likely accept the fallibility of others. This often leads to a very fast disarming of the parent. This can be part of Steps 2 and 3.

3. Remember Who Should Be the Focus of the Conversation

Regardless of what the parent is saying, this conversation is not about the other students in the class. Nor is it about your teaching. It is about the parent's child. Compassionate listening includes recognizing that all the parent really wants from you is for you to help them help the child. When listening to the parent with this attunement, you are looking for ways to accomplish this. This idea is part of Steps 3 and 4.

4. Take Notes but Don't Lose Visual Contact

In Step 4, we suggested asking the parent if they would be comfortable with you taking notes while the parent is talking. While this shows the parent how seriously you are taking the concerns being expressed, it backfires when the parent is now talking to the top of your head as you focus on the paper in front of you! Write just enough to remember what was being talked about. You are not trying to make a transcript of the conversation. Having a written reminder of the action plan from Step 5 is important for the final two steps of our approach.

5. Don't Be Afraid to Involve Others

Sometimes, despite your best efforts, a parent may not want to relinquish red energy and move into the blue. In these cases, the situation is usually not about you, your teaching, or the school in general. Sometimes, such parents just want to be able to tell others how they dominated the situation because it makes them feel better about themselves. Thankfully, these parents are rare. However, when one does show up, you do not have to take the abuse being heaped upon you. When a compassionate communication approach does not work, you have the right to ask for help from someone with more authority or from another person. You can even end the conversation politely and leave the room. Compassionate communication is not about being someone's doormat. It is about mutual respect and caring. When one of the people involved in the conversation is not interested in pursuing this outcome, it is time to end the conversation.

CHAPTER 10

Compassionate Communication: A Key Aspect of Partnering with Parents of Students with Disabilities

Kyle Robinson and Nancy L. Hutchinson

LEARNING OBJECTIVES

1. To understand the concept of compassionate communication as developed in the work of Noddings (1984, 2005, 2012), as well as Burrows (2004) and Woolfolk Hoy (2013).
2. To understand the importance of using compassionate communication in future relationships and meetings with parents of students with disabilities.

INTRODUCTION

"The teacher and I write notes back and forth every day, which I just love! She writes about what is happening with all the students ... and then this side here is just specific to Noah." Dorothy is proud of her son Noah and works hard to be a well-informed parent. She attends conferences about Down syndrome and believes that this helps her to create opportunities for Noah. Noah's kindergarten teacher appreciates that Dorothy passes along information about relevant websites and loans books that she has gathered. Dorothy expects others to share information with her in return. She recalls that the week before Noah was going to begin attending kindergarten, the school had still not contacted her about the supports that Noah would receive in a regular classroom: "I needed someone to call me and let me know that everything was going to be okay. So when no one called, I went to the school and asked my questions."

Melissa lives in the country, and her daughter Mandy attends a small, rural school. Mandy has fragile health, severe hearing loss, and autistic tendencies with little expressive language. The team of therapists who worked with Melissa and Mandy through Mandy's preschool years say, "Melissa would speak up for Mandy. She would ask questions when she was not sure what was going on and say, 'This is what is happening; what do you think we should do?'" Melissa prepared a handbook for the teacher each year because she believed there was a lot of information that needed to be shared about Mandy's medical needs and vulnerabilities. This year, when she didn't receive any response from the school, she wasn't sure whether the teacher had read it. When Melissa told Mandy's teacher that she would like frequent communication, the teacher chose, without consulting with Melissa, to use a communication book. Melissa thought, "I don't express myself well in writing. I would prefer brief conversations by phone and in person. I am worried about misunderstanding. There is such a small space to write—only room for a few words." One day, Melissa arrived at the school during recess to drop off Mandy's lunch, which had been forgotten, and observed Mandy alone on the playground while all her classmates were playing on climbing structures located at the top of a small rise. Mandy could not climb the hill, so she was forced to play by herself. Melissa decided it was time for her to speak up and request an opportunity to ask questions and talk regularly with the teacher rather than exchange terse written notes.

Two parents, each seeking respectful, informative exchanges of information with a classroom teacher about their child with special needs. And each with a different idea about what constitutes **compassionate communication**. Increasingly, **students with disabilities** are learning in inclusive classrooms and being taught by teachers who are not specialists in **special education** (People for Education, 2017). Participating in all facets of society, including educational institutions, is a fundamental right of all Canadians. When the *Canadian Charter of Rights and Freedoms* was passed, Canada became one of the first countries to guarantee rights to people with disabilities in its constitution, and we have grown increasingly inclusive in the intervening decades.

We believe compassionate communication is a key aspect of educators' partnering with parents of students with disabilities. We have three goals in this chapter about compassionate communication: (1) to make the case for teachers' engaging parents in compassionate communication; (2) to develop the concept of compassionate communication; and (3) to provide descriptions and examples to enable educators to communicate with parents in a manner that is both effective and compassionate (all with an emphasis on building trusting, respectful relationships with parents of children with disabilities).

PARTNERSHIPS AND COLLABORATION BETWEEN TEACHERS AND PARENTS

One implication of **inclusion** of students with disabilities in regular classrooms is that teachers are learning about these students from their parents, especially when the children are young or lack the communication skills to advocate for themselves (Wright & Taylor, 2014). Recent research has reported on both similarities (e.g., Burke et al., 2018) and differences (e.g., Lalvani, 2015) in the perspectives of parents and educators about collaborating for students with disabilities. Lalvani (2015) found in an interview study that elementary teachers were more likely to view disability as residing in individual minds and bodies and to question the effectiveness of collaborating with parents. By contrast, parents "were more apt to locate disability not solely in their children, but also in the contexts" of school and society (p. 389), and to advocate for contexts in which they felt their children would experience "belongingness," as well as for greater collaboration (p. 385). Burke and her colleagues reported that, in separate focus groups, parents (of students aged 3 to 16 with social-communication needs) and school professionals provided similar descriptions of how parents advocated and similar views on the importance of parents' knowledge about their children, their rights at school, and communication strategies. Both groups perceived that the quality of the parent-teacher relationship affected parental advocacy.

A number of Canadian studies have contributed to our understanding of partnership, collaboration, and communication between professionals and parents. Villeneuve and her colleagues described the experiences of parents as their children with developmental disabilities transitioned into kindergarten (2013). In three case studies, the families valued frequent and informative meetings with teachers but found it challenging to arrange meaningful exchanges of information with the school. They reported that they had to initiate contact with educators if communication was to take place; and they expected "more details from teachers about their child's inclusion at school because their children could not communicate this to them" (p. 32). By contrast, Villeneuve and Hutchinson (2012) described a case study of an elementary student with learning disabilities in which professionals moved from cooperation to collaboration by developing a shared focus, identifying a leader, prioritizing time for formal meetings, and committing to effective communication that included parents. Starr and Foy (2012) analyzed responses by parents of children with autism spectrum disorders (ASD) to open-ended questions on a survey. Parents were asked for their perceptions of and satisfaction with the education of their children (who were 4 to 18 years of age). One of the prominent themes in their responses focused on the importance of effective communication and collaboration between parents and schools. Parents often described their roles as advocates, with one suggesting that the source of a "supportive and understanding" school might have been "my husband's and my approach to the school and [our son's] needs [that] has helped foster the accepting, positive attitudes there" (p. 211). A number of parents expressed frustration with having to "educate their child's teacher each year" about their child, but also about ASD and "programming" for children with ASD (p. 212). Clearly, communication between parents and educators is critical to effective **parental advocacy**.

Some studies argue that trust is the most important contributor to family-professional relationships (Angell, Stoner, & Shelden, 2009), while others suggest that collaborative problem-solving is key (Kuhn, Marvin, & Knoche, 2017). Shultz, Able, Sreckovic, and White (2016) recommend that teachers have "careful conversations" with parents and speak "in a very sensitive manner" (pp. 348–349), while Burke et al. (2018) focus on the need for parents to be respectful in their communication, as well as knowledgeable. One professional interviewed by Burke sums it up nicely: "If everyone is really listening to what everyone else is saying and really respecting different areas of expertise that are brought to the table, that helps" (p. 198). In a landmark publication, Turnbull and colleagues (2015) review the history of the role of parents of children with disabilities to frame parental aspirations for the future, including to foster empathy, dignity, and compassion. We argue that helping educators to engage in compassionate communication with parents will enhance parental advocacy, make schools more effective in educating children with disabilities, and move us closer to fulfilling important aspirations for empathy, dignity, and compassion for all.

DEVELOPING A MODEL OF PARENTAL ADVOCACY

Historically, parents of students with exceptionalities have played many roles in their children's lives. In the early years of the 20th century, when students with exceptionalities[1] were not allowed to attend school, parents played the role of teacher in addition to their typical duties (Sandiford, 1924). As time progressed, students with exceptionalities began attending neighbourhood schools. Now, rather than be segregated, students with exceptionalities are spending more time in inclusive, regular classrooms. This has changed the role of parents in their exceptional children's education dramatically. Since those early days of auxiliary (special) education, parents have been seen as the source of their children's problems (Turnbull et al., 2015); recipients of professionals' decisions (Bezdek, Summers, & Turnbull, 2010); service developers (Scheerenberger, 1984); and educational decision-makers (Epley, Summers, & Turnbull, 2010). While these roles have been fluid, and parents have found themselves shifting through all of them (sometimes concurrently), what is becoming clear is that parents of children with exceptionalities are becoming increasingly involved in their children's education. This may be in part due to shifting understandings of the potential of these students and their legal rights.

Many parents face barriers to advocacy. Mental health issues can arise from the stress of advocacy (Jamieson, 1999), which may stem from a need to assume, at times, an adversarial role with medical and educational professionals (Bennett, Deluca, & Bruns, 1997; Trainor, 2010). Socioeconomic status can become a barrier, as lower-income families might be unable to pay for private assessment. When parents need to request testing through the school, their child can remain on a waiting list for a long time. If the child does not receive appropriate services during this wait, parents' frustrations can lead to conflicts with educators and to the parents being labelled as "difficult" (Coots, 1998). Lower-income families may also face logistical issues—schools may schedule last-minute meetings, or meetings during time slots that leave parents with little ability to change work schedules (such as those working shift work) and unable to attend Individual Education Plan (IEP) meetings at which parents and educators set goals and discuss means of helping exceptional students to work towards those goals (Lareau & Shumar, 1996; Linan-Thompson & Jean, 1997). A combination of many factors has led to a need for parents to become educational advocates for their children to ensure that the education system provides the best possible services for their child.

Many scholars have written about the importance of parents and educators collaborating and about the key role that communication plays in parental advocacy, and yet there is no adequate model of parental advocacy to guide practice and research in this important area. Recently, researchers have proposed that developing effective advocacy in parents can be supported by using current models of self-advocacy in exceptional children. The Conceptual Framework of Self-Advocacy (CFSA), a model of self-advocacy (Test et al., 2005), has been viewed as a potential starting point for identifying the components of parental advocacy (Clemens, Shipp, & Kimbel, 2011; Hutchinson et al., 2014). Test and colleagues (2005) developed the model through a review of 150 studies on self-advocacy of stakeholders including parents, teachers, researchers, and students with exceptionalities. CFSA has four components: (1) knowledge of self (knowing what you can do and what you need to do it); (2) knowledge of rights (knowing what you are entitled to receive through law or an IEP); (3) communication (effectively asking, negotiating, or asserting knowledge of self and rights); and (4) leadership (developing advocacy skills for others after developing them for oneself).

Examining the applicability of the CFSA for developing a model of parental advocacy, Hutchinson and colleagues (2014) modified the CFSA and applied it to three case studies of parents with children who have developmental disabilities. The model still has four components: knowledge of the child; knowledge of rights; communication; and leadership. Each case contained clear instances of the first three components; parents described reading about their child's disability prior to birth (knowledge of the child), consulting health care professionals for educational advice (knowledge of rights), and requesting various forms of communication about their child's educational progress (communication). The fourth component, leadership, was explicitly found in only one case, with one parent forming a moms' group to provide support for other parents in similar situations. This lack of explicit examples of leadership in the other cases is not a limitation of applying self-advocacy models to parental advocacy because, as Johnson (1999) notes, strong advocacy does not require taking a leadership role. However, several others suggest that leadership is important for advocacy at the system level (Martin, Huber-Marshall, & Maxson, 2003; Test et al., 2005).

Hutchinson et al. argue that the CFSA "has potential for informing conceptual and practical work on parental advocacy" (2014, p. 360). They are careful to note that, from a conceptual standpoint, self-advocacy and parental advocacy are different, as a parent does not personally experience the social, academic, and physical effects of a disability. However, parental advocacy is substituted for self-advocacy in many cases, especially for young children or for children unable to advocate for themselves. The authors suggest that additional components, such as the parents' knowledge of themselves, are beneficial for our understanding of parental advocacy. Further research needs to be conducted on the efficacy of this model when applied to parental advocacy, and further research is needed to identify other potential components. Possible components include parents' willingness to engage in ongoing interactions with professionals (e.g., to seek legal advice or to collaborate with specialists).

THE LIM FRAMEWORK FOR EDUCATIONAL ADVOCACY BY PARENTS OF STUDENTS WITH EXCEPTIONALITIES: LEARNING, IMPLEMENTING, MAINTAINING

When noting the impact that parental advocacy has on strengthening the inclusion of youth with exceptionalities in educational settings, Carter and colleagues call for research "that identifies potential indicators that can be used to document the longer-term impact" of parental advocacy programs (2012, p. 21). This call served as the stimulus for Robinson's (2017) LIM framework for educational advocacy by parents of students with exceptionalities, while the research of Hutchinson and colleagues (2014) and Duquette, Stodel, Fullarton, and Hagglund (2012) serves as the base. The three dimensions of the advocacy model are learning, implementing, and maintaining (LIM). Each dimension is composed of several facets that represent tasks parents typically engage in during that dimension. Table 10.1 shows each dimension and its facets. None of the parent participants in the literature on parental advocacy report using all nine facets contained within the framework, although they do report using at least one facet from each of the three dimensions.

Table 10.1: The Dimensions and Facets of the LIM Framework for Educational Advocacy by Parents of Students with Exceptionalities

Dimensions	Facet
Learning	Discovery
	Knowledge of the child
	Knowledge of rights
	Communication skills
Implementing	Building relationships
	Open communication
	Case management
Maintaining	Leadership
	Parental involvement

Source: Robinson, 2017.

Although there are nine facets, the rest of this chapter focuses on two of the facets, which are both part of the "implementing" dimension: building relationships and open communication. Although communication skills initially appear to fit thematically with the purpose of this chapter—specifically, discussing communication between educators and parents—that particular facet deals more with the specific methods of communication parents choose to use in their attempts to advocate; for example, parents may choose to negotiate or compromise rather than demand a specific accommodation for their child. Building relationships and open communication responds to the need for sensitive or compassionate communication.

COMMUNICATING WITH PARENTS

Communication is, for many teachers, a key aspect of their practice (see, for example, Duta, Panisoara, & Panisoara, 2015). Effective communication can have an impact on students' motivation (Lambrechts et al., 2013), as well as on a teacher's ability to meet the learning needs of students (Majid, Jelas, Azman, & Rahman, 2010). It also has an impact on a parent's ability to advocate for their child, and communicating compassionately is a straightforward way to meet the needs of parents.

Many parents in studies preferred an open communication style between themselves and educators, especially those educators who had a direct role in their child's everyday education. However, this proved difficult to obtain for many parents, as educators often reported they did not have the time to discuss specific information. One parent in Hess, Molina, and Kozleski noted that because her son had difficulty verbally communicating, she wished she could "call that teacher after school and say, 'Hey, what kind of a day did my son have?'" (2006, p. 154). Parents also listed "communicated more" as one of their top needs in advocating at school (Leyser & Kirk, 2011, p. 79). Kraft and Rogers (2015) examined an intervention where teachers delivered one-sentence individualized messages to parents once a week, finding that the messages decreased the percentage of students failing from 15.8 percent to 9.3 percent. In Trainor's study of approaches to parental advocacy, parents noted the importance of constant, open communication with teachers, even if teachers perceived these parents as "aggressive" (2010, p. 43). A lack of open communication on the part of a teacher fostered feelings of distrust among the parents participating in a study by Stoner and colleagues (2005). As well as noting the feelings of distrust on the part of the parents that can emerge from a lack of open communication, parents in

Stoner and colleagues' study further noted that any communication needs to be "honest. You can't be told that everything is going to be rosy" (2005, p. 46).

Parent advocates often discuss the need to build relationships with professionals and educators during the process of advocating. Fathers navigating the intricacies of inclusion and special education found this to be especially important, as Mueller and Buckley (2014) noted that fathers reported their number one role in the process as being a partner with their children's education team. Some fathers went as far as to define good teachers as those who want to partner with parents to "succeed together" (p. 44). Other parents talked about the importance of the relationship between themselves and the school board and district administration (Leyser & Kirk, 2011), while noting how difficult it is to maintain such a relationship on account of how frequently parents and teachers need to interact (Hess, Molina, & Kozleski, 2006). Finally, parents in both Rehm, Fisher, Fuentes-Afflick, and Chesla (2013) and Bacon and Causton-Theoharis (2013) discussed how important it was to create relationships with "people who hold high positions in the school district" (Bacon & Causton-Theoharis, 2013, p. 694). Parents were able to wield these relationships as bargaining chips within IEP meetings: when they could mention that the superintendent had already informally approved a request, they had more success. Similarly, some parents requested that those high-ranking administrators with whom they had excellent relationships attend IEP or transition meetings in order to provide extra support (Rehm, Fisher, Fuentes-Afflick, & Chesla, 2013).

COMPASSIONATE COMMUNICATION

What do we mean by compassionate communication? Compassionate communication has previously included notions of emotional intelligence and awareness, engagement, genuine relationships, and listening (Burrows, 2004). We expand on these ideas and develop the concept of compassionate communication by building on Noddings's (2005) ethic of care and Woolfolk Hoy's (2013) impassioned reflection on the "place of emotion in teaching." We emphasize that building trusting, respectful relationships with parents of children with disabilities creates a solid basis for communication and collaboration.

In her writing on compassionate communication, Burrows (2004) reminds us that parents often experience strong emotions when facing difficulties with the education of their children with disabilities. These emotions can include grief, anger, frustration, confusion, and feeling powerless in the face of an ingrained system. However, the language those working in schools are encouraged to use with parents has tended to focus on professionalism and accountability in education without getting "to the heart of it" (Hargreaves, 2001, p. 1057). In spite of the professional and sometimes distant language that teachers often use when communicating with parents, many researchers have reported on the emotions teachers feel, including their self-perceptions of inadequacy about meeting the needs of every student (e.g., Winograd, 2003).

Todd argues that there is a need for teachers to "uncover the personal, subjective, and affective" (2007, p. 134), and Woolfolk Hoy (2013) wrote an impassioned plea that we all pay more attention to how emotions and relationships affect life in classrooms. Woolfolk Hoy wrote about emotional labour, that is, the emotional regulation required for a professional role; on the job, one expresses emotions deemed appropriate to the context and suppresses other emotions in spite of what one is feeling. She contrasts this with emotional work, which is also emotional regulation, but that which is carried out in a private, unpaid context and in the presence of family and friends (for elaboration on these notions, see Schutz, Aultman, & Williams-Johnson, 2009). Woolfolk Hoy argues that for many teachers, their classroom is "a kind of extended family" and they see their role as including "creating a feeling of community" where people "respect and care for each other" (2013, p. 257). She adds, "That teachers often use metaphors and images of 'our class as a family' means that some of what might be considered emotional labour, done to fit the requirements of employment, can become for many teachers the emotional work of maintaining caring relationships among family members" (p. 257).

For many years, Noddings has written about the ethic of care (e.g., 1984, 2005, 2012). She describes a caring person during an encounter as attentive—that is, as listening, observing, and being receptive to the needs of the other. In addition, caring individuals direct their energy towards the "projects" of the other and respond positively as long as they have the resources and will not hurt anyone else. If responding positively would hurt someone else, then a caring person tries to find a way to respond that preserves the caring relationship.

Reciprocity is an important part of the ethic of care and involves mutual recognition and appreciation. Noddings (2012) addresses what we must do when there is some "disruption" in the relationship, and this characterizes many exchanges between parents of exceptional learners and teachers. She suggests that we must "ask what we would do if we were at our caring best or if this other were not so difficult" and goes on to elaborate that we respond with the intent to "restore the preferred condition of natural caring" (2012, p. 54).

Noddings describes the result of being receptive and attentive as "feeling something as a result of the encounter" (2012, p. 54) and suggests that such feeling, combined with understanding, produces empathy. While Woolfolk Hoy has long emphasized the importance of relationships in the classroom to the well-being of students, she has recently begun to consider the importance of such relationships for the well-being of teachers (Woolfolk Hoy, 2013). She describes the importance of teachers who are strongly committed to developing coping and emotional self-regulation skills to ensure their own well-being. They experience intense relationships not only with their students, but also with the parents of many of their students. Being able to communicate with parents, especially parents who may be emotional (and may even produce "disruption"), is essential to teachers' well-being and to thriving in teaching. Compassionate communication enables teachers to build trusting, respectful relationships with parents, as well as students, and creates a solid basis for partnering with the parents of students with disabilities.

CONCLUSION

Increasingly, students with disabilities are learning in inclusive classrooms. This has contributed to the parents of these students assuming a greater and greater role as advocates, especially for young children and students whose disabilities prevent them from advocating for themselves. Communication is a key component of parental advocacy. While all parents are seeking respectful, informative exchanges with teachers, the anecdotes that open this chapter illustrate that some parents have specific preferences, and some of the reviewed research reminds us that exchanges with parents can include "disruption." A recently developed model of parental advocacy emphasizes communication as a key component (Robinson, 2017). We focus on two of the nine facets of this model—building relationships with parents and open communication—as we develop the construct of compassionate communication. Building on the writings of Burrows (2004), Noddings (2005, 2012), and Woolfolk Hoy (2013), we characterize compassionate communication between teachers and parents as attentive, receptive, and responding positively to the "projects" of others; and we remind ourselves to be at "our caring best" even when facing disruption. Engaging with parents in this way not only enables them to advocate effectively for their children with disabilities, but it also enables teachers to ensure their own well-being through coping and emotional self-regulation. When teachers and parents experience compassionate communication, they can build trusting, respectful relationships, partnerships that enable everyone to thrive—students with disabilities as well as their parents and teachers.

QUESTIONS FOR CRITICAL THOUGHT

1. What is the difference between "regular" communication and compassionate communication? Is all communication not compassionate?
2. Besides compassionate communication, how else can teachers help parents to advocate for their child at school? What facets of Robinson's (2017) model would teachers be involved in?
3. How else might teachers use Noddings's concept of "ethic of care"? Can this be applied to more than just communication?

GLOSSARY

Compassionate communication: An approach to communication that involves the creation of trusting, caring partnerships between two people.
Inclusion: The act of including all students, including those with disabilities, in all educational contexts.
Parental advocacy: A set of acts by parents to influence the education of their children.
Special education: The process of accommodating, modifying, and differentiating teaching and learning strategies for students with disabilities.
Students with disabilities: A term referring to any students diagnosed (or identified) with physical, intellectual, or developmental disabilities. These conditions tend to be drawn from the American Psychological Association's *Diagnostic and Statistical Manual of Mental Disorders* (DSM-V).

NOTE

1. This chapter uses the terms *students with exceptionalities* and *students with (developmental) disabilities* interchangeably since various parts of Canada and the US use either term.

REFERENCES

Angell, M. E., Stoner, J. B., & Shelden, D. L. (2009). Trust in education professionals: Perspectives of mothers with disabilities. *Remedial and Special Education*, 30, 160–176.

Bacon, J. K., & Causton-Theoharis, J. (2013). "It should be teamwork": A critical investigation of school practices and parent advocacy in special education. *International Journal of Inclusive Education*, 17, 682–699. https://doi.org/10.1080/1360 3116.2012.708060.

Bennett, T., Deluca, D., & Bruns, D. (1997). Putting inclusion into practice: Perspectives of teachers and parents. *Exceptional Children*, 64, 115–131.

Bezdek, J., Summers, J. A., & Turnbull, A. (2010). Professionals' attitudes in partnering with families of children and youth with disabilities. *Education and Training in Developmental Disabilities*, 45, 356–365.

Burke, M. M., Meadan-Kaplansky, H., Patton, K. A., Pearson, J. N., Cummings, K. P., & Lee, C. (2018). Advocacy for children with special-communication needs: Perspectives from parents and school professionals. *Journal of Special Education*, 51, 191–200.

Burrows, L. (2004). Compassionate communication with parents of children and young people with learning disabilities. *Australian Journal of Learning Disabilities*, 9(4), 12–20.

Carter, E., Swedeen, B., Cooney, M., Walter, M., & Moss, C. K. (2012). "I don't have to do this by myself?" Parent-led community conversations to promote inclusion. *Research & Practice for Persons with Severe Disabilities*, 37, 9–23. https://doi. org/10.2511/027494812800903184.

Clemens, E. V., Shipp, A., & Kimbel, T. (2011). Investigating the psychometric properties of School Counselor Self-Advocacy Questionnaire. *Professional School Counseling*, 15, 34–44. https://doi.org/10.5330/psc.n.2011-15.34.

Coots, J. J. (1998). Family resources and parent participation in schooling activities for their children with developmental delays. *Journal of Special Education*, 31, 498–520. https://doi.org/10.1177/002246699803100406.

Duquette, C. A., Stodel, E. J., Fullarton, S., & Hagglund, K. (2012). Educational advocacy among adoptive parents of adolescents with fetal alcohol spectrum disorder. *International Journal of Inclusive Education*, 16, 1203–1221. https://doi.org/10.1080/13 603116.2011.557445.

Duta, N., Panisoara, G., & Panisoara, I. (2015). The effective communication in teaching: Diagnostic study regarding the academic learning motivation to students. *Procedia–Social and Behavioral Sciences*, 186, 1007–1012.

Epley, P. H., Summers, J. A., & Turnbull, A. (2010). Characteristics and trends in family-centred conceptualizations. *Journal of Social and Family Work*, 13, 269–285.

Hargreaves, A. (2001). Emotional geographies of teaching. *Teachers College Record*, 103, 1056–1080.

Hess, R. S., Molina, A. M., & Kozleski, E. B. (2006). Until somebody hears me: Parent voice and advocacy in special educational decision making. *British Journal of Special Education*, 33, 148–157. https://doi.org/10.1111/j.1467-8578.2006.00430.x.

Hutchinson, N. L., Pyle, A., Villeneuve, M., Dods, J., Dalton, C. J., & Minnes, P. (2014). Understanding parent advocacy during the transition to school of children with developmental disabilities: Three Canadian cases. *Early Years*, 34, 348–363. https://doi.org/10.1080/09575146.2014.967662.

Jamieson, J. S. (1999). *Advocacy, stress and quality of life in parents of children with developmental difficulties* (Doctoral dissertation). Lakehead University, Thunder Bay, ON, Canada. Retrieved from ProQuest Dissertations and Theses database (UMI No. MQ52718).

Johnson, J. R. (1999). Leadership and self determination. *Focus on Autism and Other Developmental Disorders*, 14, 4–16. https://doi.org/10.1177/108835769901400102.

Kraft, M. A., & Rogers, T. (2015). The underutilized potential of teacher-to-parent communication: Evidence from a field experiment. *Economics of Education Review*, 47, 49–63. https://doi.org/10.1016/j.econedurev.2015.04.001.

Kuhn, M., Marvin, C. A., & Knoche, L. L. (2017). In it for the long haul: Parent-teacher partnerships for addressing preschool children's challenging behavior. *Topics in Early Childhood Special Education*, 37, 81–93.

Lalvani, P. (2015). Disability, stigma, and otherness: Perspectives of parents and teachers. *International Journal of Disability, Development, and Education*, 62, 379–393.

Lambrechts, W., Mulà, I., Ceulemans, K., Molderez, I., & Gaeremynck, V. (2013). The integration of competences for sustainable development in higher education: An analysis of bachelor programs in management. *Journal of Cleaner Production*, 48, 65–73.

Lareau, A., & Shumar, W. (1996). The problem of individualism in family-school policies. *Sociology of Education*, 69, 24–39.

Leyser, Y., & Kirk, R. (2011). Parents' perspectives on inclusion and schooling of students with Angelman syndrome: Suggestions for educators. *International Journal of Special Education*, 26, 79–91.

Linan-Thompson, S., & Jean, R. E. (1997). Completing the parent participation puzzle: Accepting diversity. *Teaching Exceptional Children*, 30(2), 46–50.

Majid, N. A., Jelas, Z. M., Azman, N., & Rahman, S. (2010). Communication skills and work motivation amongst expert teachers. *Procedia–Social and Behavioral Sciences*, 7, 565–567.

Martin, J., Huber-Marshall, L., & Maxson, L. (2003). Transition policy: Infusing self-determination and self-advocacy into transition programs. *Career Development for Exceptional Individuals*, 16, 53–61. https://doi.org/10.1177/088572889301600105.

Mueller, T. G., & Buckley, P. C. (2014). The odd man out: How fathers navigate the special education system. *Remedial and Special Education*, 35, 40–49. https://doi.org/10.1177/0741932513513176.

Noddings, N. (2012). The caring relation in teaching. *Oxford Review of Teaching*, 38, 771–781. https://doi.org/10.1080/03054985.2012.745047.

Noddings, N. (2005). *The challenge to care in schools: An alternative approach to education* (2nd ed.). New York: Teachers' College Press.

Noddings, N. (1984). *Caring: A feminine approach to ethics & moral education*. Berkeley: University of California Press.

People for Education. (2017). *2017 annual report on schools: Competing priorities*. Toronto: People for Education.

Rehm, R. S., Fisher, L. T., Fuentes-Afflick, E., & Chesla, C. A. (2013). Parental advocacy styles for special education students during the transition to adulthood. *Qualitative Health Research*, 23, 1377–1387. https://doi.org/10.1177/1049732313505915.

Robinson, K. (2017). *Towards an understanding of parental advocacy: A preliminary framework* (Unpublished manuscript). Queen's University, Kingston, ON, Canada.

Sandiford, P. (1924). The selection of pupils for auxiliary classes. *The School*, 13(3), 184–189.

Scheerenberger, R. C. (1984). *A history of mental retardation*. Baltimore, MD: Brookes.

Shultz, T. R., Able, H., Sreckovic, M. A., & White, T. (2016). Parent-teacher collaboration: Perceptions of what is needed to support students with ASD in the inclusive classroom. *Education and Training in Autism and Developmental Disabilities*, 51, 344–354.

Schutz, P. A., Aultman, L. P., & Williams-Johnson, M. R. (2009). Educational psychology perspectives on teachers' emotions. In P. A. Schutz & M. Zembylas (Eds.), *Advances in teacher emotion research* (pp. 195–212). New York: Springer.

Starr, E. M., & Foy, S. (2012). In parents' voices: The education of students with autism spectrum disorders. *Remedial and Special Education*, 33, 207–216.

Stoner, J. B., Bock, S. J., Thompson, J. R., Angell, M. E., Heyl, B. S., & Crowley, E. P. (2005). Welcome to our world: Parent perceptions of interactions between parents of young children with ASD and education professionals. *Focus on Autism and Other Developmental Disabilities*, 20, 39–51. https://doi.org/10.1177/10883576050200010401.

Test, D. W., Fowler, C. H., Wood, W. M., Brewer, D. M., & Eddy, S. (2005). A conceptual framework of self-advocacy for students with disabilities. *Remedial and Special Education*, 26, 43–54. https://doi.org/10.1177/07419325050260010601.

Todd, L. (2007). *Partnerships for inclusive education: A critical approach to collaborative working*. New York: Routledge.

Trainor, A. (2010). Diverse approaches to parent advocacy during special education home—school interactions: Identification and use of cultural and social capital. *Remedial and Special Education*, 31, 34–47. https://doi.org/10.1177/0741932508324401.

Turnbull, A. A., Turnbull, H. R., Erwin, E. J., Soodak, L. C., & Shogren, K. A. (2015). *Families, professionals, and exceptionality: Positive outcomes through partnerships and trust.* Boston: Pearson.

Villeneuve, M., Chatenoud, C., Hutchinson, N. L., Minnes, P., Perry, A., Dionne, C., & Weiss, J. (2013). The experience of parents as their children with developmental disabilities transition from early intervention to kindergarten. *Canadian Journal of Education*, 36, 4–43.

Villeneuve, M., & Hutchinson, N. L. (2012). Enabling outcomes for students with developmental disabilities through collaborative consultation. *The Qualitative Report*, 17(97), 1–29.

Winograd, K. (2003). The functions of teacher emotions: The good, the bad, and the ugly. *Teachers College Record*, 105, 1641–1673.

Woolfolk Hoy, A. (2013). A reflection on the place of emotion in teaching and teacher education. In M. Newberry, A. Gallant, & P. Riley (Eds.), *Understanding how the hidden curriculum influences relationships, leadership, teaching, and learning* (pp. 255–270). Bingley, UK: Emerald.

Wright, A. C., & Taylor, S. (2014). Advocacy by parents of young children with special needs: Activities, processes, and perceived effectiveness. *Journal of Social Service Research*, 40, 591–605. https://doi.org/10.1080/01488376.2014.896850.

CHAPTER 11

Viewing with Compassion: Religious Responsiveness in Canadian Schools

David C. Young and Kendra Gottschall

LEARNING OBJECTIVES

1. To develop an awareness of the place of religion in Canadian education, including the issues surrounding responsiveness and accommodation.
2. To understand and appreciate the role a compassionate teacher can play in creating inclusive classrooms where diversity is embraced and celebrated.

INTRODUCTION

Canadian schools, as a microcosm of the larger Canadian society, are characterized by diversity. Although diversity takes many forms, this chapter will focus on religion, and more specifically, religious responsiveness on the part of educators. The chapter will be guided by examining reasonable religious accommodation, as well as by considering how teachers who embrace a compassionate attitude realize said accommodation within their classrooms. Certainly, all educational institutions must continuously strive to be inclusive and accommodating, but both principles can at times be difficult and tenuous to enact. Thus, this chapter will offer suggestions for how educators can work towards creating inclusive and accommodating spaces. In addition, this chapter will examine the nature and history of public education, with consideration given to policies that have shaped this debate. Finally, as the courts have been drawn into this arena, relevant litigation involving the intersection of religion and education will also be highlighted.

THE LONG ARM OF HISTORY

Writing in 1986, Milner cogently asserts that "it would be foolish to attempt any kind of comprehensive historical survey of ... education in one short chapter, nor would it serve any useful purpose" (p. 10). Yet, history tends to have a long arm, and contemporary events can often be traced to specific or general antecedents.

As reflective practitioners, those involved in teaching must draw on what has come before in order that we might improve what lies ahead. Oftentimes, teachers struggle with forging links between history and its impact on the classrooms in which they will teach. This is certainly natural, and it is safe to assume that not every aspect of history will have a direct bearing on one's daily practice. In large measure, modern education is a product of the past, and while many educators may not consciously realize the pervasive role that history plays in their daily practice, this reality is unquestionable. As Dewey pointed out in *Democracy and Education: An Introduction to the Philosophy of Education*, "the past ... adds a new dimension to life, but on condition that it be seen as the past of the present and not as another and disconnected world" (1966, p. 115).

In thinking about Canada, it is important to note that religion's fingerprints are imbued throughout the educational history of this country. Early European immigration to North America, chiefly French Catholic and British Protestant settlers, brought with them their own views on religion. This religious divide between the Catholic and Protestant faiths was an attendant feature of pre-Confederation Canada. The 1867 *British North America Act*, which provided the legal and administrative framework upon which Canada was founded, guaranteed via section 93 that education would be a provincial responsibility, and furthermore, that if a province joined Confederation with religious or **denominational** rights and privileges intact, then these rights and privileges would be essentially "frozen in time." In the years since Confederation, religion has remained as one of the most important issues in the realm of education.

Although there are numerous examples throughout this country's history that point to the fact that "religion and education are inextricably intertwined" (Sears & Christou, 2011, p. 342), a fully exhaustive examination is beyond the scope of this chapter. However, to illustrate the dynamic and oftentimes tenuous divide between religion and education, a few examples will be offered.

The Manitoba School Question was a firestorm of controversy involving the intersection of religion and language. In 1871, Roman Catholic and Protestant boards had been established in Manitoba. However, over the next several years the increased migration of English-speaking Protestants had transformed the demographic profile of the province, to the point where in 1891, only one-fifth of the population was Catholic. In a time of increasing polarization between Catholics and Protestants and between French and English spurred on by the 1884 Métis rebellion and the hanging of Louis Riel in 1885, the Manitoba government, led by Liberal Thomas Greenway, passed the *Manitoba Public Schools Act* in 1890 (Manzer, 1994, p. 60). Arriving on the heels of earlier legislation that had abolished French as an official language of the province, the *Public Schools Act* eliminated Roman Catholic school districts. From this point forward, there would only be one nonsectarian school system, and only this system would receive funding. Although the Act did not prohibit Roman Catholic schools, these institutions would be private and not entitled to government money. Supporters of these private schools would be forced to have their tax dollars directed to the public school system (Titley, 1990, p. 59). In seeking judicial relief, Roman Catholics appealed to the courts. In its ruling of 1891, the Supreme Court of Canada declared the act to be *ultra vires* (that is, the power to pass such a law was outside of the scope of the province's authority). However, on appeal to the Judicial Committee of the Privy Council (a British court that was at that time the highest court in Canada), the decision of the Supreme Court was reversed in 1892 (Giles & Proudfoot, 1994, pp. 27–29). After numerous appeals by Roman Catholics for federal involvement, a compromise was reached in 1897 between Premier Greenway and Prime Minister Laurier. This arrangement was to be known as the Laurier-Greenway compromise.

> The agreement provided for the same non-sectarian school system supported by universal taxation, but there were important concessions to the minority. Religious teaching could be conducted between 3:30 and 4:00 p.m. by any Christian clergy or delegate if requested by parents of at least ten children in a rural school or at least twenty-five children in an urban school or if authorized by the board. Attendance during religious teaching was optional, as indeed was school attendance generally. Provision was made for the employment of a minority teacher, Catholic or non-Catholic, when requested by parents of at least forty children in urban schools or at least twenty-five children in rural schools. Finally, there were guarantees of Roman Catholic representation in the education administrative structure and of bilingual instruction for minority language children. (Bezeau, 1995, p. 37)

Although the Laurier-Greenway compromise was reached in 1897, the religion clauses in Manitoba's education legislation still reflect the tenets of this agreement.

Residential schools are an extremely sad historical chapter in the interplay between religion and education in Canada. Following the passage of the 1876 *Indian Act*, the federal government began to investigate the possibility of using residential schools as a means of providing for Indigenous education. Although most of the earlier treaties stipulated that day schools on reserves would be the norm, problems with attendance, as well as a general feeling that these types of institutions were generally ineffective in assimilating First Nations youth, led to a change in approach. Nicholas Flood Davin, a member of parliament, who had been dispatched to the United States to investigate the use of these schools in that country, recommended in an 1879 report that Canada also embrace the residential school model (White & Peters, 2009, p. 17). As a result, church-run residential schools were established across the country, with the exceptions being New Brunswick, Newfoundland, and Prince Edward Island. At their peak, there were some 139 residential schools in operation in this country, with the main goal of these institutions being the assimilation of Indigenous children into the new Canadian society. The legacy of the residential schools is appalling and serves as a stark reminder of the dark side of Canada's educational history.

Another important signpost in the relationship between religion and education is the patriation of the Constitution in 1982. Interestingly, the 1867 *British North America Act* was a British law and could only be amended by the parliament at Westminster. For a developed nation such as Canada, this was indeed an odd arrangement, and *patriation* was the term given to the process by which the Constitution would be "brought home." As a means of background, Quebec had experienced a referendum in 1980, in which the citizens of the province were asked if they wished to remain part of Canada or become a sovereign country. During the referendum campaign, Prime Minister Pierre Trudeau promised constitutional renewal if Quebec voted against separation. In the end, roughly 60 percent of the electorate voted against separation in the 1980 referendum. After much political wrangling, including involvement of the Supreme Court of Canada, a deal was brokered, and patriation was achieved. More importantly for our current discussion, the *Canadian Charter of Rights and Freedoms* was enshrined in the Constitution. The Charter is particularly important in that it guarantees freedom of conscience and religion (section 2) as well as prohibiting discrimination based on religion (section 15). Further, section 29 of the Charter permits for denominational rights and privileges—which can still be found in Ontario, Saskatchewan, and Alberta—to take precedence over even the Charter itself (Buckingham,

2014, p. 21). As section 29 states: "Nothing in this Charter abrogates or derogates from any rights or privileges guaranteed by or under the Constitution of Canada in respect of denominational, separate or dissentient schools."

In post-Charter Canada, religion has continued to play an important role in education. In Ontario, denominational rights and privileges existed at the time the province joined Confederation. However, compared to the public school system, the Roman Catholic system was disadvantaged in that public funding extended to only the end of Grade 10. Until the 1950s, the shortfall in revenue was alleviated by the fact that members of religious orders provided much of the instruction in schools. By the 1960s, this solution was unworkable. Soaring enrollment in Roman Catholic schools, not to mention the fact that boards were increasingly having to hire lay teachers who demanded competitive salaries, pushed the system to a near-breaking point. In response, members of the Catholic community began to pressure the government for access to corporate property taxes, as well as for the extension of public funding for Grades 11 to 13. Finally, in 1984, Premier William Davis announced that legislation would be introduced guaranteeing full public funding for Roman Catholic schools. Although Davis had hoped the legislation would satisfy everyone, much rancorous debate ensued, pitting Protestants against Roman Catholics. After public hearings, as well as a reference to the Supreme Court of Canada, in 1986 *Bill 30* was passed by the government of then-Premier David Peterson (Gidney, 1999, pp. 124–141). This Bill guaranteed public funding of separate Roman Catholic schools to the end of Grade 13 by adding a grade level to the system each year. This drew to a close "the most divisive conflict over an educational issue in Ontario since the middle decades of the nineteenth century" (Gidney, 1999, pp. 124–125).

It's also worth noting that, in the 1990s, a reorganization of school boards occurred in Quebec and Newfoundland and Labrador. In regards to Quebec, religion, especially since the Quiet Revolution of the 1960s, had declined in importance. Concurrently, language had become a central identifying theme in the province. Roman Catholic and Protestant school boards were often considered anachronistic and not attuned with the modern realities of Quebec society. As a result, in 1997, via an amendment to the Constitution, denominational school boards were eliminated and replaced by English- and French-language boards. It is interesting to note that the transition from denominational to linguistic education was relatively smooth, and in fact, not even the Catholic or Protestant churches voiced great opposition to the change (Young & Bezeau, 2003). In Newfoundland and Labrador, four different denominations enjoyed legal rights and privileges, thus resulting in a Roman Catholic system, a

Pentecostal system, a Seventh Day Adventist system, and an Integrated system that drew from the Anglican, United, and Presbyterian churches, as well as from the Salvation Army. Despite strong resistance from the Catholic and Protestant churches, declining enrollments, not to mention a weak economy, facilitated the 1998 reorganization of the Newfoundland and Labrador education system along non-sectarian lines. Thus, a complex multi-denominational arrangement that pre-dated 1949, when Newfoundland joined Confederation, disappeared from the landscape.

EDUCATION AND RELIGION: A VOLATILE LEGAL MIX

In thinking about religion and education, an important point to keep in mind is that "expression of one's reasonable and legitimate beliefs needs to be accommodated in our public schools to promote toleration and respect for diversity" (Clarke, 2005, p. 373). And this is certainly consistent with the religious freedom safeguards found in the Charter. Yet it is worth noting that the duty to accommodate is not absolute but rather is only required to the point of "**undue hardship**." Essentially, "undue hardship" arguments can be advanced on various grounds, including financial and safety concerns (Bowlby & Reesor, 2017, pp. 281–282).

In the 1985 case of *R. v. Big M Drug Mart Ltd*, the Supreme Court of Canada defined religious freedom as "the right to entertain such religious beliefs openly and without fear of hindrance or reprisal, and the right to manifest belief by worship and practice or by teaching and dissemination" (as cited in Buckingham, 2014, p. 24). Various cases that have followed in the wake of the *Big M Drug Mart* decision have further shaped the debate surrounding religion and education. *Zylberberg v. Sudbury Board of Education* (1988), *Corporation of the Canadian Civil Liberties Association v. Ontario (Minister of Education) and Elgin County Board of Education* (1990), and *Adler v. Ontario (Minister of Education)* (1992–1996) all involve challenges to religious polices and funding; in totality, these cases are referred to as "the trilogy." For Dickinson and Dolmage (1996), the addition of *Bal v. Ontario* (1994) and *Islamic Schools Federation of Ontario v. Ottawa Board of Education* (1997) has transformed the "trilogy" into a "quintet."

In *Zylberberg*, a group of atheistic, Jewish, and Muslim parents challenged a provision requiring that public schools in Ontario open and close each day with religious exercises, which could consist of reading scripture or reciting the Lord's Prayer. The policy further stated that a student could be exempted from the religious exercise on the grounds of religious objection, provided a parental request was received. Ultimately, in 1988 the Ontario Court of Appeal found the provision to be contrary to section 2 of the Charter (Young, 2008). The court noted that one religion cannot be given primacy, and that opening or closing exercises in schools must be consistent with the multicultural nature of Ontario society (Brown & Zuker, 1994, p. 110).

The case of *Corporation of the Canadian Civil Liberties Association v. Ontario (Minister of Education) and Elgin County Board of Education* also illustrates the contentious nature of the interplay between religion and education. The crux of this court challenge was an allegation that a provision that mandated two periods of religious instruction per week in public schools, while allowing an exemption for students whose parents objected to their participation in such classes, coerced minority children into taking part in religious education classes designed for the majority religion—Christianity. A further contention was that the Elgin County School Board's curriculum on religious instruction exhibited a Christian point of view, thus resulting in a form of indoctrination. On appeal from the Divisional Court, in 1990 the Ontario Court of Appeal found that both the provision mandating religious instruction and the curriculum itself smacked of religious indoctrination and violated religious freedom as guaranteed in section 2 of the Charter (Young, 2008). Amendments by the government made in light of the court's decision "permitted school boards to offer courses about religion and world religions, but specifically forbade any form of indoctrination in any one religion. In short, public schools were to be secular" (Dickinson & Dolmage, 1996, p. 370).

In *Adler v. Ontario (Minister of Education)*, two groups of Jewish and Christian Reformed parents opted, on religious grounds, to send their children to **independent schools**. The parents argued that it was discriminatory to not provide public funding to independent schools. In 1996, the Supreme Court of Canada rejected the argument advanced by the parents, stating that there was no infringement of Charter rights. It is worth noting that the Court did not expressly prohibit the funding of independent schools, rather leaving this decision to the discretion of individual governments (Young, 2008). According to some observers (Farmy, 2004; Ogilvie, 1997), the decision in *Adler* to deny rights to certain individuals or groups that are enjoyed by other citizens is *prima facie* discriminatory.

The case of *Bal v. Ontario* arose in response to a decision by the Ontario government that religious classes could not promote indoctrination and, further, that no one religion could be given primacy. As such, public schools were to be secular (Foster & Smith, 2001, p. 49). According to the applicants, who were parents from the Sikh, Hindu, Christian Reformed, Muslim, and Mennonite communities, the government decision was tantamount to infringement of their right to freedom of religion and conscience and freedom of expression, as guaranteed by the Charter (Dickinson & Dolmage, 1996, p. 371). In the end, the *Bal* court found there was no Charter violation, as "parents, teachers, and students could hold and express whatever religious views they wished; however, they could not use the public schools to promote these beliefs" (Dickinson & Dolmage, 1996, p. 373).

The 1997 *Islamic Schools Federation of Ontario v. Ottawa Board of Education* case is the final piece of litigation in the "quintet." Much like the others, this case involved the intersection of religion and education. The main issue at play was a decision by the Ottawa Board of Education to adjust the start date of the school year so as not to commence on Rosh Hashanah, the feeling being that this would cause undue hardship for Jewish students and employees. In response, the Islamic Schools Federation of Ontario requested that schools be closed on the Muslim holy days of March 3 and May 11, 1995. When the board did not acquiesce to this request, an application for judicial review was brought by the Islamic Schools Federation of Ontario, in which it asked the Ontario Divisional Court to require the Ottawa school board to close its schools on the Muslim holy days, where numbers warranted. The Islamic Schools Federation also argued the organization of the school year contravened sections 2 and 15 of the Charter because it provided tacit recognition to various Christian holy days in the establishment of school holidays. In 1997, the Ontario Divisional Court rejected the claim, noting religious holidays such as Christmas and Easter were in fact secular holidays or common pause days. The court further posited that there was no Charter violation because students are permitted to be absent from school on holy days (Young, 2008).

A 2006 Quebec case, *Multani v. Commission scolaire Marguerite-Bourgeoys*, is an example of how the law is moving beyond the "quintet." In this litigation, Gurbaj Singh Multani, a Khalsa Sikh student, was told by his school principal that he would not be permitted to wear his kirpan (ceremonial dagger) while at school. However, his religious beliefs dictated that Gurbaj wear his kirpan at all times, including while at school. On appeal from the Quebec Superior Court, in 2006 the Supreme Court of Canada, in a unanimous judgment, set aside the decision of the Quebec Court of Appeal, and in so doing, struck down the decision by the school board to prohibit the wearing of a kirpan while at school (Smith, 2006). The Supreme Court based its decision on a violation of Multani's freedom of religion as guaranteed by section 2 of the Charter (Young, 2008).

Certainly, the Canadian mosaic is a delicate balancing act of competing interests. Each of the aforementioned cases is relevant in that it sheds some light and clarity on the place of religious freedom and accommodation in education. In a very interesting piece, Burton (1992, p. 202) argues that when we add education to the inevitably heated discussion about politics and religion, we are left with a "concoction of extreme volatility."

RELIGIOUS RESPONSIVENESS AND THE COMPASSIONATE TEACHER

The Canadian classroom of today is very unlike that found in the one-room schoolhouse of years gone by. Historically, the student body, as well as the nature of teaching and learning, was very homogeneous. While homogeneity may have been the norm in the past, heterogeneity is the cornerstone of the contemporary classroom. If one were to visit a typical school in Canada, it would not be surprising to see a classroom composed of children who are different. These differences might be of a physical, intellectual, social, or cultural nature, to name but a few, but the fact remains that Canadian schools are characterized, to an ever-increasing degree, by diversity. And, arguably, this diversity is amplified in urban settings across the country.

As the heterogeneous nature of Canadian schools continues to evolve, public education has responded to these emerging realities by working towards creating a system that addresses the unique needs of students from a variety of backgrounds, including but not limited to language; socioeconomic class; sexual orientation; ability/disability; gender; race/culture; and religion. Yet in her year-long study of religion and schooling in Canada, Sweet (1997) found that most religious communities felt there was no space or avenue for their religion or religious beliefs to be embedded within schools. Even though Sweet's work is more than two decades old, and the law- and policy-makers of this land have provided some semblance of clarity to the place of religion and education, there remains much work to be done. Noddings notes that "religion plays a significant role in the lives of individuals. … We cannot remain silent on this vital topic and still claim to educate" (2008, p. 386).

Teachers, and perhaps more specifically compassionate teachers, occupy a position of prime importance in undertaking this remaining work. We recognize, to a large degree, compassionate teachers for what they do. If, for example, you were asked to describe a compassionate teacher, you might list such characteristics as passionate, fair, considerate, helpful, and so on. For Noddings, compassionate teachers "steadfastly encourage responsible self-affirmation in their students" (1988, p. 222). Unquestionably, each of these characteristics is important and their impact far-reaching. However, besides these observable and concrete features of what makes a compassionate teacher, there are other less visible factors that are nonetheless important. For example, compassionate teachers also possess an understanding of the system in which they work. Compassionate teachers recognize that education does not exist in a vacuum and is context-dependent on myriad factors. Among the factors that serve as a driver for education, law and policy remain as constituent features of the landscape. Although it is neither assumed nor expected that teachers be lawyers or policy-makers, it is incumbent upon compassionate teachers to have a healthy respect and appreciation for the manner in which law and policy impact education.

In discussions of religion and education, the argument has been that the imprint of the law is pervasive. It has been argued that teachers need to possess an adequate level of legal literacy (Young, Kraglund-Gauthier, & Foran, 2014). As Reglin notes, "teachers must have a strong working knowledge, beyond common sense, of education law" (1990, p. 17). As the old saying goes, "ignorance of the law is never a legal defense." The preceding discussion has pointed out that religious accommodation is a legal expectation, so it stands to reason that compassionate teachers are at least somewhat familiar with what this exactly entails.

To instill within teachers this familiarity with the policy landscape, both pre-service and in-service education can do much to equip educators with the foundational knowledge they require. Similarly, specific attention to infusing the notion of compassion into curriculum expectations could go a long way to instilling within teachers the attributes associated with being a compassionate individual. As Noddings points out, "Teachers, like students, need a broad curriculum closely connected to the existential heart of life and to their own special interests" (2005, p. 178).

Compassionate teachers also embrace, or in some cases exude, a positive attitude. In fact, they may well epitomize what we might term "attitudinal caring." Their over-arching philosophical standpoint is focused on creating classroom communities where all feel welcome and respected. Simply put, compassionate teachers devote attention to creating inclusive learning environments, and here the reference is to the broad notion of inclusion that moves beyond the focus on exceptionalities. To some degree, a teacher's commitment to inclusion might be a personal choice, but almost certainly, the fact remains "that everyone deserves to be included fairly in all systems and practices of school and society" (Ryan, 2006, p. 15). As such, compassionate teachers make inclusion a non-negotiable aspect of their pedagogy and practice. And this is reasonable and appropriate, especially when we consider "inclusion's alter ego is exclusion" (Ryan, 2006, p. 19).

Of course, schools, much like society in general, can often be characterized by dominant discourses, often stemming from or imposed by those who enjoy a privileged position of power. As Fraser and Shields put it, "Power resides with those whose social status places them in a privileged and superior position that is rarely questioned in any explicit fashion, but rather accepted as the normal state of affairs" (2010, p. 7). As a result, silence and marginalization, especially for those who may not fall within mainstream religions, becomes commonplace. Compassionate teachers are not satisfied with accepting this reality but rather work towards troubling these dominant discourses so as to empower all students. In sum, they treat the "other" in "absolute regard" (Starratt, 1991).

In addition, compassionate teachers recognize that inclusion should not be an individual experience. Too often, teachers enter their classroom and close the door to the outside world. This makes education truly isolating, and for inclusion to work well, educators must take a team approach. Compassionate teachers rely on other teachers, and they remember that asking questions is not a sign of weakness, but rather demonstrates commitment and compassion to the children under their charge. Within any given school, there exist educators who possess a wealth of knowledge, and it is only through dialogue and interchange that we as compassionate teachers can provide for our students the most optimal and inclusive learning environment. Thus, compassionate teachers take to heart and recognize the value that can emerge when the "collective we [emerges] from the shared norms, beliefs, and values of a disparate group of I's" (Vibert, Portelli, Shields, & Larocque, 2002, p. 110).

Compassionate teachers also recognize the distinction between equality and equity, with the former referring to an arrangement where all receive similar treatment, and the latter denoting a situation where one receives what one actually needs. Put another way, equality might mean that we all receive a pair of shoes, but equity would involve receiving a pair of shoes that actually fit. In regards to religion and education, compassionate teachers know the difference between majority and minority, and work towards embracing and celebrating religious diversity. Here, the compassionate teacher reflects on the concept of "othering," in which minority groups are singled out from the majority (Rawls & David, 2005). Thus, equality seems a rather hollow tool to employ in promoting the cause of diversity, and as such, the compassionate teacher relies on the principle of equity to advance the cause.

The compassionate teacher also draws on pedagogical constructs to address issues of religion and education. One of the chief vehicles compassionate teachers can use to tackle these issues is that of multicultural education:

> Multicultural education is committed to the goal of providing all students— regardless of socio-economic status, gender, sexual orientation or ethnic, racial, or cultural backgrounds—with equal opportunities to learn in school. Multicultural education is also based on the fact that students do not learn in a vacuum—their culture predisposes them to learn in certain ways. And finally, multicultural education recognizes that current school practices have provided, and continue to provide, some students with greater opportunities for learning than students who belong to other groups. (Parkay, Hardcastle Stanford, Vaillancourt, & Stephens, 2009, p. 162)

There are various approaches to multicultural education that a compassionate teacher might adopt. For example, according to one method, you might choose to value religious diversity fully and above all else, and in so doing, you demonstrate that you do not see any one religion as being superior to others. In this regard, compassionate teachers may opt to recognize religious diversity with reference to the larger social world (inclusion by omission), or they may choose to reflect the religious diversity as specifically found in their classroom (inclusion by identification) (Hillier, 2014).

According to the tenets of multicultural education, a compassionate teacher might adopt a stance whereby the values of the majority religion are stressed, thus equipping students with an opportunity to engage with and function within this dominant religion. Or a compassionate teacher may opt to employ a synthesizing approach that emphasizes the values of both the dominant religion as well as that of diversity. This is certainly the most contemporary view of multicultural education, and although it explores the possibilities open to students, it also stresses the acquisition of knowledge, skills, and behaviours that will permit them to assume meaningful positions in the world (Edmunds & Edmunds, 2010, p. 248).

In thinking about the role of a compassionate teacher, there is no agreed-upon approach to multicultural education. However, Banks (2001) offers some insight into the subject that may be important to consider. For him, multicultural education, and by extension its use in being responsive to religious realities within today's classrooms, involves the following components:

1. helping students understand the role cultural assumptions play in shaping knowledge;

2. identifying the features of racial attitudes, and detailing how these might be changed through education;
3. creating a school culture that allows all students to become empowered;
4. teaching in a manner that respects and addresses the unique needs of all students in an equitable manner; and
5. using examples from a variety of cultures in your teaching.

Each is certainly quite applicable to the issue of religion.

As compassionate teachers, we should welcome the concept of multicultural education and strive to make it part of our professional practice. In so doing, the classroom will be one where diversity is respected and embraced, and hopefully this will transmit to the students we are teaching. In this regard, remember that the curriculum we deliver should be anti-racist and anti-discriminatory. As well, diversity should be an openly visible part of the school and of individual classrooms. However, as a caveat, remember that as compassionate teachers, we do not want to trivialize the process. Too often, teachers with good intentions attempt to celebrate difference by employing hollow gestures. In addition, compassionate teachers need to be diligent in raising the level of cultural consciousness of their students (Kanu, 2002). By doing this, the ultimate goal is to produce citizens who will strive to enact just principles in their life and work. And finally, as compassionate teachers, we need to be sensitive to the background of parents. Keep in mind that sometimes, because of lived experiences, parents from diverse backgrounds may have mixed or even negative sentiments towards education. Your role as compassionate teachers will be to invite parents to be partners in their child's educational experience and to encourage their full participation (Santrock et al., 2007, p. 150). In this sense, we are giving the "other" a sense of voice as representation and influence, whereby "one's concerns, experience, and analysis of the world are heard, taken seriously, and accounted for within a given context" (Vibert, Portelli, Shields, & Larocque, 2002, p. 105). As Noddings (2006) points out, compassionate teachers listen and are responsive, and in giving voice to those who may have been silenced in the past, we are doing our part to transform dominant cultures, thereby making schools a better place for all.

CONCLUSION

Throughout this chapter, the focus has been placed largely on the interplay between religion and education. This interplay is long-standing and actually predates the birth of this country in 1867. Although policy and legal decisions have assisted in carving out a space where these two often countervailing forces (religion and education) might mutually and happily coexist, tension is still an ever-present feature. In trying to create inclusive classroom spaces where accommodation is the norm, and conflict is absent, educators can and must play a central role. But even more importantly, teachers must embrace compassion as a constituent feature of their pedagogy. As Noddings notes, "teachers not only have to create caring relations in which they are the carers, but that they also have a responsibility to help their students develop the capacity to care" (2005, p. 18). In so doing, not only are teachers responsive to the needs of those under their charge, but at a more macro level, they facilitate the development of future generations that are all equipped with an ethic of compassion. Of course, this is not an easy task, and perhaps not for the faint of heart, but the stakes are simply too high to accept anything less than complete success. Now is the time for compassionate teachers to step up and assume the mantle of leadership within schools.

QUESTIONS FOR CRITICAL THOUGHT

1. Can schools be truly secular and yet still accommodate various religions?
2. In thinking about religious accommodation, how would you as a teacher enact an ethic of caring within your practice?

GLOSSARY

Denominational: Relating to the tenets of a particular religion or religious denomination.

Independent school: Sometimes referred to as private schools, independent schools operate parallel to the public school system and are usually funded by means other than taxpayer contributions.

Undue hardship: Exempting an individual or an organization from a legal expectation on the basis that such accommodation would create an unreasonable burden.

REFERENCES

Banks, J. A. (2001). *Cultural diversity and education: Foundations, curriculum, and teaching* (4th ed.). Boston: Allyn & Bacon.

Bezeau, L. M. (1995). *Educational administration for Canadian teachers* (2nd ed.). Toronto: Copp Clark.

Bowlby, B., & Reesor, L. (2017). Special education law in Canada. In D. C. Young (Ed.), *Education law in Canada: A guide for teachers and administrators* (pp. 259–285). Toronto: Irwin Law.

Brown, A. F., & Zuker, M. A. (1994). *Education law.* Toronto: Carswell.

Buckingham, J. (2014). *Fighting over God: A legal and political history of religious freedom in Canada.* Montreal: McGill-Queen's University Press.

Burton, J. W. (1992). Legal status of religion in Canadian schools. In W. F. Foster (Ed.), *Education & law: A plea for partnership* (pp. 202–214). Proceedings of the Annual Conference of the Canadian Association for the Practical Study of Law in Education.

Clarke, P. (2005). Religion, public education and the Charter: Where do we go now? *McGill Journal of Education, 40*(3), 351–381.

Dewey, J. (1966). *Democracy and education: An introduction to the philosophy of education.* New York: Free Press.

Dickinson, G. M., & Dolmage, W. R. (1996). Education, religion, and the courts in Ontario. *Canadian Journal of Education, 21*(4), 363–383.

Edmunds, A., & Edmunds, G. (2010). *Educational psychology: Applications in Canadian classrooms.* Don Mills, ON: Oxford.

Farmy, M. (2004). The private school funding debate: A second look through Charter first principles. *Education & Law Journal, 13*(3), 397–431.

Foster, W. F., & Smith, W. J. (2001). Religion and education in Canada: Part II—An alternative framework for the debate. *Education & Law Journal, 11*(1), 37–67.

Fraser, D. F. G., & Shields, C. M. (2010). Leaders' roles in disrupting dominant discourses and promoting inclusion. In A. L. Edmunds & R. B. Macmillan (Eds.), *Leadership for inclusion: A practical guide* (pp. 7–18). Rotterdam, Netherlands: Sense.

Gidney, R. D. (1999). *From hope to Harris: The reshaping of Ontario's schools.* Toronto: University of Toronto Press.

Giles, T. E., & Proudfoot, A. J. (1994). *Educational administration in Canada* (5th ed.). Calgary: Detselig.

Hillier, C. (2014). "But we're already doing it": Ontario teachers' responses to policies on religious inclusion and accommodation in public schools. *Alberta Journal of Educational Research, 60*(1), 43–61.

Kanu, Y. (2002). In their own voices: First Nations students identify some cultural mediators of their learning in the formal school system. *Alberta Journal of Educational Research, 48*(2), 98–121.

Manzer, R. A. (1994). *Public schools and political ideas: Canadian educational policy in historical perspective.* Toronto: University of Toronto Press.

Milner, H. (1986). *The long road to reform: Restructuring public education in Quebec.* Kingston & Montreal: McGill-Queen's University Press.

Noddings, N. (2008). The new outspoken atheism and education. *Harvard Educational Review,* 78(2), 369–390.

Noddings, N. (2006). Educational leaders as caring teachers. *School Leadership and Management,* 26(4), 339–345.

Noddings, N. (2005). *The challenge to care in schools: An alternative approach to education* (2nd ed.). New York: Teachers College Press.

Noddings, N. (1988). An ethic of caring and its implications for instructional arrangements. *American Journal of Teacher Education,* 96(2), 215–230.

Ogilvie, M. H. (1997). Adler v. Ontario: Preconceptions, myths (or prejudices) about religion in the Supreme Court of Canada. *National Journal of Constitutional Law,* 9(1), 79–95.

Parkay, F. W., Hardcastle Stanford, B., Vaillancourt, J. P., & Stephens, H. C. (2009). *Becoming a teacher* (3rd Can. ed.). Toronto: Pearson.

Rawls, A. W., & David, G. (2005). Accountability other: Trust, reciprocity and exclusion in a context of situated practice. *Human Studies,* 28(4), 469–497.

Reglin, G. L. (1990). Public school educators' knowledge of selected Supreme Court decisions affecting daily public school operations. *Research in Rural Education,* 7(1), 17–22.

Ryan, J. (2006). *Inclusive leadership.* San Francisco: Jossey-Bass.

Santrock, J. W., Woloshyn, V., Gallagher, T., Di Petta, T., & Marini, Z. (2007). *Educational psychology* (2nd Can. ed.). Toronto: McGraw-Hill Ryerson.

Sears, A., & Christou, T. (2011). Religion and education. In J. Arthur & A. Peterson (Eds.), *The Routledge companion to education* (pp. 341–349). New York: Routledge.

Smith, W. J. (2006). Private beliefs and public safety: The Supreme Court strikes down a total ban on the kirpan in schools as unreasonable. *Education & Law Journal,* 16(1), 83–112.

Starratt, R. J. (1991). Building an ethical school: A theory for practice in educational leadership. *Educational Administration Quarterly,* 27(2), 155–202.

Sweet, L. (1997). *God in the classroom: The controversial issue of religion in Canada's schools.* Toronto: McClelland & Stewart.

Titley, E. B. (1990). Religion, culture and power: The school question in Manitoba. In E. B. Titley (Ed.), *Canadian education: Historical themes and contemporary issues* (pp. 45–77). Calgary: Detselig.

Vibert, A. B., Portelli, J. P., Shields, C., & Larocque, L. (2002). Critical practice in elementary schools: Voice, community, and a curriculum of life. *Journal of Educational Change,* 3(2), 93–116.

White, J. P., & Peters, J. (2009). A short history of Aboriginal education in Canada. In J. P. White, J. Peters, D. Beavon, & N. Spence (Eds.), *Aboriginal education: Current crisis and future alternatives* (pp. 13–31). Toronto: Thompson.

Young, D. C. (2008). Education law and multiculturalism: Beyond the quintet. In J. M. Mangan (Ed.), *Social foundations of education coursebook, 2008–2009* (pp. 197–203). London, ON: The Althouse Press.

Young, D. C., & Bezeau, L. M. (2003). Moving from denominational to linguistic education in Quebec. *Canadian Journal of Educational Administration and Policy*, 24.

Young, D. C., Kraglund-Gauthier, W. L., & Foran, A. (2014). Legal literacy in teacher education programs: Conceptualizing relevance and constructing pedagogy. *Journal of Educational Administration and Foundations*, 24(1), 7–19.

CHAPTER 12

The Radicalization of Youth in the West: How Can Canadian Teachers Effectively Approach This Issue in Their Classrooms?

Dilmurat Mahmut, Helal Hossain Dhali, and Ratna Ghosh

LEARNING OBJECTIVES

1. To better understand the link between education and radicalization and violent extremism.
2. To be able to see the connection between care in education and moral disengagement that would lead to violent extremism, through the case study presented in this chapter.

INTRODUCTION

The menace of extremism has been spreading at an unprecedented speed throughout the world, including Canada. With increasing frequency, young people in Canada, the United States, and many other Western countries have been involved in violence instigated by extremist ideologies (Neumann, 2017). This means the extremist groups have become increasingly sophisticated and powerful in luring Western youth into their radical and violent ideologies and moral paradigms. For example, according to Public Safety Canada, by August 2016, Canadians who were fighting with foreign terrorist groups in the Middle East increased to 190 (Public Safety Canada, 2017) from 130 in early 2014 (Tasker, 2016). Right-wing extremism in Canada has been on the rise as well in recent years, with the cases ranging from protests against refugees and immigrants (Public Safety Canada, 2017) to violent events such as the Quebec mosque attack that resulted in the loss of six innocent lives in early 2017.[1] According to the Canadian Incident Database, right-wing extremists had perpetrated an average of 3.3 violent incidents per year in Canada between 2003 and 2016, with increasing frequency (Parent & Ellis, 2016). The recent situation has been even more alarming (Goujard, 2018).

Apparently, those who are most susceptible to adopting extremist ideologies tend to be youth who seek to uncover their own identity, look to bolster self-confidence, and are in search of meaning in their lives (Samuel, 2012). Some typical Canadian examples of this reality are Damian Clairmont[2] from Calgary; John Maguire and several other radicalized Canadian youth from Ottawa;[3] the famous seven Montreal CEGEP[4] students who all went to join ISIS from 2012 to 2015;[5] Brad Galloway,[6] the ex-leader of Volksfront, a neo-Nazi group based in the West coast; and Alexandre Bissonnette,[7] a right-wing extremist and the Quebec mosque shooter. Overall, the number of young people being radicalized in the West has been alarming in recent years.

Psychologically, school or college students are in an age group that tends to be impulsive, action-oriented, and characterized by higher risk-taking. Moreover, they lack experience; they are still in the process of forming their ideological positions and are, therefore, ready to experiment with new values and identities (Silke, 2008). This makes it likely that they are more vulnerable to extremist or radical world views or ideologies (Neumann, 2017). Moreover, young Canadians and Americans have been increasingly disengaged from the mainstream civic sphere since the 1960s (Ménard, 2010). Therefore, it is crucial that we quickly work to uncover how this demographic has been positioning itself regarding extremist or radical world views and ideologies, which are readily available and widespread both in online and offline settings in the West.

With this background, this chapter attempts to elucidate to what extent Canadian secondary school teachers have been playing a positive role in cultivating resilience among their students against **violent extremism**. Given that incidences of extremism still occur, we provide data from an ongoing study on extremism and give some recommendations on how to improve the status quo. Conceptually, the chapter highlights the importance of caring education (Noddings, 1984, 1992, 2001) in preventing students from being marginalized and morally disengaged (Bandura, 1999, 2002), and therefore easily attracted to alternative and destructive world views or ideologies propagated by violent extremist groups. The lack of healthy moral values—a direct result of being excluded or marginalized in society—is an essential precondition for leading youth to radicalization. Literature indicates that among the factors that push youth towards radicalization, a sense of "not belonging" or marginalization of students is an important cause that needs to be seriously addressed (Ghosh et al., 2016). Thus, teachers must play a critical role in providing care and compassion so that no child feels excluded or marginalized.

EDUCATION AND VIOLENT EXTREMISM

When discussing violent extremism, very few people think about the role of education in countering such a destructive turn. This is not surprising, given the fact that the focus of the leading global rhetoric on countering violent extremism has been primarily on using coercive and aggressive state measures that include military strategies and security tactics—*hard power*. Education, as a *soft power* that can be used to make young people resilient against extremist and destructive ideologies and world views, has been severely overlooked. However, extremist groups have been widely employing their own forms of education to spread their radical ideologies in Western societies.

This means education is a double-edged sword that can be used to either counter violent extremism or, conversely, fuel violent radical ideology or social forces. There are many cases in which various extremist individuals or groups have been using education, especially informal education online, to attract Western youth to their extremist ideologies (Ghosh et al., 2016). One typical example would be the above-mentioned John Maguire, who was believed to have been radicalized by listening to the online lectures of Anwar al-Awlaki[8] (Duffy and Harley, 2015). Damian Clairmont was also believed to have been exposed to his lectures (Bell, 2015). Despite his death in 2011, al-Awlaki has been the key instigator of many major terrorist attacks and plots that happened in the West in recent years (Bergen, 2015). The Counter Extremism Project (CEP) (2017) documented nearly 90 extremists in the United States and Europe with ties to al-Awlaki, whose lectures had been largely available online. Unfortunately, his lectures are still available on the internet today.

Indeed, informal education like that illustrated above is the primary source that has been radicalizing many vulnerable young people in the West. Some other forms of informal education that have been contributing to the same phenomenon include the influence of peer groups (Baaken & Schlegel, 2017); the influence of radical religious or community leaders (Bergen, 2015); enticing media stories and messages evoking sympathy and affiliation via social media and the internet (Neumann, 2017); and offline or online recruitment (Braniff, 2015).

Several extremist groups have largely shifted to online recruitment in recent years. In 2014, approximately 90 percent of extremist recruitment activities were believed to have been carried out through social media (Weimann, 2014). One can imagine the number would be even higher today, as the world has been increasingly interconnected through social media. Among those extremist groups, ISIS has become particularly sophisticated in using various platforms to propagate their ideologies and attract young followers. It is estimated that in 2015, ISIS alone was using 46,000 Twitter accounts (Casciani, 2015). Apart from these mainstream platforms, ISIS has been utilizing some anonymous websites and encrypted messaging apps to further disseminate their extremist propaganda to Western audiences (Milton, 2016). Moreover, ISIS has been publishing online magazines such as *Rumiyah* (previously *Dabiq*) in various languages including English, French, German, Russian, Indonesian, and Uyghur in order to reach out to a wider audience more effectively (McKernan, 2016).

Right-wing extremist groups in the West have also been using similar strategies to recruit young candidates. According to a report that discovered this commonality between ISIS and right-wing extremists, "White nationalists and Nazis outperformed ISIS in average friend and follower counts by a substantial margin" in using Twitter accounts to attract members to their groups (Berger, 2016, p. 17). Accordingly, Public Safety Canada (2017) reminds us that right-wing extremists in Canada have been predominantly active in cyberspace, creating and spreading a culture of fear, hatred, and distrust through chat forums and online networks. The recent rise of right-wing extremism and terrorist attacks, such as the Quebec mosque shooting in early 2017, is in line with the rapid increase of online activities of such radical groups.

Apart from lone actors or extremist groups who have been directly trying to radicalize Westerners through their informal education, as Ghosh and colleagues (2016) reveal, the formal and non-formal educational systems of some nations have been directly or indirectly contributing to the radicalization of their own young people. For example, the education system of Pakistan has become increasingly exclusive of religious minorities and deeply Islamic in nature since the 1970s by making Islamic studies a compulsory subject for all disciplines, including engineering and medicine. At the same time, it has introduced radical ideologies that emphasize the importance of jihad as part of the nation's security policy (Khan, 2018). Another example is Saudi Arabia, which has been using its formal education system in a manner similar to Pakistan and which has the capacity to radicalize its own young citizens (Ghosh et al., 2016). Recently, a study conducted by the United States Commission on International Religious

Freedom (USCIRF, 2018) shows that, although the Saudi government has been engaged in textbook reform for the last 15 years, little progress has been achieved in terms of eliminating intolerant content, such as jihad, or fighting against non-Muslims; not prescribing execution of apostates, or those who critique the prophet; and not degrading non-Muslims or seeing them as enemies.

All this indicates that education has a contradictory relationship with violent extremism. On the one hand, it can be utilized as a positive tool to cultivate resilience against violent ideologies amongst young people. On the other hand, extremist groups or social institutions have been radicalizing innocent youth, using their own very powerful forms of education. The lack of education that develops resilience against violent extremism itself can create a precondition that makes young people vulnerable to extremist propaganda.

EDUCATION IN NORTH AMERICA AND COUNTERING VIOLENT EXTREMISM (CVE)

Since young people spend most of their time in schools, and schools are the central spaces that influence the development of their identities and world views, it is highly important to look into the realities of educational institutions. However, in North America, unlike the European Union,[9] very little attention has been paid to the role of education in countering radicalization and violent extremism. Currently, topics such as extremism and terrorism are not addressed within the North American formal education systems despite the rise in extremist incidents (religious or right wing). Under such circumstances, young students have been largely left on their own to explore the complex phenomena of radicalism and violent extremism and build their resilience against the seduction of such ideologies and alternative moral values.

Thus, it is crucial to identify how North American school teachers have been effectively working towards building resilience against radicalization and violent extremism among their students given that there are no deliberate, specific, and formal educational programs designed for the students for countering violent religious extremism (CVE). This is an urgent necessity when increasingly more school-aged youth have been attracted to or lured by the radical and violent extremist world views and ideologies widely circulating in various lifelong-learning spaces.

At the same time, while the literature on violent extremism, radicalization, and terrorism is growing, there is no significant North American literature connecting educational efforts to preventing violent extremism and violence, despite reports of increasing youth involvement in extremist groups. In response, this chapter tries to contribute to the theoretical and empirical knowledge on education's role in the prevention of violent extremism among Canadian youth, and more specifically, it aims to explore what kind of education would be effective for CVE, which will hopefully have wide global applications.

We acknowledge that prevention of violent extremism must be a multi-dimensional effort in which numerous educational and other approaches are needed. While there are no specific or focused formal educational programs in North America addressing radicalization and violent extremism that can be evaluated, we try to explore some other factors, including how educators themselves understand the phenomenon of radicalization and extremism, how they respond to and dialogue with their students when there is a need to discuss such issues in the classrooms, and how effectively they care about their students regarding their ethical and emotional development. Engaging with these factors is essential to building student resilience against violent extremism.

CONCEPTUAL FRAMEWORK: THE INTERSECTION OF MORAL DISENGAGEMENT AND COMPASSIONATE EDUCATION

The argument of this chapter is based on the assumption that radicalization or violent extremism is a result of certain individuals being disengaged from the mainstream or from healthy moral values in society. What distinguishes violent extremism from other kinds of violence, such as gang or drug activity, is the moral factor. It is the moral justification of violence as being acceptable and even necessary for the ultimate cause that makes violent extremism different. In other words, violent extremists create and/or follow some radical ideologies that can justify their harmful actions towards other groups of people. This sort of "ideological resort to destructiveness is of greatest social concern but, ironically, it is the most ignored in psychological analyses of people's inhumanities toward each other" (Bandura, 1999, p. 207). After the September 11 terrorist attacks in the United States in 2001, the ideological sources of violence, which are the ethical justifications of violence based on alternative and disengaged moral paradigms, seem to be increasingly attracting the attention of academics, the media, and policy-makers. However, how this sort of **moral disengagement** occurs at the ideological level and how to address or remedy it is still a relatively unexplored area of study.

At the centre is the concept of moral agency, which "is an individual's ability to make moral judgments based on some notion of right and wrong and to be held accountable for these actions" (Taylor, 2003, p. 20). This is a human capacity that enables individuals to choose ethical positions according to certain forms of rational thinking. This being said, moral agency can be used for either good or evil. In the words of Bandura, it "is manifested in both the power to refrain from behaving inhumanely and the proactive power to behave humanely" (2002, p. 101). The exercise of moral agency has dual aspects—*inhibitive* and *proactive* (Bandura, 1999, 2002); this, too, is a double-edged sword.

Resorting to the *inhibitive* form of moral agency or moral disengagement is a gradual process, in which the subject gives up their "self-censure" step-by-step (Bandura, 2002, p. 110). As Wilner and Dubouloz (2011) point out, it is a transformative learning process in which a series of psychological and cognitive shifts occur: it is the development of alternative personal belief systems provoked by specific triggering factors. This can be better explained by Moghaddam's (2005) use of the "Staircase to Terrorism" theory as illustrated in Figure 12.1, which we have fashioned to describe the specific phases one may go through before becoming a terrorist.

Moghaddam notes that at the third floor "a gradual engagement with the morality of terrorist organizations" may occur (2005, p. 162), which, on the other side of the coin, is a gradual disengagement from the healthy and mainstream moral values in society; in Bandura's (1999, 2002) words, it is resorting to the *inhibitive* form of moral agency. And as Samuel (2012) explains, this signals a paradigm shift that would make violence morally acceptable.

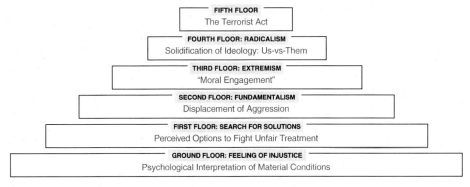

Figure 12.1: The Staircase to Terrorism

Source: Ghosh et al., 2016.

To prevent such a process of moral disengagement, which could lead to violent extremism, and instead to work towards constructing a civilized world, we need to build "social systems that uphold compassionate behavior and renounce cruelty" (Bandura, 2002, p. 116). To this end, it is necessary to develop education systems that can cultivate individuals who are ethically healthy and resilient against moral disengagement. However, as Noddings (1992, 2002) argues, schools always emphasize the academic achievements or merits of their students, neglecting care. Yet care is one of the key human capacities essential to building a better world. In most industrialized nations and in the developing world, education systems have been focusing on developing cognitive skills, while largely neglecting the affective and ethical skills of their students (Fenstermacher & Richardson, 2010; Noddings, 2002). Cognitive and affective domains are not mutually exclusive; they can both be developed by reinforcing each other.

According to Noddings (1992, 2001), caring pedagogy or compassionate education is needed to effectively address the affective and ethical domains of human development. **Care in education** is not solely an action or behaviour; rather, it is more about an attitude, a positive reciprocal relationship between the teacher and student, who both give and receive. As Noddings further argues, care in education is a quality that "provides the motivation for us to be moral" (1984, p. 5). This means that, as an affective domain of human life, caring can form a dynamic social force that embodies our collective sense of justice (Noddings, 2002). Methodologically speaking, Noddings (1988, 2002) proposes four components in applying care to education: modelling, dialogue, practice, and confirmation. Each of these components reinforces one another and, ultimately, works towards cultivating morally and ethically superior students. This also indicates that **teacher education** that can produce highly competent, caring teachers is essential; however, it is very difficult to achieve (Cornelius-White, 2007) because care and compassion cannot be taught.

Care also leads to a healthy expansion of social capital. Through experiences of being cared for, students will learn to care about others. This process may start from their friends and family members and gradually extend outwards— "learning first what it means to be cared for, then to care for intimate others, and finally to care about those we cannot care for directly" (Noddings, 2002, p. 31). Positive moral agency that upholds social justice can only be developed through such social interactions, as "people do not operate as autonomous moral agents" (Bandura, 1999, p. 207).

Based on such a link between caring education and moral disengagement, we highlight some possible reasons behind the radicalization of youth in the

West in recent years. The lack of caring in education that would emotionally disconnect students from teachers—who should be positive role models, and who are supposed to guide their students affectively and morally—could contribute to the alienation of many students from mainstream and healthy social norms and values. Therefore, some of those students can be easily attracted to the alternative and destructive rhetoric and narratives of various extremist groups. In this regard, the absence or inadequacy of care in education could be seen as one of a number of push factors that could lead to radicalization of youth in Western contexts (for parallel factors, see Ghosh et al., 2016). One way to develop care and empathy is to discuss real situations that are often controversial, but that can connect the students to what is being studied so that knowledge is not disconnected from their lives. It is with this in mind that the present empirical study sought to explore how Canadian teachers have been approaching controversial topics such as radicalization and violent extremism in their classrooms, and to consider to what extent their care has been able to cultivate positive or *proactive* moral agency among their students—a force that could make them resilient against extremist moral values and world views.

CONTROVERSIAL ISSUES, CARING EDUCATION, AND STUDENTS' RESILIENCE AGAINST EXTREMISM

Summarizing Bandura (2002), Noddings (1984, 1992, 2002), and Ghosh and colleagues (2016), this chapter suggests that a lack of caring education can morally disengage some students and lead them to radicalization or violent extremism. It analyzes how Canadian secondary school teachers approach controversial issues like radicalization and violent extremism and to what extent they support the students who want to learn about these topics in their classrooms. This chapter also tries to explore to what extent the students feel included in classroom discussions and connected to their teachers affectively.

This chapter is part of a five-year project titled Countering Violent Extremism through Education in Multicultural Canada, which is funded by the Social Sciences and Humanities Research Council of Canada. Methodologically, a phenomenological research design is used to uncover how Canadian students, especially secondary school students in four major cities across Canada, make meaning of their lived experiences concerning the ideological threat of radicalism and violent extremism in society. Given the delicate nature of the topic, phenomenological research is most appropriate, as it effectively allows in-depth examination of phenomena. More specifically, the qualitative data given here are from one city and based on a small number of semi-structured interviews (14) with 13 students and a teacher, along with a Focus Group Discussion (FGD) with parents.

The interviews and FGDs with the students, teachers, and parents have resulted in four significant findings:

1. teachers do not discuss controversial issues such as radicalization or violent extremism in the classroom;
2. students discuss controversial news items and have some ideas of their own about radicalization or violent extremism;
3. students who belong to different groups have different experiences and different viewpoints; and
4. teachers do not encourage diverse views from students.

In the following sections, these themes are discussed more in detail.

Students' Understanding and Perception of Extremism and Radicalization

The interviewed students or their parents are mainly immigrants who came from a range of locations around the world. Some of them had some educational background in their country of origin, and some of them are children of immigrants. This chapter selected participants from three different school boards in the studied city.

We began the interviews with a question about their understanding of radicalization. One student (FS1) defined extremism as a devotion to a particular religion, which means they regard any devoted followers of a religion as extremists:

> Someone who is religiously extreme … devotes their whole life towards a religion, like a priest, you know, Dickens, whatever all those people's different religions … devote their entire life … I consider like other people like myself … have the faith but I am not … devoting my whole life to it. (Participant FS1, Semi-Structured Interview)

However, for other students, devotion by itself is not extremism. When devotion becomes manipulation, then it might turn into extremism, according to participant LS3:

> Religion is supposed to guide you to do the right things, and supposed to help us in our lives and to allow us to accept others … however, when we talk about

religious extremism, it's one certain group of people, typically minorities try to manipulate religion into their own ways, so they can attract the attention of others through their horrific acts, and we see the stand with ISIS nowadays. They try to manipulate and go around some roles and their interpretations. (Participant LS3, Semi-Structured Interview)

Thus, some students know that devotion to a particular religion is not extremism or radicalization. When people are in a binary position and belong to a right or wrong, yes or no position, that is the extremist position. However, another interviewee (FS2) thinks that when one uses religion as their basis of violent acts, then it is extremism:

My understanding is that it's when people use religion … as a basis for their violent acts. … It's either you are using your religion as an excuse or when they do those violent acts because of their religion, like, they are supporting the religion. That's my kind of understanding of it. (Participant FS2, Semi-Structured Interview)

These participants give us a clear impression that students are aware of religious extremism. In some cases, they are not only aware of it but also have their own perspectives on it. Another student (LS2) sees extremism as an outcome of binary (e.g., either good or bad) thoughts:

It has taken the religion to, like a different, an entire whole level … like everything you will have to do, you will have to bring back through religion … each religion is an open topic, it's not like a "yes" or "no." Extremism is "yes" or "no," you are right, or you are wrong. That's it. They don't have exceptions … like binary … they don't understand and saying everything they follow is so strict. "Yes" or "no," "yes" or "no" is all they have—that's extremism. (Participant LS2, Semi-Structured Interview)

In summary, students' understandings of extremism or radicalization vary to some extent. Different students have different viewpoints on this topic. The discussion revealed that all of our interviewed students had some understandings of the term, although they were different, and some could mark non-extremist religious people as extremists. Thus, we need to know what role the schools play in developing the students' understandings or misunderstandings of extremism. For this purpose, the next section discusses how teachers deal with topics of radicalization and violent extremism in class.

Teachers Dealing with Controversial Issues in Classrooms

According to participant LS 4/5,

> [Education] opens your mind to different perspectives, things may be, that
> you know, like aware of and…. It is taught around the world what is going on,
> what people think and what example like they list them to do whatever they do,
> but sometimes it's not always like that. (Participant LS 4/5, Semi-Structured
> Interview)

However, our interviews have revealed that the students do not discuss any of
the things related to extremism or gangs or any violent behaviour in class or in
their families.

> *Interviewer:* … so, you said, you did not discuss any of the things related to
>   extremism or gangs or any violent behaviour with your parents?
> *FS5:* No.
> *Interviewer:* In class, you don't do that either?
> *FS5:* No.

That these issues are not discussed in class is not always true, as students in some
schools can discuss these issues in their social studies class. According to LS4/5,

> I feel no one is afraid to speak about their opinion because here [in social
> studies class], teachers are like indeed understanding, and even if you have a
> different perspective on something, they still allow that. (Participant LS 4/5,
> Semi-Structured Interview)

However, the teachers do not go into detail, although they talk about extremism
in their class. For example, they do not talk about the specific people leaving
their daily routines to join foreign extremist groups. Student FS2 stated:

> We don't talk about the reasoning behind those actions, and we don't talk about
> the radicalization of people, and that's all. We talk more about the news of it,
> and we talk about more of the popular version of the story; but we don't go deep
> into the psychology, or the reasoning behind it, or we don't go into the reason-
> ing why some people are being radicalized. (Participant FS2, Semi-Structured
> Interview)

One student (LS3) talked about the reasons behind not discussing any controversial issues in the class:

> If we mean ISIS, we definitely do not talk about that in class, I don't think anyone has that comfort to do so. [They] wouldn't bring up this in class discussions at all because … it would bring down the school, [people may misunderstand that some] student from the school joined ISIS and that would be ruining the reputation of the school. [People would be] saying oh you have students going to ISIS, [and so] you are a really bad school, and we should not send our children here. (Participant LS3, Semi-Structured Interview)

However, the teachers' resistance to raising such topics in the classroom could not stop students from discussing those issues among themselves. According to participant FS1,

> [We do discuss] not in class but with friends … we talk about it a lot, we talk about it all the time. (Participant FS1, Semi-Structured Interview)

Thus, from the students' responses, it is clear that the schools in our studied city sometimes discuss the issues related to religious extremism in class; however, they do not encourage analyzing the current issues in more detail and from a critical perspective. Schools are not comfortable developing critical perspectives for two possible reasons: (1) they are afraid of encouraging interest among the students in those controversial ideologies; and (2) they are discouraged by the parents who are opposed to the discussion of these issues in classrooms.

Teachers Handling Students with Different Experiences and Views

Students come to school from different backgrounds and with different experiences. They are likely to have different viewpoints as well. Siblings of a student (LS1) we interviewed had gone through some negative experiences at their school, and because of those experiences, the student left that school. According to LS1,

> I don't want to be there because my brother went to that school. … Now he is not even in that school because his name is Osama, and so, they [were] making fun of him and they [were] putting him down and specially his name too. … Now, he is like doing so many bad things, and he got involved in drugs, and

this and that. … When he was young, he was bullied because of the name. … Even my sisters, you know, don't wear their hijab because they are scared. (Participant LS1, Semi-Structured Interview)

Thus, school is not a "safe" place for all students. In **Canadian schools**, some students have negative experiences, which might make them feel depressed and lead them to oppositional or anti-social behaviour. Some students may feel they are "othered" or excluded due to their names, attires, and different viewpoints. Consequently, if teachers do not care about, or are not compassionate enough towards, those excluded students, that might lead some of those young people to anti-social behaviours, radicalization, or even violent extremism. Therefore, we tried to find out how the teachers deal with the students who are different and to what extent they care for those students.

Caring and Empathy in Education

Caring and empathy in education, in this context, refers to dealing with recently emerged controversial issues that might embarrass or negatively affect some students in schools. We asked some students about the role of teachers and schools in keeping students grounded and deterring them from being attracted to extremist ideologies. One of the participants (LS7) denied the positive role of schooling: "I don't think schools have a lot to do with this… ." Although some of them acknowledged that they could bring up their views on extremism in class, in reality, they could not because there was no opportunity to analyze and discuss the topic. If they discuss such issues, their parents may get a call from the school principal.

I never discussed this really in depth and like run over. I told exactly, what I told you guys [my views on extremism], I told my social teacher in class and [my mom] got a call from the principal saying [your son] wants to become [an] extremist. (Participant LS7, Semi-Structured Interview)

Even though some teachers are interested in discussing controversial issues like violent extremism, and although they allow different views and different perspectives in class, there are many teachers who do not want to do so. This is because they fear that discussing those topics might attract some of their students to radicalization and violent extremism. As stated by participant FS1,

I think it's more of a news item because, at the same time, I think differ-ent teachers have different perspectives. I know teachers who will talk about this … however, there are other teachers who prefer not to talk about it. You are talking about the negatives, you know, other people may become interested in it. (Participant FS1, Semi-Structured Interview)

In sum, students are aware of the controversial events happening around the world, and they discuss those issues among themselves—even at their schools, with their peers. Nevertheless, teachers are reluctant to raise this topic for discus-sion in the classroom. Furthermore, most of the teachers are often not comfort-able discussing controversial issues. In some cases, they are very skeptical about those students who raise alternative views on those controversial issues. For ex-ample, the teachers see a student with alternative views as a potentially radicalized person; instead of being empathetic to those with differences and trying to dia-logue with them, teachers tend to identify them as potential extremists. Moreover, many teachers rarely address "bullying" against minority students and rarely take care of them when they are treated as "others" or excluded by their classmates. This means many teachers are not compassionate enough towards their students, or there is a need for them to be more caring in how they dialogue with students. Examining controversial topics in class in a caring atmosphere is required ur-gently, as those young students are generally more susceptible than adults to moral disengagement that could lead them to radicalization and violent extremism.

A Brief Profile of a Young Extremist in Canada

Born into an Acadian French-Canadian Catholic family, Damian Clairmont went through depression and identity crises in his teen years. Apparently, he did not get any help in school, which led him to drop out of formal education. He started home schooling, but it didn't last more than a few months. He felt des-perate and even attempted to commit suicide at the age of 17. Soon after, in his search for some meaning in his life, he converted to Islam and took the name of Mustafa al-Gharib. He was greatly influenced by the messages of some ex-tremist figures such as al-Awlaki on the internet, which steered him towards radicalization and gave him a feeling of belonging to a group. In 2012, he left Canada to join ISIS and was killed in Syria in 2014.

Since his death, his mother has been actively involved in advising parents of the push factors that may lead to the radicalization of youth.

CONCLUSION AND RECOMMENDATIONS

In conclusion, the aim of this chapter is not to examine in detail the vulnerabilities of the interviewed students respecting radicalization, but to find some factors existing in Canadian secondary schools that might draw some students to radical ideologies or violent extremism. The analysis of 14 interviews and two focus group discussions indicates that, despite Canada's being a multicultural country with a constitutional policy of multiculturalism, schools in Canada might not be effectively ensuring open discussions of controversial issues. Students are generally aware of recent terror attacks and controversial issues, such as radicalization and violent extremism, but they cannot openly or freely discuss those topics in class, as the teachers are reluctant to raise them in the classroom. In some cases, students who have different viewpoints on such controversial issues are not well accepted, and students with differences are generally discouraged from expressing opposing views.

Although the teachers in some social studies classes in schools are open to accepting different views, they generally avoid discussing controversial issues—in particular, radicalization and violent extremism. There is often a lack of care or consideration among the teachers about developing a critical understanding of what their students feel or want to know about pressing issues that are very often in the news. According to Bandura (2002), this situation can negatively affect students and make them disengage morally from schools, a most influential social institution. Although the youth participation rate in extremism is not high in Canada, youth engagement in different forms of extremism has been growing. Therefore, ensuring a caring environment in schools is necessary. To cultivate a caring environment in schools, we recommend the following:

1. Teachers should be better prepared to respond to controversial issues such as radicalization, extremism, and terrorism when they engage in classroom discussions. This is not easy for teachers without proper training. Therefore, not only does the curriculum of secondary-level education require change, but teacher training and professional development programs need to be updated accordingly.
2. Every school should have a particular mechanism for identifying the reasons behind the marginalization of some students. Student counselling centres can be given this responsibility, or the assigned teachers for all courses should be offered proper training on this subject. However, teachers need to avoid isolating some students from the mainstream in

the name of addressing or identifying marginal or disengaged students. This should be practiced through being more caring and compassionate towards the students.

3. Caring and compassionate relationships cannot be cultivated automatically; they require time and practice, gaining the trust of students and giving them a sense of agency. Teachers should try to develop a positive self-concept among all students in an equitable manner.

4. Teachers should also be careful about their behaviour when approaching marginalized or minority students so that their attitudes do not hamper the development of a positive self-concept of those students (Ghosh & Abdi, 2013).

5. Teachers should be well informed about the concept of critical multiculturalism and try to become positive role models for social justice, as this can greatly influence their students.

QUESTIONS FOR CRITICAL THOUGHT

1. Why do we say that education is a double-edged sword regarding violent extremism?

2. What do you think about Canadian students' understanding of the phenomenon of violent extremism?

3. How do you think Canadian teachers are approaching controversial topics like radicalization and violent extremism in their classrooms? Why might they be approaching these topics in this way?

GLOSSARY

Canadian schools: In this chapter, Canadian public secondary schools.

Care in education: Generally, refers to a positive attitude as well as reciprocal interaction or relationship between the teacher and student, who both give and receive care (Noddings, 1992, 2001).

Moral disengagement: A process in which an individual, step by step, gives up healthy and mainstream moral values and resorts to alternative and destructive world views (Bandura, 2002).

Teacher education: Any formal educational training programs designed and delivered by higher educational institutions for future or current teachers.

Violent extremism: "Those activities and beliefs which are used to advocate, engage in, prepare, or otherwise support ideologically-motivated violence to further socio-economic and political objectives" (Mirahmadi, Ziad, Farooq, & Lamb, 2015, p. 2).

NOTES

1. The mosque attack occurred amidst the anti-Muslim rhetoric and infamous Muslim ban initiated by the newly elected US President Donald Trump in early 2017. The perpetrator, Alexandre Bissonnette, was a follower and supporter of Donald Trump, as indicated in his online activities.
2. Damian Clairmont was 20 when he joined ISIS in 2012.
3. These were all college students who were in their early or mid-20s when they were radicalized.
4. CEGEP is an acronym for Collège d'enseignement général et professionnel, which refers to general and vocational colleges. CEGEPs are *publicly* funded pre-university and technical colleges in the educational system of the province of Quebec.
5. These Montreal students were in their late teenage years when they left Montreal to join ISIS.
6. Brad Galloway was in his early 20s when he started to get involved in right-wing extremist groups in Toronto.
7. Alexander Bissonnette was 28 when he perpetrated the mosque attack and was a political science student at Université Laval in Quebec City.
8. Anwar al-Awlaki was a US-born Islamist cleric who was the leader of external operations for Al-Qaeda in the Arabian Peninsula (AQAP).
9. In many parts of Europe, including the Netherlands, Germany, and, more recently, France, national and local governments have teamed up with educational institutions to develop and promote inclusive education in schools for CVE purposes. However, in North America, counter-terrorism policies have not involved the educational sector. *Building Resilience against Terrorism: Canada's Counter Terrorism Strategy* does not even mention the word *education* (see https://www.publicsafety.gc.ca/cnt/rsrcs/pblctns/rslnc-gnst-trrrsm/index-en.aspx).

REFERENCES

Baaken, T., & Schlegel, L. (2017). Fishermen or swarm dynamics? Should we understand jihadist online-radicalization as a top-down or bottom-up process? *Journal for Radicalization*, 18(13), 178–212.

Bandura, A. (2002). Selective moral disengagement in the exercise of moral agency. *Journal of Moral Education*, 31(2), 101–119.

Bandura, A. (1999). Moral disengagement in the perpetration of inhumanities. *Personality and Social Psychology Review (Special Issue on Evil and Violence)*, 3, 193–209.

Bell, S. (2015, January 25). Jihad becoming 'as Canadian as maple syrup' says Calgary man who joined armed extremists in Syria. *National Post*. Retrieved from https://nationalpost.com/news/canada/abu-dujana-al-muhajir-says-fighting-jihad-becoming-as-canadian-as-maple-syrup.

Bergen, P. (2015, January 12). The American who inspires terror from Paris to the U.S. *CNN*. Retrieved from http://www.cnn.com/2015/01/11/opinion/bergen-american-terrorism-leader-paris-attack.

Berger, J. M. (2016). Nazis vs. ISIS on Twitter: A comparative study of white nationalist and ISIS online social media networks. *Program on Extremism*. Retrieved from https://cchs.gwu.edu/sites/g/files/zaxdzs2371/f/downloads/Nazis%20v.%20ISIS%20Final_0.pdf.

Braniff, B. (2015). Understanding terrorism and the terrorist threat: Module 5. In *National Consortium for the Study of Terrorism and Responses to Terrorism (START)* [massive online open course]. Retrieved from https://www.coursera.org//learn/understandingterror.

Casciani, D. (2015, May 12). The battle of the e-Muftis. *BBC News*. Retrieved from http://www.bbc.com/news/magazine-32697424.

Cornelius-White, J. (2007). Learner-centered teacher–student relationships are effective: A meta-analysis. *Review of Educational Research*, 77(1), 113–143.

Counter Extremism Project (CEP). (2017). Anwar al-Awlaki's violent legacy continues years after his death [Press release]. Retrieved from https://www.counterextremism.com/press/anwar-alawlaki%E2%80%99s-violent-legacy-continues-years-after-his-death.

Duffy, A., & Harley, M. (2015, February 7). From JMag to Jihad John: The radicalization of John Maguire. *Ottawa Citizen*. Retrieved from http://ottawacitizen.com/news/local-news/from-jmag-to-jihad-john-the-radicalization-of-john-maguire.

Fenstermacher, G. D., & Richardson, V. (2010, May 26). What's wrong with accountability? *Teachers College Record*. Retrieved from https://www.tcrecord.org/content.asp?contentid=15996.

Ghosh, R., & Abdi, A. (2013). *Education and the politics of difference: Select Canadian perspectives* (2nd ed.). Toronto: Canadian Scholars' Press.

Ghosh, R., Manuel, A., Chan, W. Y. A., Dilimulati, M., & Babaei, M. (2016). *Education & security: A global literature report on countering violent religious extremism (CVE)*. London: Tony Blair Faith Foundation.

Goujard, C. (2018, April 1). Worried by rise of far-right groups, Canada puts millions into anti-racism effort. *The Washington Post*. Retrieved from https://www.washingtonpost. com/news/worldviews/wp/2018/04/01/worried-by-rise-of-far-right-groups-canada -puts-millions-into-anti-racism-effort/?utm_term=.5652d5952a1d.

Khan, R. (2018, April 1). Extremism and our educational institutions. *The Express Tribune*. Retrieved from https://tribune.com.pk/story/1674324/6-extremism-educational -institutions.

McKernan, B. (2016, September 6). Isis' new magazine Rumiyah shows the terror group is "struggling to adjust to losses." *Independent*. Retrieved from https://www.independent. co.uk/news/world/middle-east/isis-propaganda-terror-group-losses -syria-iraq-a7228286.html.

Ménard, M. (2010). *Youth civic engagement*. Background Paper No. 2010-23-E. Library of Parliament. Retrieved from http://www.parl.gc.ca/Content/LOP/ ResearchPublications/2010-23-e.htm.

Milton, D. (2016). *Communication breakdown: Unraveling the Islamic State's media efforts*. West Point, NY: Combating Terrorism Center at West Point. Retrieved from https:// ctc.usma.edu/app/uploads/2016/10/ISMedia_Online.pdf.

Mirahmadi, H., Ziad, W., Farooq, M., & Lamb, L. (2015, January). *Empowering Pakistan's civil society to counter global violent extremism*. Washington, DC: Center for Middle East Policy at Brookings. Retrieved from http://www.brookings.edu/~/media/ research/files/papers/2015/01/us-islamic-world-forum-publications/empowering -pakistans-civil-society-to-counter-violent-extremism-english.pdf.

Moghaddam, F. M. (2005). The staircase to terrorism: a psychological exploration. *American Psychologist*, 60(2), 161–169.

Neumann, P. R. (2017). *Countering violent extremism and radicalisation that lead to terrorism: Ideas, recommendations, and good practices from the OSCE region*. London, UK: International Centre for the Study of Radicalisation (ICSR).

Noddings, N. (2002). *Starting at home caring and social policy*. Berkeley: University of California Press.

Noddings, N. (2001). The caring teacher. In V. Richardson (Ed.), *Handbook of research on teaching* (pp. 99–105). Washington: American Educational Research Association.

Noddings, N. (1992). *The challenge to care in schools: An alternative approach to education*. New York: Teachers College Press.

Noddings, N. (1988). An ethic of caring and its implications for instructional arrangements. *American Journal of Education*, 96(2), 215–230.

Noddings, N. (1984). *Caring: A feminine approach to ethics & moral education*. Berkeley: University of California Press.

Parent, R., & Ellis, J. O. (2016). *The future of right-wing terrorism in Canada*. TSAS (Canadian Network for Research on Terrorism, Security and Society) working paper no. 16-12.

Public Safety Canada. (2017). *2017 public report on the terrorist threat to Canada*. Retrieved from https://www.publicsafety.gc.ca/cnt/rsrcs/pblctns/pblc-rprt-trrrst-thrt-cnd-2017/index-en.aspx.

Samuel, T. K. (2012). *Reaching the youth: Countering the terrorist narrative*. Kuala Lumpur, Malaysia: Southeast Asia Regional Center for Counter-Terrorism (SEARCCT).

Silke, A. (2008). Holy warriors: Exploring the psychological processes of jihadi radicalization. *European Journal of Criminology*, 5(1), 99–123.

Tasker, J. P. (2016, August 25). More Canadians travelling abroad to join ISIS, other terrorist groups, report says. *CBC News*. Retrieved from http://www.cbc.ca/news/politics/terrorism-threat-report-1.3735434.

Taylor, A. (2003). *Animals & ethics: An overview of the philosophical debate*. Peterborough, ON: Broadview Press.

USCIRF. (2018, March 24). *Study reveals numerous passages in Saudi textbooks inciting violence and intolerance*. Retrieved from http://www.uscirf.gov/news-room/press-releases-statements/uscirf-study-reveals-numerous-passages-in-saudi-textbooks.

Weimann, G. (2014). *New terrorism and new media*. Washington, DC: Commons Lab of the Woodrow Wilson International Center for Scholars. Retrieved from http://www.wilsoncenter.org/publication/new-terrorism-and-new-media.

Wilner, A. S., & Dubouloz, C. J. (2011). Transformative radicalization: applying learning theory to Islamist radicalization. *Studies in Conflict & Terrorism*, 34(5), 418–438.

CHAPTER 13

Compassion in High-Poverty Schools: Socially Just Educational Leadership in Action

Pam Bishop

LEARNING OBJECTIVES

1. To identify a variety of ways in which teachers in high-poverty schools show compassion to support students' social and academic learning.
2. To draw on an evidence base (i.e., research, theory, and practice) to articulate understandings about "socially just" teaching in high-poverty schools.

INTRODUCTION

Accounts of highly successful principals and teachers in Western countries show that apart from being knowledgeable and skillful, they evidence a variety of attitudes and values—some of which pertain to being compassionate in one form or another (Bishop, 2014; Mulford, 2007; Peterson, 2017). The fact that those principals' and teachers' contributions in schools are informed by a valuing of empathy, an ethic of care, and kindness or other aspects of compassion is not surprising, given that the teaching profession's intergenerational gift to school students pivots on enhancing their life chances. Indeed, it is the teaching profession which understands better than most professions how important it is to ensure students learn effectively in schools in order that they, as children and youth, are positioned to "find out what they are good at, what they would like to do with their lives, and how to live responsible and fulfilling lives" (Noddings, 2013, p. 66).

The purposes of education identified by Noddings (2013) are similar to those illuminated by Greene (1986), namely that education is for freedom—a freedom which enables every person to be the best human being they can be, someone who understands they are part of a community and world that requires self-understanding, thoughtful actions, and consideration of others. Such a quest is a massive undertaking in schools across a province or territory (or state), let alone a nation or beyond. That all Canadian provinces and territories have created many thousands of schools which have actively nurtured students' senses of themselves; helped clarify current and future interests; and developed literate, numerate, and empathetic students is a tribute to the teaching profession, parents, and our democratic systems of governance. Whilst there is little doubt about the achievements and calibre of most schools in Canada, many that serve large numbers of students who live in poverty have not enjoyed such widespread or enduring success. Certainly, particular "**high-poverty schools**" have done well over time or for a limited number of years (Harris, 2006). However, schools that serve large numbers of students who live in poverty have faced a raft of structural and cultural challenges which other schools typically do not confront (Leithwood & Day, 2007). In addition, high-poverty schools have been underfunded relative to their educational needs. For example, the level of funding needed for on-reserve schools to comprehensively attend to students' academic and social learning needs has been chronically lacking from successive federal governments for many decades, according to First Nations education directors (Mai `Stoina Eagle-Speaker & Bishop, 2015).

Although many funding shortfalls can be—and have been—made up for by extra dedication and work from principals and teachers, the complexities faced by high-poverty schools are such that additional effort and care are vital but insufficient for sustainable improvements to student learning to be achieved. Nonetheless, one way highly successful teachers and principals support students in high-poverty schools is by showing care, kindness, empathy, and other forms of compassion in their engagements with each student.

This exploratory case study (Yin, 2018) captures some of the efforts involved in enhancing one Ontario high-poverty school structurally and culturally so as to improve student academic and social learning. The school was selected because of its socioeconomic status and location, plus recent successes in provincial literacy tests (as a board source pointed out during the planning stage of the research). The unit of analysis was the principal and teachers. Semi-structured interviews for up to 90 minutes were individually conducted with 10 teachers and for four hours with the principal. Transcriptions of the interviews were returned to each participant for review and possible amendment. No amendments were requested by any participant. Informal observation notes were also kept to assist with the researcher's contextual understandings. Those notes included details about the library facilities, school grounds, students' displayed work, and art. The data were analyzed thematically. The following key questions were asked of the data: What evidence of compassion is apparent in the principal and teachers' work at Cedar Hills Public School? How might we understand the term *compassion* as it is enacted at Cedar Hills Public School by the principal and teachers? In this chapter, compassion was operationalized as those practices, values, and dispositions by the principal and teachers that evidence empathy, kindness, care, and actions to improve students' academic and social learning. Although the data were obtained as part of another study, taken as a whole, the case study demonstrates multiple ways in which compassion was evident in the purposes, efforts, and achievements of the principal and teachers at Cedar Hills. The case demonstrates many aspects of the complex work of the principal and teachers, and how their values and day-to-day work are enmeshed with aspects of compassion towards students.

A SNAPSHOT OF CHILD POVERTY IN CANADA

At present, official counts of child poverty in Canada suggest that nearly one in five children lives in poverty (Statistics Canada, 2017). Low-income households of four people living in poverty in 2016 had a total household after-tax income of less than $44,266 (Statistics Canada, 2017). The median after-tax income of Canadian households in 2016 was $57,000. By way of comparison, in the provinces (not including territories), the median after-tax incomes of households in 2016 were as follows:

- Alberta: $70,200
- British Columbia: $56,800
- Manitoba: $57,000
- New Brunswick: $50,900
- Newfoundland: $55,800
- Nova Scotia: $49,700
- Ontario: $59,400

- Prince Edward Island: $51,600
- Quebec: $49,500
- Saskatchewan: $59,700

Census data from 2016 also showed lone-parent families with children were three times more likely to be low-income households than were two-parent families (Statistics Canada, 2018).

Canada Without Poverty (2017) argues that 40 percent of Indigenous children live in poverty and, for those children who live on reserves, the figure increases to 60 percent. These data suggest that poverty is raced, with disproportionate numbers of Indigenous children (compared to non-Indigenous children) growing up in poverty. As well, poverty in Canada, like in many countries, is gendered: women head most sole-parent households that have children. Moreover, women often earn lower wages than men in the same occupations (Statistics Canada, 2018). Against those data, it is perhaps not surprising that parental unemployment and sole parenthood are viewed as the two key determinants of childhood poverty (Saunders, 2005).

As Dorling claims, "social inequality within rich countries persists because of a continued belief in the tenets of injustice" (2015, p. 15). Moreover, Dorling argues those tenets include elitism, social exclusion, prejudice, greed, and despair. In Dorling's view, "people are poor because they cannot afford to take part in the norms of society, and those norms only become unaffordable because the better-off have been allowed to become better off" (p. 30). Similarly, it can be argued that children and youth, who live in poverties of one sort or another, whether in Canada or elsewhere, have been placed **at risk** by society (Deil-Amen & De Luca, 2010; Epstein, 2001). Part of that risk is manifest in the emotional and financial stresses of living in poverty, which negatively impact family life and the process of parenting (Saunders, 2005). In turn, Brandon (2015) and Saunders (2005) suggest that those disruptions contribute to both immediate and long-term damage to the lives of children who live in poverty, such as child neglect or abuse.

In a democratic country as economically and socially prosperous as Canada, it is difficult to accept that any children should have to live in poverty. Yet oftentimes, the parents of children who live in poverty are blamed for the circumstances they find themselves in rather than any other explanations being considered, such as the historical and profoundly destructive factors of colonization in Canada, hiring or labour market responses to a "knowledge era," and the types of work now commonly available to those who did not complete Grade 12.

In Noddings's book *Education and Democracy in the 21st Century*, she argues that "schools can help students to achieve satisfying lives in three great domains: home, occupation, and civic life" (2013, p. 11); teachers, principals, school boards, and systems should progress teaching and learning towards those three domains. According to Noddings, recognizing or largely pursuing only one domain—as some schools do—is problematic for students and, ultimately, for society. Not only can a concentration on one domain require (or embed) a narrow curriculum, but it also potentially underserves many important immediate and longer-term learning needs of students—for example, being able to collaborate well, being highly relational, and being able to appreciate differences between one another.

COMPASSION: A MULTI-DIMENSIONAL CONCEPT

According to Coles, compassion is linked to three components: "the recognition of a person's or a group's suffering; an empathetic response to that suffering; and, an active determination to alleviate the distress and, where possible, the causes of that distress" (2015, p. 4). In a similar vein, Kohler-Evans and Barnes (2015) suggest, "compassion begins with the emotional response but adds an authentic desire to help" (p. 16). Compassion is a "basic emotion" (Nussbaum, 1996, p. 1) and a capacity that all (or nearly all) humans are capable of exercising in some form or other (Peterson, 2017). Although research into school-based manifestations of compassion is limited, studies that reveal its existence may help school systems and faculties of education better understand its potential benefits for students. Peterson suggests that empathy is but one of several elements of compassion. Kindness, care, and emotional intelligence are additional elements of what Peterson suggests compassion can embrace.

Teachers who show respect and care for students in schools should not be diminished or accused of being "egoistic" for doing so (Noddings, 2002, p. 151). Those enactments of an ethic of care enrich and strengthen both parties. Noddings's advocacy of teachers demonstrating an ethic of care with students is linked to larger questions about how and why schools need to cultivate students' moral capacities.

In her classic text *The Right to Learn*, Darling-Hammond (1997) argued that, if they achieved nothing else, teacher education programs should teach pre-service students about empathy. Darling-Hammond's argument was that empathy needed to be a capacity that inheres in teachers and school students. Even very young students starting out in school should be encouraged to literally put themselves "in the shoes of another." Darling-Hammond made little mention of compassion but located empathy as an essential element of what students could develop in order for them to ultimately become thoughtful, caring human beings. Compassion can be difficult to extend to others when what may be required involves a great deal of work or emotional distress for oneself (Rabois, 2016). Nonetheless, Rabois posits, "if you are a teacher who wants to stimulate student learning and increase prosocial behaviour in the classroom, one of the best things you can do is act with empathy and compassion with your students" (2016, p. xi).

CASE STUDY

Cedar Hills Public School (a pseudonym, as are all names used in this paper) is located in Southwestern Ontario and known amongst district teachers and principals as a "high-poverty" school. The K-8 school is set amidst houses and apartments that were mostly built in the 1940s, 1950s, and 1960s. Cedar Hills is a suburb of a large city and a place where rents are usually lower than in surrounding areas. Many families stay in Cedar Hills for brief periods of time. Some residents know there is a stigma to the name "Cedar Hills"—it is stereotyped as a place often marked by domestic violence, poverty, sub-standard housing, high unemployment, and young families.

Cedar Hills is on the "wrong side of the tracks" according to one of the school's teachers, who grew up in the area but now lives in an affluent part of the city. The area has a long history of being viewed as poverty-stricken and marginalized by wealthier city dwellers because of who lives, visits, or passes through Cedar Hills. But the 130-year-old school is disrupting that stigma. Five years ago, a new school principal was appointed by the district school board because of system concerns about student achievement outcomes—too many students were struggling to learn literacy and numeracy. As they progressed into higher grades in the school, many students fell further and further behind in their learning. With the appointment of the new principal, she set forth, with teachers in particular, to improve the school so that more Cedar Hills students would prosper.

The decision to transfer Principal Angela Howard to Cedar Hills Public had been carefully thought through by the school board director, Jim Rainsford. Historically, Rainsford was widely respected amongst the 8,000 principals and teachers and known, amongst many, for having been an engaging and expert-level teacher earlier in his career. As Rainsford "rose through the ranks" to become a principal and later superintendent, he worked collaboratively with many principals and teachers who were based in high-poverty schools. That "political capital" was needed when Rainsford phoned Howard at her home late one evening to indicate she would soon be transferred to Cedar Hills Public School. The phone call didn't immediately take Howard aback—but the location did. She was a 20-year veteran happy in her present role. Howard told Rainsford that she knew Cedar Hills reputationally. Not long after she began at Cedar Hills, she realized how little she knew of the school:

> When I came here, I was literally blown out of the water. … I had been at Rye Grove Public for a year and a half, and its lower socioeconomic—lots of poverty. But it's not the same [at Cedar Hills]. This is dire. There is a lot of high needs in terms of behaviour and mental health, and even with the parents.

The contrast identified by Howard between Rye Public and Cedar Hills Public was supported by demographic data from the city council's social statistics department. Cedar Hills's 230-plus student population typically lived in households where there was no car and the family lived in rental accommodation. Unemployment was prevalent throughout Cedar Hills, and that situation and the lack of cash flow placed strains on parents as well as their children. Often, parents were unable to easily access medical care or sufficient food for themselves and their children. Howard elaborated:

> Many parents need to go to the doctor or to the food bank: Between myself and some staff members, we will drive them. We will pick up kids; we will take them to the doctor. We meet families who are walking to the doctor. We will go to the doctor just to be an advocate for them because many of our parents aren't strong advocates for the kids; they don't know how to "voice."

Prior to Cedar Hills, Howard's experience of teaching and working with so many parents who consistently flouted school rules had been very limited. She said:

> Attendance was very poor, and I came in "guns-a-blazing" wanting everybody to follow the rules, and it was like "who do you think you are," and so yeah, I struggled at first. I remember Jim Rainsford came in here the first week, he did that [because of a nearby shooting] and he came again because he heard I was struggling, I said, "Oh yeah, I'm struggling." I said, "I don't know what you were thinking putting me in here," and he said, "Because you can do this job," and I said, "I don't know where you see that, because I am really struggling, the children are telling me to f-off, the parents I've phoned to suspend [their child] they're saying f-you, you're a problem." I didn't know what to do.

Openly unsupportive, and in some instances abusive, comments from many parents were not the only daunting challenge that Howard faced as soon as she arrived at Cedar Hills Public School:

> I went into the classrooms, and they [students] were running on top of the desks and playing football and the teachers were looking at me for guidance, I'm thinking oh my god I don't know what to do.

Situations in schools where students are able to defy and, in effect, dominate teachers or the principal are usually extremely challenging for educators because they undermine their authority and school orderliness. As a result, in collaboration with all of the teachers, Howard focused on creating a system to support teaching and learning, and creating safety in classrooms:

> So we did a lot of suspensions that first term from January into June. We came up with a behaviour sheet, and if students didn't follow those rules and expectations, they were sent to the office. We had a huge amount of office referrals during those six months, but I think they got used to it. Some of the parents knew they [students] couldn't behave that way. We had lots of police involvement, we called the police frequently to say, "You know what, this is not normal behaviour in the school and we're changing this around."

According to Howard, her view then, and since, was:

> Our children can do better, will do better, and they deserve better than what they're getting in here. Teachers cannot teach in a building where their children are behaving that way in the classroom, so my rule is if you can't behave in the classroom and you can't behave in the office, you're going home.

Whenever a vacancy arose at Cedar Hills, Howard opted to hire teachers who were known to her as being committed and effective. "The teachers that we have hired in the last few years are super passionate and they want to be here," she said. Teachers appreciated working at Cedar Hills with their principal. Across the board, teachers recognized the recent successes of the school. Erika, who had been teaching for six years, commented:

> I think it is a combination of many factors. I think that leadership is number one—we have a wonderful, wonderful principal who is building a team, and she is keeping us together. And we have also a team of teachers who really truly

care. We have high expectations for children. I don't believe that just because children are coming from difficult circumstances they should cut them slack every time they are late or they don't do something. We should expect them to perform well, and we should provide conditions in the school that allow them to do well.

According to Erika, teachers and the principal knew about a raft of conditions that would help students. Not all of them were affordable for a school that was the size of Cedar Hills. However, some conditions could be created. Erika's approach was to

> provide security, structure, [and] routine so that they [students] can trust us, so they can believe that, whatever they do, there will be the same metre applied to everybody, and I think that makes them successful. Because they can rely on, "This is the consequence—this is the positive consequence, this is the negative consequence—if I do this, this is going to be the result." They don't have that in their home environment at all. I think they thrive on high expectations and follow-through [from teachers and the principal].

Data pertaining to the school's improved academic outcomes over the previous year were pleasing to the Cedar Hills principal and teachers. The improvements signalled, at least to some extent, that their combined efforts had been successful. The teaching had directly impacted learning in most classrooms, and teachers viewed the principal's leadership as indirectly, yet crucially, contributing to the outcomes.

The emphasis on having high expectations of students in terms of their behaviour as well as their learning was a valuable strategy by Angela Howard and the school's teachers. Howard and her colleagues understood the need to maximize the time for learning, and to achieve that, students had to be ready, willing, and able to learn. Further, she explained:

> First and foremost, we provide things at the school, above and beyond Ministry curriculum, and delivering of the curriculum—feeding the kids, working on their social skills, their social development, and providing them parenting. I think all of that goes into it—clothing, clothing drives, things of that nature. I think all of that and sometimes even I think the Ministry curriculum gets put to the back burner at times, and it needs to, it has to, because of other needs— basic needs aren't being met, and until you meet those needs, you can't deliver them the other stuff.

In many of the upper-grade Cedar Hills classrooms, teachers encouraged high-level conceptual thinking in students by employing topics that were relevant to them. "Real world" problems and aspects of what students valued (e.g., the environment, music, technology) were considered, and math, literacy, and art then linked to the topic. Teachers adapted aspects of their teaching to enable students to improve their learning "buy-in" rather than simply teaching in ways they had done in other schools. The principal's "heads-up" guidance to newly appointed teachers to be both flexible and prepared for students who were dramatically different to those in other schools was subsequently found to be astute guidance by teachers. As one teacher put it,

> I remember Angela was wonderful; she actually came to see me teaching before she hired me, and one of her comments I will remember forever, she said, "You will have different children at Cedar Hills; it's going to be different for you because these children are so different," and it's true, so that's the biggest difference I see between schools.

The caution from Howard to teachers was not intended to position students in a negative light. Rather, her compassion for students was focused on their learning needing to be dramatically elevated. For that to occur, teachers needed to respect, value, and affirm students wherever appropriate. Teachers also needed to work with their students to consistently create peaceful and engaging classrooms. As well, a key part of teachers' work required them to address relevant provincial learning requirements. As one teacher noted, the differences in context and circumstances spoke to the lives of students and their learning needs:

> I started off in a middle-class suburban school, and that was the opposite end of the spectrum—the kids came well-fed, well-dressed; so many of them had rich extracurricular experiences, travelling with mom and dad, or sports and stuff like that. All of that is missing here, so what they experience here at school is much more intense because you're providing that enrichment. This is it—the field trips, the learning opportunities, the food, feeding them nutritional food, health aspects, liaison with community support, and coaching parents on good hygiene.

Jane, who had been teaching at the school for three years, said:

> The population of children that are coming—and I know the educators are adjusting to that—means you have to be a much stronger educator here than

you have to be at different schools because it's just so much easier [in the other schools]. Most of our staff are in it for the right reasons—we're not in it because of its vacation time, we're not in it because it's easy, people flock to the easy schools. In those schools, kids are going to get better at reading. I [as a teacher] have a small contribution to make re: how these kids are going to do in reading, but the foundation is already there and they are going to progress in the reading and math because of the family foundations. We don't have that here.

Although the school had a reputation for serving families who live in poverty, there was a strong sense amongst teachers that their efforts were successful. Terry, who had taught in the upper grades for six years, stated:

The reasons we're highly successful is because we have teachers who are relentless—teachers who care, teachers who are really knowledgeable about their craft, and teachers who are passionate, and that's the "how" that makes the "why" possible.

Terry later added:

Further, everybody here understands what kind of building we're in, we're all living in reality, and it's a different kind of support that we offer everybody. This is my fourth school, and the difference is I've had more conflicts—there have been more conflicts, disagreements, in this building with this staff, than all the other schools I've been at combined, but it's because we work in a really, really stressful environment—really stressful environment. There are just more collisions between staff members because we care so much here and we fight—we fight about what's going to be best for this kid, we fight about how we are going to handle that parent who is out of control, we have disagreements about where that money we got is best used, so they're good productive fights.

Teachers and the principal demonstrated care, empathy, and compassion as they responded to various key challenges—in order to ultimately support students' academic and social learning. The responses from the teachers below show the challenges faced by students to also be extremely compelling:

I think it's the family. The family structure, alcohol and drug abuse in the family, that's one BIG problem that we have, and I don't want to hurt their feelings or anything, but many people here are almost proud of their being dependent on society. They almost present that, "Oh well, somebody will pay for that, or my kid will get a breakfast, I don't have to feed her." [Students] are late because they sleep in; well of course if their parents are sleeping in, they are sleeping in. They don't do their homework because they don't care. If their parents don't care about school, why would the children, because as a child, you copy what you see. So if they see and hear inappropriate language, they use it because that's what they know. I think that the major challenge is what they are getting from the family.

Kids getting enough food, a consistent home life—is someone going to be there when I get home, someone who loves me when I get home? Are the parents encouraging them enough, are the parents trying to turn the kids against the teachers and the support staff because mom and dad have had bad experiences with the education system themselves? Are mom and dad very angry at how their lives turned out so they are taking it out on the teachers, or taking it out on the kids, or taking it out on both?

Our biggest challenge is that they come to school from the conditions of poverty with a belief system and their self-image as learners—as "I can't." That is a really huge thing, and they don't persist on tasks. ... You can just see the language: "I'm stupid," "I can't," "I'm not worth it," and so on. One of our biggest challenges here is always to change their image of themselves to "I can." So that's where the differentiation helps, it says, "Oh, I can; if I work a little harder, I can get this." I know it sounds like jargon, but it's very much that growth mindset that they don't have. They shut down so quickly, you can see it in some of our Grade 8 kids. It's almost like the pain of having to acknowledge that they can't right now makes them vulnerable. It's just not worth the trip for them, because for them it's "I can't right now and I never will be able to, so then what's the point?"

I see the haves and the have-nots. I see children like my own and the children here and how unfair it truly is. Some of those children in the North end should come here and see what it's really like. ... Because they need to learn life is hard for some people and yeah, you know that they live in poverty and their moms don't have jobs and it doesn't make them any less better than you.

The social outcomes have to come first; the social challenges are first because academics can't improve if the social challenges haven't been met. They don't see sharing and getting along at home and they don't have parents that really care at home, and parents are either working or not really caring about the kids, yelling and getting their own way.

DISCUSSION

It was evident in this exploratory case study that the principal and teachers at Cedar Hills Public School recognized the suffering of many—especially students and their families. They also possessed and responded to "an appreciation for human fragility, empathetic distress, the principle of care and compassionate action" (Peterson, 2017, p. 142). The principal and teachers wanted for the students of Cedar Hills what many of their own children had experienced in life—genuine opportunities to learn and prosper by working in jobs and living and working harmoniously with others amidst the trials and successes of life.

By and large, the compassion displayed at Cedar Hills Public School was built on an affirming view of their students as "deserving" human beings. The views of the principal and teachers were focused on satisfying current student needs in terms of both academic and social learning needs. As well, there was recognition of the potential of students to progress and lead prosperous lives. There was also a sense that, as young Canadians, students had the right to be cared for and strongly supported by schools, families, and society: students deserved good learning and life chances. The pursuit of a good life was made more viable as a prospect for some Cedar Hills Public School students as an outcome of what the principal and teachers collaborated to achieve with students at Cedar Hills.

Education is central to eradicating future poverty (Palmer, MacInnes, & Kenway, 2006). At the very least, what happens in schools can blunt some of the marginalizing and exclusionary aspects that students who live in poverty can experience: being able to take part in school excursions, camps, and sports (that require specific outfits or equipment) are examples of experiences that should be available to all students—not just those whose parents can afford such outlays (Morris, Barnes, & Mason, 2009).

Why Cedar Hills Public School warrants being viewed as a school that had a principal and teachers who, by and large, were compassionate in multiple ways is due to several factors. Principal Angela Howard and her colleagues worked with "where the students were at"—they listened to, observed, talked with, and asked questions of students. The curriculum was adapted to capture more of students' interests for the purpose of giving them more of a voice in their learning and engaging them more in class. Some of the literacy and numeracy aspects of the school program were redeveloped to improve knowledge and skill acquisition and be more coherent and developmental. The teachers actively shared curriculum and pedagogy ideas with one another, and most expanded the variety of teaching offered to better support a range of student learning styles. Overall, the principal and teachers were very respectful of students and deeply empathetic about the punishing aspects of poverty they endured.

Angela Howard and Cedar Hills Public School teachers worked with their school board to enhance student achievement in terms of academic and **social learning**. In that respect, the principal and teachers were mindful of the need to use and show data-based evidence of students' improved learning to the school board and ministry. Further, suspension and allied data were kept and analyzed by the principal and teachers to help them better understand how to support students. For example, they checked the data to see whether any patterns of absences or behaviour challenges were evident and illuminating.

At every opportunity, the principal promoted learning amongst teachers for the purpose of capacity building. Even in situations where the school was not scheduled to take part in the school board's professional learning, Howard doggedly advocated for, and was often successful, at gaining Cedar Hills Public School teachers access to such learning opportunities.

The attention given to offering a planned and relevant curriculum as well as social learning classroom experiences were markers of the principal's and teachers' commitment to school-based social justice efforts. In an allied way, efforts by the principal and teachers to provide food, delousing, and clothes washing at the school demonstrated significant care and respect for the health and dignity of students. Howard's successful grant writing ensured that school trips were heavily subsidized or free, so students could visit places they had rarely or never been to within the province.

As part of social learning, a five-point framework was used to guide student behaviour. It drew "buy-in" from all teachers as well as Howard. The principal and teachers knew that they needed to be consistent with the implementation of the framework as it was essential to sending a clear message about high expectations to students. Behaviour expectations, in particular, applied to classrooms and the schoolyard, and were designed to create safe, welcoming, and peaceful spaces for students to learn and play in during each school day. The tactic ultimately worked for most students most of the time.

The principal and teachers modelled peaceful ways of working with students— and oftentimes families—to negotiate resolutions to difficult problems. In the course of those dealings, sometimes family members did not agree with the problem-solving and verbally bullied the principal or a teacher with abuse.

At Cedar Hills Public School, the principal and teachers were clear in understanding they had an obligation to cultivate student learning. They realized that students' academic learning was linked to their social learning. For example, by taking every chance to explicitly praise students when they achieved in class, many teachers hoped to build student self-esteem. All of the teachers and Howard believed their efforts were "the right thing to do." They were also pragmatic in realizing that not all students would respond fully to those efforts and achieve as strongly as many classmates. However, there was a resolve that the collective effort of teachers and the principal was the only highly efficacious way forward for the students' learning to be notably advanced.

Elevating students' academic outcomes is critical in all schools and evident in schools throughout the world. Improving the academic achievements of students who live in poverties of one sort or another remains a crucial part of the core work of principals and teachers. High-poverty schools are extremely challenging places to work. In part, the complexities faced by children and youth with backgrounds of disadvantage are related to a set of complexities that principals and teachers encounter in high-poverty schools. Although there is heightened awareness amongst the teaching profession in many countries regarding the need to provide engaging learning, it is often difficult to offer engaging teaching in some high-poverty schools.

Students who come from the poorest of the poor families are as incredible as any other students. However, the amount of support made available for these students in schools that they attend is often remarkably insufficient. The factors and conditions that students face to get to the gate of a high-poverty school are often dramatically different to what most students in mainstream schools experience. The extent of those factors and conditions is one of the reasons why teaching effectively in high-poverty schools is complex, and often emotionally demanding, work. Arguably, the most effective teachers in high-poverty schools are those who respect and greatly appreciate the humanity of their students. The appreciation of students' worth—and their rights to excellent schooling—can act as a relationship anchor with teachers when a class or school day is not working well for one or both parties. As Cedar Hills Public School teachers' and the principal's comments showed, their recognition of students' prior learning was not an indication of their learning potential. The students' grasp of academic learning was usually not at grade level (according to provincial data from the ministry). However, with a flexible and affirming yet consistent approach to student behaviour in the classroom, many students focused on their academic learning with genuine interest.

CONCLUSION

Because of its relevance and importance to schools, the term *compassion* and what it means to be a compassionate teacher or principal requires further consideration by scholars, educational leaders, and members of the teaching profession. In high-poverty school settings, compassion can communicate a strong commitment to students from their teachers and principal, as happened at Cedar Hills. Enactments of compassion at Cedar Hills happened alongside other activities including student behaviour initiatives, a revitalized curriculum, and the provision of food and personal hygiene care to numerous students. In that respect, the principal and teachers were acutely aware of their obligation to respond to the harsh conditions created by poverty. The affection and respect towards students as individuals underpinned relations with teachers and also helped more broadly with teaching and learning in classrooms.

In the 21st century, poverty presents more risks for children than it did in much of the 20th century. Protracted periods of time living in poverty may deny children opportunities to experience happy childhoods and/or reach their true potential. Children's health and capacity to learn and prosper during their years in school may also be reduced. One of the core purposes of education is to create freedom—for individuals and communities (Greene, 1986). Yet poverty restricts the development of capabilities that enable freedom to be fully realized (Nussbaum, 1996; Saunders, 2005; Sen, 1999). The matter of child poverty pertains to matters of human rights: All children in Canada should enjoy the freedom to reach their potential. Canadian school students such as those at Cedar Hills Public School should not have their human rights restricted by inadequate food, housing, and clothing. Public schools that actively and compassionately support students who live in poverty (of whichever sort) should be given additional financial resources to continue to do so. For example, if a Grade 3 student can read only to the level of an end-of-year kindergarten student, the class size at a school such as Cedar Hills would need to be reduced in order to enable teaching and learning to occur that effectively bridges the achievement gap.

Compassion, empathy, kindness, and care from principals and teachers are a vital part of what develops successful schools for students living in poverty. However, those fundamental qualities from principals and teachers must be matched by significantly improved funding. If school boards and ministries of education are not going to systemically change who typically ends up being a teacher in high-poverty schools (typically those beginning their teaching careers), then that aspect alone means additional monies are needed for professional learning and allied capacity building. It is not equitable to allow disproportionate numbers of expert-level (Bishop, 2004, 2014) teachers to work in middle-class schools. The values underlying those existing policies are too accommodating of social disadvantage being located to particular Canadian individuals, groups, and communities.

As is frequently the case for Canadian students who live in poverty, having clothing that is ill suited to the season was apparent at Cedar Hills Public School. The ongoing efforts of the principal and teachers to ensure "students who were without" received warm clothing were impressive. Not surprisingly, the school had no control over the quality of dwellings that students lived in (e.g., not having a lot of books, furnishings such as a desk, or heating and cooling arrangements). However, the school actively provided food for many students so that they had a nutritious breakfast and lunch.

The compassion evident from the principal and teachers at Cedar Hills Public School pertains to their values as both professionals and formal and informal educational leaders. Their multiple efforts demonstrated numerous elements of Coles's (2015) view of compassion. The degree of compassion exhibited towards the students spoke to what the principal and teachers believe are obligations of the teaching profession. Although not mentioned much by this chapter's participants, the respect, affirmation, care, empathy, and overall compassion hint at the sort of community they viewed as important for Canada.

QUESTIONS FOR CRITICAL THOUGHT

1. Many teachers never teach in high-poverty schools over the course of their careers. That may be preferable if there is a lack of interest in or regard for improving the life chances of students who live in poverty. Nonetheless, 21st century universities, and in particular those involved in pre-service teacher education, are well placed to offer courses that develop deep understandings of poverty, exclusion, marginalization, and inequities—most notably in Canada but elsewhere, as well. Based on your reading of this chapter, what knowledge, skills, values, and dispositions might be developed in teacher education programs to help Bachelor of Education students start their teaching careers as compassionate and effective teachers in high-poverty schools?

2. Darling-Hammond (1997) was correct to assert that the teaching profession—incredible as it is overall—can play a pivotal role in creating schools that allow students to be fully appreciated and nurtured as human beings with potential and talent amidst burdens such as poverty. Why, and in what ways, are students in high-poverty schools often stereotyped and seen as less worthy of receiving a quality education than students from materially well-off backgrounds?

3. It is clear that schools cannot—on their own—ameliorate poverty. However, schools remain a key part of any systematic approach to improve the learning and life chances of students who live in poverty. Why might schools like Cedar Hills be one of the last institutions that can provide strong support to students who live in poverty? Explain why that matters in terms of social justice in Canada.

GLOSSARY

At-risk students: Students who are likely to fail at school without temporary or ongoing intervention.

High-poverty schools: Schools where 25 percent or more of students live near or below the poverty level.

Social learning: Learning new behaviours, values, or attitudes by observing others.

REFERENCES

Bishop, P. (2014, November). *Leadership for collective efficacy and meaning* [Keynote address]. Paper presented at the annual conference of the Ontario Principals' Council, CPC, ADFO, Curriculum Services Canada & Student Achievement Division (Education Ministry) Toronto, ON.

Bishop, P. (2004). *Stories from within: Leadership, learning and lives in a high-poverty school.* Paper presented at the annual conference of the Australian Assocation for Research in Education, Melbourne, Australia.

Brandon, M. (2015). In what ways might poverty contribute to maltreatment? In E. Fernandez, A. Zeira, T. Vecchiato, & C. Canali (Eds.), *Theoretical and empirical insights into child and family poverty* (pp. 257–271). New York: Springer.

Canada Without Poverty. (2017). *Just the facts.* Retrieved from http://www.cwp-csp.ca.

Coles, M. (2015). Changing the story, altering the paradigm. In M. Coles (Ed.), *Towards the compassionate school: From golden rule to golden thread* (pp. 1–22). London, UK: UCL Institute of Education Press.

Darling-Hammond, L. (1997). *The right to learn: A blueprint for creating schools that work.* San Francisco: Jossey-Bass.

Deil-Amen, R., & DeLuca, S. (2010). The underserved third: How our educational structures populate an educational underclass. *Journal of Education for Students Placed at Risk*, 15(1–2), 27–50. https://doi.org/10.1080/10824661003634948.

Dorling, D. (2015). *Injustice: Why social inequality still persists* (Rev. ed.). Chicago: Policy Press.

Epstein, J. L. (2001). Building bridges of home, school, and community: The importance of design. *Journal of Education for Students Placed at Risk*, 6(1–2), 161–168. https://doi.org/10.1207/S1532761ESPR0601-2_10.

Greene, M. (1986). *The dialectic of freedom.* New York: Teachers College Press.

Harris, A. (2006). *Improving schools in exceptionally challenging circumstances: Tales from the frontline.* New York: Continuum.

Kohler-Evans, P., & Barnes, C. (2015). *Civility, compassion, and coverage in schools today.* London, UK: Rowman and Littlefield.

Leithwood, K., & Day, C. (2007). What we learned: A broad view. In C. Day & K. Leithwood (Eds.), *Successful principal leadership in times of change: An international perspective* (pp. 189–203). Dordrecht, Netherlands: Springer.

Mai ʼStoina Eagle-Speaker, D., & Bishop, P. (2015). *The complex administrative, economic and political contexts of education directors' work in First Nations in Alberta, Canada.* Paper presented at the 20th Annual Values and Leadership Conference, University Park, PA.

Morris, K., Barnes, M., & Mason, P. (2009). *Monitoring poverty and social exclusion.* Portland, OR: The Policy Press.

Mulford, B. (2007). Successful school principalship in Tasmania. In C. Day & K. Leithwood (Eds.), *Successful principal leadership in times of change: An international perspective* (pp. 17–38). Dordrecht, Netherlands: Springer.

Noddings, N. (2013). *Education and democracy in the 21st century.* New York: Teachers College Press.

Noddings, N. (2002). *Educating moral people: A caring alternative to character education.* New York: Teachers College Press.

Nussbaum, M. (1996). Compassion: The basic emotion. *Social Philosophy and Policy*, 13, 27–58. Retrieved from https://doi.org/10.1017/S0265052500001515.

Palmer, G., MacInnes, T., & Kenway, P. (2006). *Monitoring poverty and social exclusion.* York, UK: Joseph Rowntree Foundation.

Peterson, A. (2017). *Compassion and education: Cultivating compassionate children, schools, and communities.* London, UK: Macmillan.

Rabois, I. (2016). *Compassionate critical thinking.* Lanham, MD: Rowman & Littlefield.

Saunders, P. (2005). *The poverty wars: Reconnecting research with reality.* Sydney, Australia: University of New South Wales Press.

Sen, A. K. (1999). *Development as freedom*. New York: Anchor Books.

Statistics Canada. (2018). *The income of Canadians*. Catalogue No. 11-627-M2018006. Retrieved from http://www150.statcan.gc.ca/n1/pub/11-627-m/11-627-m2018006 -eng.pdf.

Statistics Canada. (2017). *Census in brief: Children living in low-income households: Census of population 2016*. Catalogue No. 98-200-X2016012. Retrieved from http://www12.statcan.gc.ca/census-recensement/2016/as-sa/98-200-x/2016012/98 -200-x2016012-eng.pdf.

Yin, R. (2018). *Case study research and applications: Design and methods* (6th ed.). Thousand Oaks, CA: Sage Publications.

CHAPTER 14

Racism in Schools and Classrooms: Towards an Anti-Racist Pedagogy of Power and Systemic Privilege

George J. Sefa Dei and Rowena Linton

LEARNING OBJECTIVES

1. To develop an understanding of the importance of the relationship between theory and praxis in anti-racism education.
2. To identify and analyze the pertinency of race and its continued impact on education, schooling, and other aspects of governance in social life.
3. To reflect critically on social positions(s) and teaching philosophy when teaching in today's diverse schools and classrooms.

INTRODUCTION

A major problem in society today is the intellectual and public hypocrisy about race and racism and the open refusal to see how issues of race and social difference connect to White privilege and White supremacy. White supremacy is often understood as individual acts. Recently, the racial climate in Canada and its neighbour down south has worsened; both nations have experienced a rise in racial incidents. In Charlottesville, White supremacists fought to maintain power, terrorized **anti-racism** protesters, and killed innocents. They were afforded the privilege to hold their rallies undisturbed by the police while innocent Black bodies continue to be targeted by the system, through policing, in the name of safety. Yet we often fail to see how White supremacy is embedded within our institutions and systems as a set of ideas and practices that are hegemonic and script our everyday lives. Though White privilege is an institutionalized phenomenon, it is similarly encoded on particular bodies, even as racialized bodies assume the markers of this privilege (e.g., conceptions of excellence and the sense of entitlements). We believe that society should operate on a level playing field, with hard work and merit serving as an equalizer or key to success. Oftentimes we fail to aim attention at how powerful ideas and practices have become hegemonic to the extent that they script our lives and become the modus operandi of our institutions. Ideologies promoting fairness, excellence, hard work, individual responsibility, freedom, choice, and liberty (among others) have limited, if not cancelled, any discussion of institutional responsibility and complicity in the creation of social and racial inequities.

But why is race a major issue in schooling and education? The racial politics of schooling includes discussion of race and knowledge production; identity; embodiment and links with schooling experiences; race and representation in terms of physical body presence; and the many overt, covert, and myriad ways race undergirds the climate, environment, and culture of schools. Because of the range of complex and sensitive subjects, educators in today's classrooms struggle with how to teach race and racism. This is usually explained in terms of a perception of race as a hot button issue or a taboo subject (Tatum, 1992). Our diverse classrooms offer many possibilities for learners, educators, and school administrators; such diversity should be seen as a source of strength rather than a challenge. Diversity entails recognizing our different contributions to knowledge production and also appreciating the knowledge base each individual brings to the school setting. Our classrooms are demarcated by race, gender, class, sexuality, (dis)ability, language, and sexual differences. Recognition of this requires more than the lip service of tolerance, appreciation, and accommodation. Educators must come to terms with the critical questions of power, privilege, representation, identity, and difference constructions. The contemporary educator must acknowledge the strengths and challenges of the classroom and what it means to urge our learners to come to the classroom proud of their myriad identities. Teachers need more than compassion. They must acknowledge their power and privileged positions to be interacting with diverse groups of learners with different stories and experiences to share. Learners must also be equipped to appreciate and to draw on the community of learners with whom they are interacting. The critical teacher is aware of the complexities of educators' and learners' lived realities. The lived reality of race and racism is one such example.

In many instances, some educators may deny race as meaningless or irrelevant and then proceed to act as if bringing attention to race is in fact the problem. However, we must be able to have honest conversations about race and difference as sites of privilege and oppression. Race is an important identity just as class, gender, sexuality, and (dis)ability are important identities. Importantly, each of these identities maintains their full effect when linked with each other. In other words, race does not stand alone. If we highlight race, it is because race is often ignored, which we excuse by claiming that bringing attention to race fosters a problem. By not speaking about race and its connections to racism, we continue to perpetuate racial oppression in our classrooms. Race in itself is not a problem. Our understanding of what race signifies and our inaction about this understanding is much of the problem (Dei, 1996). Our conversations cannot be sanitized as if race is non-existent in society. Race is about Black(ness), White(ness), Asian(ness), and **Indigeneity**. Racialized learners have to contend with sites of exclusion and marginalization in our classrooms and school settings. Yet these learners are also active resisters who are engaged in making change happen in classrooms, in schools, and, subsequently, in society. They continually resist their oppressions, and sometimes their resistance is only confronted with more oppression and harm. As educators, we need to engage race, its complex and myriad meanings, and talk about how it is linked with racism and other oppressions. Racism is institutionalized; it is not just the result of the actions of bigoted individuals. Racism is embedded in White supremacist thinking and capitalist logics of schooling.

In this chapter, our goal is to begin a discussion about concrete practices related to what classroom educators can do to bring race into the centre of classroom discussions. Race cannot be the elephant in the classroom; instead, it must be openly discussed in order to uncover any fears, anxieties, pains, and suffering we harbour or have experienced. Clearly, discussing race is not easy. Thus, we must be prepared to face anger, risk, consequences, and violent contestations. These discussions are not going to be over a "cup of tea," since feathers are going to be ruffled as people defend their power and privileges. Nevertheless, putting race on the table is to call for people and institutions to account for actions. It is a critical time for educators to show and use compassion to promote healthy learning environments in Canadian classrooms. We see parallels between the anti-racist educator and the compassionate educator—in fact, it is the compassionate educator who will address race, racism, power, and systemic privilege in the classroom. At the same time, we maintain healthy skepticism that teaching with compassion is done with genuine commitment to social change and transformative learning and not as lip service.

CONCEPTUALIZATIONS

Equity has become an elastic concept—very contested, fluid, and not bounded. Generally, equity is concerned with the practice of, or pursuit of, fairness and justice. Employing the social categories of race, gender, class, (dis)ability, language, and sexuality can serve as entry points to address questions of identity, representation, power, access, and control over resources. Similarly, *social justice* is also a paradoxical term with no fixed meanings. However, it constitutes a prism and involves a degree of social advocacy to respond to inequities and unfairness along the lines of race, gender, class, sexuality, (dis)ability, language, and religion, among others. Social justice is fundamentally about an awareness and a desire to address the harmful ways power relations manifest inequities structured around interstices of difference.

Moreover, considering that the definition of race can be contested, educators must have working definitions with which to operate. Race is a signifier of difference; it is a social relational category determined by socially selected physical and cultural characteristics (e.g., skin colour, language, culture) (Dei, 1996; Henry & Tator, 2005; Omi & Winant, 2015). What this definition means is that while race is often understood as being all about skin colour, it also expands to include culture, language, and religion. These, too, are distinguishing racial factors. Responding to race directly is racism. Racism becomes a concrete practice (individual or institutional) that works with a hierarchy of social groups, subjecting people on the lower social strata to differential and unequal treatment. What this operationalization of racism signifies is the importance of racial markers defined through the lens of race as a signifier of difference. While we may quibble over the scientific and analytical validity of any objectified characteristics of race, what is without dispute is that race is consequential in terms of its power and its political, economic, material, and social effects. Race has currency, and it becomes a site of power, privilege, oppression, and punishment for different groups. Thus, racism is practiced using the identifiers of race. This is the basis of the idea that it is racism that makes race real. One cannot exist without the other. This also serves to debunk those who view the problem as racism rather than race and argue, therefore, that we must devote our attention to racism. We cannot fight racism without an understanding of race. We cannot wish away race and simply hope racism will likewise vanish. An argument classroom teachers need to emphasize is that it serves no useful purpose to debate the scientific relevance of race because it is racism that makes race real; on its own, it is not relevant. Furthermore, although race is biologically unreal, sociopolitically it has an impact on the lives of the racialized (Ahmed, 2012). In the end, attempting to use science to justify race may end up denying the lived realities of those who are racially oppressed.

It is vital that classroom educators emphasize race and racism as "not just a theory" (see also Simpson, 2006). Any educational approach to race and racism must have a counter pedagogical response—that is, an anti-racist educational orientation. Classroom educators cannot hope to fight racism without an understanding of anti-racist practice or a willingness to take an anti-racist approach to education. Dei (1996), building on the pioneering works of other scholars from ages past, defined (integrative) anti-racism as a concrete (action-oriented) educational strategy to deal with race and racism and its relational aspects of sexism, ableism, and classism (Abella, 1984; Lee, 1994; Thomas, 1984; Troyna, 1993). Anti-racism education is not just about theory but is fundamentally about practice; it is what we do to fight racism, and not simply a classroom discussion of racism.

Educators must also be able to discuss anti-racism as distinct from and yet related to anti-Black racism and **anti-Blackness**. There is a specificity to and salience of anti-Black racism and anti-Blackness. As argued elsewhere (Benjamin, 2003; Dei, 1996; Dei & Vasquez, 2017; Dei, 2018a), anti-Black racism is about a particular negative reading, (re)action, and concrete response to Blackness and racism directed at the Black/African body. Such reading, response, and practice is framed by racist thought (e.g., the alleged sub-humanity of the Black/African subject and our supposed roots in a dark, uncivilized, deviant, and criminalized world). This is virulent and visibly directed at the Black/African body in the everyday criminalization and denial of the mental intellectual capacity of Black personhood. Relatedly, anti-Blackness is the "socio-historical and political dimensions of Black existence that speaks to the everyday individual and systemic hostilities, violence [and victimization] mapped onto the congeniality of the Black body with profound concrete, material and spiritual manifestations of Black life [and humanity]" (Dei, 2019; see also Dumas, 2014, 2016; Dumas & Ross, 2016; Sexton, 2015). This violence is racialized, classed, gendered, and sexualized and is manifested in culture, politics, and knowledge. It is this nuanced understanding that extends the meaning of anti-Blackness beyond anti-Black racism. Basically, anti-Blackness speaks to the curious interface of body, skin, culture, race, and politics in the context of a White supremacy racism that foments and cements a breathing culture and climate of anti-Blackness (Dei, 2019; see also Dei, 2017; Sharpe, 2016). Anti-Blackness is endemic to the normal everyday functioning of a White capitalist society. It is also anchored in

White supremacy as a hegemonic thought process that affirms the superiority of Whiteness and seeks to measure Black and African humanhood in White normativity. Distinguishing anti-Blackness and anti-Black racism from other forms of racisms and oppressions as particularly characterized by the severity of issues for Black and African bodies should not be perceived as tantamount to claiming to win the "oppression Olympics." This is in itself a marker of anti-Blackness.

In teaching race and anti-racism, classroom educators must also connect race with issues of (settler) colonialisms and the question of Land and Indigeneity. Colonialism was about the appropriation of Indigenous peoples' Land and resources with implications for the knowledge processes associated with Indigenous geographic spaces. Colonialism and settler colonialism proceeded with a racist ideology of White supremacy and an imperial practice of dominating groups. The dispossession of Indigenous Lands was a deliberate act to deny their humanity. While Land has always been an acknowledgement of where we reside, it also marks an important feature and site of the historic struggles of Indigenous peoples in resisting oppression and colonial settlerhood (Simpson, 2014). Racism and colonialism are intertwining forces. A discussion of racism must necessarily distort the processes of colonization in multiple geographies. Consequently, the "Indigenous" is more than a location and connection to Land as a physical space; Indigenous is about resistance and decolonization. Land, in particular, is an embodiment of peoples' spirit and soul. It is also a recognition of consciousness as residing in bodies, spiritual and psychic memories, histories, and cultural knowledges. In teaching race and Indigeneity, learners must be exposed to the colonial processes of Land dispossession, genocide, and other colonial violence, as well as to struggles of resistance for Indigenous self-determination. As a spiritual force, Land is the source of Earth-wide teachings about community, responsibility, mutual interdependence, relationality, reciprocity, sharing, respect, and human dignity. Thus, when teachers create a link between race and Indigeneity, they bring to the classroom discussion an affirmation of the power of spiritual healing and cultural rebirth, representation of self and collective, and other themes.

It is important to note here that conversations about race must include dialogue about the intersection of various forms of oppressions. Educators teaching race, schooling, and education must also adopt a critical framework for understanding anti-Islamophobia (Zine, 2006). That is, they must adopt a framework for examining the construction of Islam as a threat, dangerous, and unwelcome, and for considering the impact such perceptions will have on Muslims. This calls for a critical discussion with students as to how nation states sanction policies aimed at targeting Muslims (e.g., Muslim ban in the US, hijab ban in

France) and how such authorization affects those with Muslim identities. Such discussions should include how people's bodies, religions, and appearance—particularly their attire (e.g., hijab, niqab, burka)—are racialized by the dominant group, regardless of the body's skin marker. There is also the impact of the intersectionality of Black, racialized, and Muslim identities with other identity markers, including gender, class, ethnicity, sexuality, (dis)ability, and dress attire. This is especially true given that the social construction of what constitutes a person who is Black, who is racialized, and who is Muslim is embedded in the dominant's imagination. All these representations affect how one is read and whether one is included or excluded as Black, Muslim, Black Muslim, or other, as well as the materialized and politized impact and consequences one endures as an individual (Dei, 2018b).

WHAT CONSTITUTES AN ANTI-RACIST PEDAGOGY?

Before suggesting some practical approaches to teaching about race, racism, and anti-racism in the classroom, we must discuss the constitution of anti-racist pedagogy. First, we begin by outlining what is *not* an anti-racist pedagogy. Within the last few years, ideologies such as multiculturalism, colour-blindness, inclusivity, and diversity have raised a deafening silence on the subject of race. Within these discourses, race becomes the subject of a disappearing act, purporting this new idea that we are all one race, or that we are living in a post-racial society. What goes hand in hand with this thinking is the idea that racism is a phenomenon of the past. Unlike these discourses, which tend to silence race, anti-racist pedagogy deals specifically with "race" and seeks to challenge racism. Anti-racist pedagogy, which is rooted in critical race scholarship, positions racism as natural—as so enmeshed in society that it appears normal (Dei, 2014; Dei & Simmons, 2010; Ladson-Billings, 2010). Therefore, anti-racism pedagogy is concerned with analyzing structural and institutionalized racism, power relations, and social justice or transformation. More than just a harmonizing intellectual discourse, anti-racism education focuses on the importance of challenging racism at all levels and seeks to primarily empower the racially disempowered. Adopting anti-racism as a framework for educational equity means exposing racism in education. This means that students and individuals must be able to identify racism beyond the conversation of what is racist and be able to articulate their experiences as linked to systemic, covert, and structural oppression. Once individuals are able to articulate their experiences, such articulations are followed by proposed solutions for addressing racial injustice in an attempt to create safer and genuine learning spaces.

An anti-racist pedagogy challenges Eurocentrism in curricula and historical approaches to education. The literature on Black students' schooling experiences in Canada confirms that the current school system and Canadian curriculum do not totally represent Black students (Linton & McLean, 2017). An anti-racist pedagogy aims to correct this by engaging and affirming both students' and teachers' identities, world views, and cultural and experiential reference points in the process of learning. Furthermore, an anti-racist pedagogy meaningfully integrates racial content into course materials, activities, teaching, and learning approaches. In so doing, it eschews the common myth that there is only one way of knowing. Instead, Indigenous knowledge and other ways of knowing are fully included, and students are also able to identify voices of privilege and bias within the text. This discredits the common classroom practice of involving a racial perspective only as an additive to, or a checkpoint on, learning outcomes within a particular section of a lesson plan, or within an activity related to a particular month or heritage/cultural week. But an anti-racist pedagogy is careful with how the racial perspective is integrated into the curriculum, education policies, and practice so as to avoid further marginalizing racialized voices, creating new trauma for racialized students or tokenism. Moreover, in classroom teachings, educators must ask about and critically explore the types of representations that tend to be centred, imposed, reified, and upheld as a singular dominant narrative. Subsequently, we must examine what is most often erased in our representations (e.g., Black/Afro-Latinxs, Indigenous peoples, Asian Indigenous, Black/Afro-Indigenous peoples, Indigenous peoples from Turtle Island, etc.). Furthermore, for peoples with South and Central American backgrounds, there is a need to unveil the nuances and complexities of Latinx identities to see how schooling impacts various groupings within Latinx communities, including Black/Afro-Latinxs, Indigenous peoples, and Black/Afro-Indigenous peoples. It is worth understanding their experiences and voices in schooling and beyond, including ways to bring liberation for all Latinx peoples (Dei & Vasquez, 2017).

Anti-racist pedagogy is an anti-colonial praxis, centralizing the question of Indigeneity, settler colonialism, and the Land. Racism and European colonization are intertwined. To challenge the powerful remnants of European colonializations, we must call out colonialism as an evil system. Colonialism is an institution that has destroyed Indigenous peoples' lives and dismissed ways of being, ways of knowing, and ways of interacting with the world. We cannot teach racism without locating relevant issues in colonialism. Anti-racist pedagogy insists on the complete overhaul of ongoing colonial structures in society. Arguably, anti-racist education marks the first crucial step to undoing the legacy of colonialism. As an anti-colonial project, and with its commitment to uncover the concealed ways in which colonialism continues to condemn Indigeneity, anti-racist education aims at a revaluing of Indigenous culture and social practices, as well as of spiritual systems that have been deemed "uncivilized." Anti-racist education resurrects voices that have been muted and stories that have been omitted. Dei and Asgharzadeh (2001) assert that the aim of anti-colonial discourse is to provide a common zone of resistance and struggle, within which variously diverse minoritized, marginalized, and oppressed groups are enabled to "come to voice," and subsequently to challenge and subvert hegemonic systems of power and domination (p. 317). This is essentially what anti-racist pedagogy sets out to accomplish.

To provide context, the term *Indigenous* is commonly used in relation to a group of people who are considered to have developed a long-term social, cultural, spiritual, and emotional relationship with the Land, where such relationships predate colonial conquests from Europe (Breidlid & Botha, 2015; Kincheloe, 2006). Colonialization uprooted people from their Lands and disrupted the relationship with their Land and environment. Yet the colonizer did not just seize Land; indeed, the process of colonization subjugated minds, spirits, people's connection to their Land, and information about their history and relationships (Asante, 2006; Kincheloe, 2006). In most instances, Indigenous people's relationship with the Land was a source of spirituality and connection. Therefore, anti-racist, anti-colonial pedagogy is also about making space for the colonized to regain the ability and motivation to live spiritually and emotionally. Furthermore, as subjects who were also displaced, non–Indigenous peoples from Turtle Island and colonized peoples also have a responsibility to Turtle Island.

As Dei (2008a, 2012) argues, we must understand the relations of political power and geographical and social spaces, as well as the strategic importance of Land as a place of affirmation of histories, identities, and cultures of resistance. Further, we must recognize the links among culture, knowledge production, and colonization of Land and space. As African diasporic subjects, our development of anti-colonial knowledge production and intellectualities should remain rooted in histories, cultures, and revolutionary political traditions of African people's radical resistance to colonialism. Anti-colonial, anti-racist pedagogy seeks not only to understand the complexities, messiness, disjuncture, contentions, and contradictions of social realities, but, importantly, to transform, recreate, and rebuild. It is important to note here that this begins with the valuing of Indigenous knowledge in our own communities and among our own peoples, for preservation and restoration, and to safeguard such knowledge from being misappropriated by colonial regimes.

An anti-racist pedagogy is participatory and action-oriented. This solution endorses an approach to teaching and learning that goes beyond what is taught to how teachers teach. It encourages a system where students are active participants in their own learning. Students taking responsibility for their own learning process involves student engagement and interaction with course materials (Kumashiro, 2003). Based on Freire's emphasis on student-centred learning, anti-racist pedagogy indicates that teachers are not the owners of knowledge; instead, they decentre authority in the classroom. In this sense, there is actually no centre in the classroom, but everyone is learning and sharing from their vantage point. Freire's (2000) problem-posing education affirms humans as beings in the process of becoming—as unfinished, incomplete beings in and with a likewise unfinished reality. Therefore, teaching and learning are processes, and teachers and students are learning together, challenging assumptions together, developing awareness together, making sense of their realities together, and creating new knowledge together. While this approach to teaching and learning might be denounced as too idealist, we believe that the pragmatisms and utopian visions associated with such pedagogy suggest a "messy utopia." This "messy utopia" is where individuals are able to actualize their hopes and dreams, without having to worry about inferior thoughts that others might hold of them—that they are less than capable, less than human, and less than intellectual because of their racial, gender, class, or sexual background (Dei, 2017).

As an action-oriented praxis, anti-racist pedagogy is an ongoing process that requires converting theory to action. While research is still underway to develop robust ways in which this might be demonstrated, essentially, an anti-racist praxis is concerned with providing the tools through which we can understand the world and challenge structural, systemic, racial, and all other kinds of oppressions. Furthermore, it seeks to establish ways for us to carefully and genuinely articulate our experiences and trajectories for the kind of future and social world we hope to create and reside in. Action resulting from an anti-racist praxis will emulate community activism, mobilization, collaborative efforts, and allyship. Beyond merely protesting or speaking out, social action, advocacy, and mobilization require sharing knowledge, creating awareness, and teaching students not only how to identify and challenge power relations but also how to engage from their individual social location. Location itself also serves as a source of knowledge.

Finally, and most importantly, *an anti-racist pedagogy is transformative.* Within an anti-racist framework, the goal is to redefine new possibilities and futures for racialized students. With the understanding that transformation will not be given, nor will it be brought about with the approval of the privileged, an anti-racist pedagogy must instead equip students with the skills necessary to achieve any form of transformation. As Freire states, "it is necessary for us to defeat these lords whose speeches promise what they know they cannot deliver" (2000, p. 44). A transformative anti-racist pedagogy will not just name the atrocities that have happened to racialized individuals, but will also include evidence of resistance, and stories of every attempt made by racialized individuals to fight for their own freedom. Furthermore, a transformative anti-racist pedagogy will help both racialized and non-racialized students understand their respective positions and responsibilities in eliminating racial disparities. While this will look different for both parties, privileged students will challenge Whiteness, acknowledging the unearned perks that come with it, and how their unmerited positions come with a disadvantage for racialized students. Racialized students will continue to name their truth, share their stories, and then come together to formulate ways to share power and achieve equity.

THE PEDAGOGY OF RACE AND ANTI-RACIST CLASSROOM EDUCATION

With the increasing diversity in Canadian society, almost all Canadian teachers will soon have to confront social justice issues in their classroom. Race continues to implicate schooling and society and remains embedded in institutional structures, policies, and practices. As such, there is a need for more public conversations on race, racism, privilege, oppression, anti-oppression, and anti-racism. It is important to pay attention to how social issues are addressed, be critical, and not be blinded or distracted by new or subtle ways in which racism is being manifested. Anti-racism education allows teachers to remain aware of issues relating to race and racism. Teachers might not always want to engage in conversations about race because they feel uncomfortable or ill-prepared to do so; however, it is important to have these conversations in the classroom. Dialogue related to race demonstrates to students that teachers care about the issues that might be affecting them and gives them an opportunity to voice their perspectives. In most diverse classrooms, teachers might not be of the same ethnicity as the majority of their students, so it is important for teachers to be aware of their own biases. In this section, we outline some practical ways in which educators can engage race, racism, and anti-racism in the classrooms.

Practical Strategy #1: Develop Self-Awareness

Self-awareness and acknowledging implicit bias are crucial first steps in talking about race in the classroom. Teachers first need to know their positions and their own beliefs, attitudes, and biases in order to better understand those of others—in this case, their students. Gaining self-awareness and consciousness requires the ability to develop an in-depth understanding of the self, knowledge of ancestry, and subjectivities. Also, these involve developing the ability to situate the self in the world—to understand how the world works and how history, structures, and systems impact the self. This is particularly true because our conception of self and world can become critical only when we appreciate the historicity of its formation (Kincheloe, Steinberg, & Hinchey, 1999). Furthermore, whether or not teachers explicitly acknowledge it, their beliefs and biases shape their teaching practices and their efforts to motivate students to excel, which subsequently affect students' success. Ladson-Billings (2006) speaks of the direct link between teachers' beliefs and their practices; she concludes that teachers who believe that society is fair and just also believe that their students are participating on a level playing field and simply have to learn to be better competitors. In contrast, teachers who are aware of their privileged positions are also aware of how race, class, and gender (for example) unfairly categorize students before they even enter the classroom. Therefore, teachers have to use their positions to ensure that all students are treated equitably. While the process of knowing and/or establishing the teaching self is beyond the scope of this chapter, we believe that there are multiple ways in which teachers can achieve this, sometimes simply by reflecting on their history and existence, and by asking critical questions about how they come to know that they know. Essentially, establishing the teaching self enables teachers to develop a deeper awareness and understanding of inequities, including those related to race. It also permits teachers to model behaviours for their students. Finally, awareness and self-reflection of our social positions must be understood within the broader context of race and power and needs to be applied beyond the individual in order to make effective institutional change (Kishimoto, 2016).

Practical Strategy #2: Create and Maintain a "Safe Space" for Learning

A "safe space" learning environment has become a buzz phrase in social justice scholarship and equity and equality endeavours. The topic of safety is emphasized as a necessity in any dialogue on race—but safety for whom? In some instances, discussions around Canada's racist past, colonization, and the involvement of people of European descent are sometimes greeted with resistance or guilt. We recall incidents in some classes in which students explicitly stated that it was their ancestors who committed the heinous crimes involving racism and not them; in other classes, Black students were offended and disparaged with the use of the N-word without a trigger warning. Other marginalized students often defended their ancestors when comments were perceived to demoralize them. This raises a number of questions: What does a safe learning environment look like? Is it the same for marginalized and non-marginalized students? Can marginalized and non-marginalized students learn in the same safe space? Can there even be any safety in race dialogues? In its typical sense, safe space discourse often champions inclusivity; the practice of being respectful; active listening; and being judgment-free, open, and tolerant. However, beyond just a harmonious setting, when we speak of a safe space in anti-racism praxis, we envision one where discomfort is a site of learning and a push for action. Racism, colonization, and imperialism are violent acts against humanity—there is not going to be a discussion on these topics that will not invoke particular emotions of anger, guilt, embarrassment, frustration, and pain. Decades ago, Fanon (1965) established that the ongoing process of decolonization is always violent. Thus, in order to maintain a respectful learning space, teachers will need to acknowledge that these are spaces that could be hostile and possibly unsafe, but that the goal is to learn about others' perspectives and experiences, with all students getting equal attention and respect, rather than prioritizing certain voices or essentializing or minimizing some students' experiences. More importantly, these spaces and this discomfort can be used as the starting point for encouraging students to each participate in the quest to tackle racism and establish new ways to coexist.

Practical Strategy #3: Establish Community

Community remains central to anti-racist pedagogy. hooks (2003) believes that the loss of a feeling of community is one of the dangers we face in our current educational systems. Educators must connect with communities in order to create the best learning experience for students.

In establishing learning communities, which is essential for students, educators must get closer to students' realities and better understand their needs. Anti-racist pedagogy seeks to cultivate a sense of identity within culture and community and calls for more effective methods of teaching diverse youth and establishing spaces where the needs of the most disadvantaged are seriously and concretely addressed. Thus, educators must collaborate with students and their families not only to develop a network of support but also to ensure that race, racism, and racialized people's truths are taken up in real ways. As a start, educators can avoid telling simple stories of historical occurrences, instead connecting with other communities in which students have membership; they can invite leaders, Elders, and other representatives to come to class and share their lived experiences. In these ways, Indigenous knowledge can be incorporated into the classroom. Also, by doing this, educators are promoting learning environments with strong ties to the community, which subsequently helps learners build their self-identities (collective and cultural) within an environment of social excellence (Dei, 2008b). It is also important for educators to dispel the myth that racialized communities are monolithic. In doing this, they can leverage opportunities to highlight the strengths and diversity that exist within these communities.

When teachers foster a sense of community in the classroom, they provide students with opportunities to learn about others, understand different perspectives, and eventually foster empathy. In this "community-classroom," students become aware of their social positions. Education here in its true sense is the equalizer, and the classroom is a space where students get a chance to share their experiences or stories. As well, students learn of other worlds outside theirs. To accomplish this, the teachers must ensure that all students have the opportunity to introduce the rest of the class to their world. Also, in this setting, the teacher has a responsibility to help students connect their experience to history and structure. An anti-racist community/classroom is also engaging. To create community concretely in the classroom, it is important to make the conversation and pedagogy relevant to all students. One way of doing this is connecting the past with the present, bringing real-life current events into the classroom, and helping students make sense of them. Making course content relevant to students also means linking theory to practice because anti-racist pedagogy prepares students to combat racism in and out of the classroom. An anti-racist pedagogy is primarily concerned with equipping students with the tools necessary to engage in critical thinking so that they can apply knowledge to practice.

Practical Strategy #4: Encourage Critical Thinking

Related to the previous point about creating and maintaining critical safe spaces, educators must try to be genuine in their approach to unearthing or making sense of continued racial violence against racialized students. It is important to note here that racism is linked to hate, so educators must speak candidly to students about hate crime and encourage students to think critically about not just racial incidents or occurrences, but also the students' responsibility, if any, to intervene. Widely used in social science and interdisciplinary discourses, critical thinking is recognized as vital to the creation of new knowledge and necessary for citizens of democratic societies. Drawing on Freire's (2000) model of critical pedagogy and the problem-posing method of learning, critical thinking is asking the right questions, exposing fallacies, and challenging the information available to solve problems. The need to engage in dialogue, or the exchange of thoughts and beliefs in order to challenge racial injustices, remains pertinent to anti-racism discourse. Anti-racist pedagogy seeks to cultivate critical thinking in, and an appreciation among, students for the lived experiences of all people. Moreover, anti-racist pedagogy can help young learners develop interrogative voices to speak about social oppressions and relations of domination, especially when oppression is multiple, interconnected, and ever-changing (Kumashiro, 2003). We can use such knowledge and action-oriented pedagogies to challenge privilege and power and to subvert the status quo. Through critical anti-racism education, we are able to clarify the functions of White power and privilege, and expose how it masquerades as normal, universal, reasonable, and natural to the extent that those punished by such power may even develop fantasies, desires, and aspirations of Whiteness (Dei, 2014). Schools and learning spaces are also sites for social change and evolution. In this manner, these sites should not only foster critical thinking in students, but more importantly, they should also teach students how to engage in actions that foster critical analytical skills to challenge and understand power relations behind racism; understand how race continues to create and justify injustices and inequalities (Kishimoto, 2016); and eventually transform their own reality.

Practical Strategy #5: Develop Racial Literacy

To develop racial literacy, we first suggest that teachers establish working definitions of race-related terms and concepts. This will help students make distinctions between a number of related terms. It is important that these working definitions acknowledge the origins of these terms and concepts. Oftentimes *race, racism,* and other relatives (e.g., *culture, Whiteness, intersectionality, implicit bias, stereotypes, institutional racism, prejudice*) may lose saliency when clustered with other race-neutral concepts. Repeatedly, these terminologies are used interchangeably or ambiguously. There is a danger in clumping all these terms together, as doing so can reduce the perception of the severity of the impact of racism on individuals. Racial literacy will help to address this and help students accept any discomfort or uncertainty related to naming race—in other words, explicitly identifying race and racism.

Furthermore, it is important to help students understand how structural and institutional racism influences individual perception and bias. As mentioned throughout this chapter, anti-racism discourse is concerned with exposing how racism is entrenched in institutional practices, structures, and systems, as well as demonstrating how it continues to reside there.

Racial literacy will also help students identify subtle racisms within the curriculum and teaching practices. Tatum (1999) states that aversive racism is present in education and that it manifests itself as institutional racism. This aversive racism is often observed in selection of curriculum and teachers, in tracking of students (especially racially marginalized students into special education classes at a disproportionate number), and in teaching practices and expectations. In race and racism conversations, if racism is merely understood only as individual prejudice, then racism embedded in institutions, like education, might be ignored. At the same time, focusing on only institutional racism allows individuals benefiting from racism to avoid any responsibility. We suggest that teachers establish working definitions of race-related terms and concepts in order to help students clearly distinguish and articulate what is racist and what is not. In the end, race neutrality or ambiguity does not necessarily challenge structures; rather, it has potential to reinforce racialized, unequal power structures and dominant ideologies.

Practical Strategy #6: Talk about White Privilege

Sometimes in conversations around race and racism, there is a common tendency to speak of race as relating only to racialized individuals—that is, to understand race as applying exclusively to so-called "people of colour." By doing this, Whiteness remains the normal, and White privilege is ignored. However, an anti-racist pedagogy seeks to bring attention to the unearned power and advantages conferred systematically upon particular individuals based on their membership in a dominant group (McIntosh, 2003). Through critical anti-racism education, educators should clarify the functions of White power and privilege, and teach how it impersonates normalcy, universality, reasonableness, and naturalness (Dei, 2014). As White privilege is institutional, the goal here is not to instigate guilt, denial, or defensiveness; rather, the goal is to help students begin to challenge their own assumptions and world views, and to disrupt some of their presuppositions about individualism and meritocracy (Kishimoto, 2016; St. Denis & Schick, 2003). Additionally, the goal is to help students develop an understanding of structural racism and the ability to analyze issues of power and privilege as they relate to race and racism. Thus, it is important that educators are genuine in their approach when teaching about White privilege to avoid undesirable and depleting reactions.

Practical Strategy #7: Teach Hope

At its core, anti-racism education is about activism, social justice, and the creation of change—all of which are intrinsically linked to hope. As an academic and political project, anti-racism education focuses on the hope that something different is possible; those who teach it believe that acting on hope will transform learning and realities for students. In the midst of White supremacy, capitalism, and patriarchal systems and structures in society—all of which continue to incriminate racialized learners—educators must consistently seek to foster a progressive, unbiased learning environment in which students will not grow weary in the fight to end racism but will continue to work collectively to shape a brighter future. Racialized youth need hope to be able to anticipate and participate positively in the future. Educators have a critical role in ensuring this—first and foremost by imagining new possibilities for their students. Such an endeavour can be emotionally and mentally draining, but at the same time necessary. Ladson-Billings (2010) warns of the risks involved and suggests that anti-racist educators operate from a position of alterity or liminality. She states:

> We will have to take bold and sometimes unpopular positions, in which we may be pilloried figuratively or, at least, vilified for these stands. Ultimately, we may have to hear our ideas distorted and misrepresented. We may have to defend a radical approach to democracy that seriously undermines the privilege of those who have so skillfully carved that privilege into the foundation of the nation. We will have to adopt a position of consistently swimming against the current. (p. 22)

Despite the risks, educators must maintain hope in order to cultivate it in their students, to help students identify clear goals (e.g., to fight racism), and to develop their own ways to achieve set goals. They must motivate students to keep pursuing their education and dreams and the fight to end racism, despite any odds against them. hooks writes that hope "empowers us to continue our work for justice even as the forces of injustice may gain greater power for a time" (2003, p. xiv). She believes that teachers often enter the classroom with hope because educating is always a vocation rooted in hopefulness. As such, teachers hope for the best for their students, both individually and collectively; they hope that through their transformative, anti-racist teaching, the world will become a better place.

Hope is also active. hooks states that "we live by hope; living in hope says to us, 'there is a way out,' even from the most dangerous and desperate situations" (2003, pp. xiv–xv). hooks states that educators who dared to study and learn new ways of thinking and teaching to ensure that the work they do does not reinforce systems of domination, imperialism, racism, sexism, or class elitism have created a pedagogy of hope (p. xiv). Based on this premise, we believe that anti-racism education in itself is a pedagogy of hope.

Conversations about race and racism are typically rare in most Canadian classrooms, despite the increasing diversity and racial disparities in students' learning outcomes. We believe that there is a dire need for more genuine and meaningful dialogues on race and its implications. By no means are we implying that such conversations are simple. Instead, we acknowledge the complexities, aversion to, and discomfort in having such conversations, especially for individuals who may not understand the complexities of race politics or who are not directly affected by race or racism. However, these conversations are not meant to be easy, nor is engaging in them a simple feat. But, without them, educators will never begin to truly understand the root causes of racial disparities and ways to challenge them. The purpose of these conversations is to show that race matters insofar as racism continues to affect racialized students. In engaging in practical conversations about race, educators must identify the role race plays in driving systems, policies, and practices. They must consider how these inform their own teaching practice and how they view their students.

CONCLUSION

We conclude by noting that anti-racist pedagogy is a complex paradigm and still requires further development. One may question how one can introduce anti-racist pedagogy in non-humanities subject areas. The answer to this lies in the anti-racist scholars' attempt to disrupt the notion that anti-racism education is an add-on or a separate subject. Anti-racism education is multidisciplinary, if not transdisciplinary, meaning it is not discipline specific. It is more than theorizing the race experience but aims to combat racism that resides in all subject structures and teaching practices. A closer look at transdisciplinary anti-racism is a focus for further research.

In addition, the concepts and practical strategies presented in this chapter are by no means exhaustive; however, we have revealed some of the basic elements that must be included in any anti-racist pedagogy. With an anti-racist pedagogy, teaching is about more than standing in front of a classroom, banking information into students, who themselves may be misperceived as "empty vessels." Moreover, the educator's roles and responsibilities extend beyond content delivery, assessment, and evaluation. The educators who take up race in the classroom must do so with compassion, and subsequently instill similar values in their students, to approach race conversations intentionally and to do so compassionately.

Our discussion fails to cover implementation of anti-racist pedagogy. Specifically, who can teach anti-racist education? At what age should we introduce anti-racist pedagogy? Should anti-racist pedagogy be a mandatory part of all pre-service teaching programs, or should it be offered as professional development for teachers who are interested? Who is best suited to train teachers to teach anti-racist education? All these are areas and questions worth further exploration. However, moving towards an anti-racist pedagogy is an ongoing process that requires collaboration, commitment, and persistence.

QUESTIONS FOR CRITICAL THOUGHT

1. Anti-racism education, as a critical race pedagogy, seeks to challenge the institutional and systemic preservation of Whiteness as normal and natural, as well as to address the issues of racism and the interlocking systems of social oppression. In most instances, anti-racism focuses on those who experience racism, while the decentring of Whiteness is often ignored. Why is Whiteness or White privilege critical to anti-racist education? Is there a place for White bodies in anti-racism education?

2. Safe space is considered vital in anti-racist education, particularly with storytelling—what stories we tell, who's telling those stories, and why we tell our stories. These spaces can also be sites of contention and discomfort. How should safe spaces be established? Can there be safe spaces in anti-racism education for divergent and oppositional voices to exist? Elaborate.

3. What is racial progress, and what role does it play in anti-racism education? How do we want to measure racial progress? When racisms and racial injustices are being manifested in new ways, are we making racial progress? How do we communicate racial progress?

GLOSSARY

Anti-Blackness: Black scholars have theorized Blackness as an identity and experience with shared, contested, and contingent histories and specific geographies. Blackness is more than racial identification. It is knowledge about Black culture and politics, and an understanding of the history of Black and African peoples' experiences, with profound implications for education.

Anti-racism: An action-oriented educational strategy intended to address racism and the intersections of difference and other forms of oppression.

Indigeneity: The ways of knowing as a body of epistemology connecting place, spirit, and body. Indigeneity is about the power of historical and cultural memory. It is about resisting the push to forget and to erase colonial occupations and White colonial settlerhood on global Indigenous Peoples' Lands.

REFERENCES

Abella, R. S. (1984). *Report of the Royal Commission on Equality in Employment.* Ottawa: Minister of Supply and Services.

Ahmed, S. (2012). *On being included: Racism in institutional life.* Durham, NC: Duke University Press.

Asante, M. (2006). A discourse on black studies: Liberating the study of African People in the western academy. *Journal of Black Studies, 36*(5), 646–662.

Benjamin, A. (2003). *The Black/Jamaican criminal: The making of ideology* (Unpublished doctoral dissertation). University of Toronto, Toronto, ON, Canada.

Breidlid, A., & Botha, L. R. (2015). *Indigenous knowledges* in education: Anticolonial struggles in a monocultural arena with reference to cases from the global south. In W. Jacob, S. Cheng, & M. Porter (Eds.), *Indigenous education* (pp. 319–339). Dordrecht, Netherlands: Springer.

Dei, G. J. S. (2019). Black theorising: Indigeneity and resistance in academia. In S. Styres & A. Kempf (Eds.), *Troubling the trickster.* Edmonton: University of Alberta Press.

Dei, G. J. S. (2018a). Black like me: Reframing blackness and decolonial politics. *Educational Studies, 54*(2), 117–142.

Dei, G. J. S. (2018b). Decolonizing education for inclusivity: Implications for literacy education. In H. Hunter, M. Honeyford, & K. Magro (Eds.), *Transcultural literacies* (Ch. 1). MERN Symposium Book Series I. Winnipeg: University of Winnipeg.

Dei, G. J. S. (2017). *Reframing blackness and black solidarities through anti-colonial and decolonial prisms*. New York: Springer.

Dei, G. J. S. (2014). The African scholar in the western academy. *Journal of Black Studies*, 45(3), 167–179.

Dei, G. J. S. (2012). Revisiting the intersection of race, class, gender in the anti-racism discourse. In Valerie Zawilski (Ed.), *Inequality in Canada: A reader on the intersections of gender, race and class* (2nd ed., pp. 3–35). London, UK: Oxford University Press.

Dei, G. J. S. (2008a). Indigenous knowledge studies and the next generation: Pedagogical possibilities for anti-colonial education. *The Australian Journal of Indigenous Education*, 37(S1), 5–13. https://doi.org/10.1375/S1326011100000326.

Dei, G. J. S. (2008b). Schooling as community: Race, schooling, and the education of African youth. *Journal of Black Studies*, 38(3), 346–366.

Dei, G. J. S. (1996). *Anti-racism education in theory and practice*. Halifax: Fernwood Publishing.

Dei, G. J. S., & Asgharzadeh, A. (2001). The power of social theory: Towards an anti-colonial discursive framework. *Journal of Educational Thought*, 35(3), 297–323.

Dei, G. J. S, & Simmons, M. (Eds.) (2010). *Fanon and education: Thinking through pedagogical possibilities*. New York: Peter Lang.

Dei, G. J. S., & Vasquez, A. (2017). The foundation of transformative anti-racism: A conversation. *Canada Education*, 57(3), 50–52.

Dumas, M. J. (2016). Against the dark: Anti-blackness in education policy and discourse. *Theory into Practice*, 55, 11–19.

Dumas, M. J. (2014). "Losing an arm": Schooling as a site of black suffering. *Race, Ethnicity and Education*, 17(1), 1–29.

Dumas, M. J., & Ross, K. M. (2016). "Be real black for me": Imagining BlackCrit in education. *Urban Education*, 51(4), 415–442.

Fanon, F. (1965). *The wretched of the earth*. New York: Grove Press.

Freire, P. (2000). *Pedagogy of the oppressed* (Myra Bergman Ramos, Trans.). New York: Continuum.

Henry, F., & Tator, C. (2005). *The colour of democracy: Racism in Canadian society*. Toronto: Thomson Nelson.

hooks, bell. (2003). *Teaching community: A pedagogy of hope*. New York: Routledge.

Kincheloe, J. L. (2006). Critical ontology and Indigenous ways of being: Forging a postcolonial curriculum. In Y. Kanu (Ed.), *Curriculum as cultural practice: postcolonial imaginations* (pp. 181–202). Toronto: University of Toronto Press.

Kincheloe, J. L., Steinberg, S. R., & Hinchey, P. (1999). *The postformal reader: Cognition and education*. New York: Falmer Press.

Kishimoto, K. (2016). Anti-racist pedagogy: From faculty's self-reflection to organizing within and beyond the classroom. *Race Ethnicity and Education*, 21(4), 540–544. https://doi.org/10.1080/13613324.2016.1248824.

Kumashiro, K. (2003). *Troubling education: Queer activism and anti-oppressive pedagogy.* New York: Routledge Falmer.

Ladson-Billings, G. (2010). Just what is critical race theory and what's it doing in a nice field like education. *International Journal of Qualitative Studies in Education*, 11(1), 7–24.

Ladson-Billings, G. (2006). Introduction. In G. Ladson-Billings & W. F. Tate (Eds.), *Education research in the public interest: Social justice, action, and policy* (pp. 1–13). New York: Teachers College Press.

Lee, E. (1994). Anti-racist education: Panacea or palliative? *Orbit*, 25(2), 22–25.

Linton, R., & McLean, L. (2017). I'm not loud, I'm outspoken. *Girlhood Studies*, 10(1), 71–88.

McIntosh, P. (2003). White privilege: Unpacking the invisible knapsack. In S. Plous (Ed.), *Understanding prejudice and discrimination* (pp. 191–196). New York: McGraw-Hill.

Omi, M., & Winant, H. (2015). *Racial formation in the United States*. New York: Routledge.

Sexton, J. (2015). Unbearable blackness. *Cultural Critique*, 90(1), 159–178.

Sharpe, C. (2016). *In the wake: On blackness and being*. Durham, NC: Duke University Press.

Simpson, J. (2006). *I have been waiting: Race and US higher education*. Toronto: University of Toronto Press.

Simpson, L. B. (2014). Land as pedagogy: Nishnaabeg intelligence and rebellious transformation. *Decolonization: Indigeneity, Education & Society*, 3(3), 1–25.

St. Denis, V., & Schick, C. (2003). What makes anti-racist pedagogy in teacher education difficult? Three popular ideological assumptions. *Alberta Journal of Educational Research*, 49(1), 55–69.

Tatum, B. D. (1999). *Why are all the Black kids sitting together in the cafeteria? And other conversations about race*. New York: Basic Books.

Tatum, B. D. (1992). Talking about race, learning about racism: The application of racial identity development theory in the classroom. *Harvard Educational Review*, 621, 1–24.

Thomas, B. (1984). Principles of anti-racist education. *Currents*, 2(3), 20–24.

Troyna, B. (1993). *Racism and education: Research perspectives*. Toronto: OISE Press.

Zine, J. (2006). Unveiled sentiments: Gendered Islamophobia and experiences of veiling among Muslim girls in a Canadian Islamic school. *Equity & Excellence in Education*, 39(3), 239–252. https://doi.org/10.1080/10665680600788503.

AUTHOR BIOGRAPHIES

Stephanie Arnott (PhD) is an Assistant Professor in Second Language Education (French and English) at the University of Ottawa. Her research focuses on methodological innovation in Canadian French as a Second Language (FSL) education, with a complementary emphasis on investigating the motivation of adolescent second-language learners.

Francis Bangou (PhD) is an Associate Professor in the Faculty of Education, University of Ottawa. His post-structural research focuses on second language (L2) teachers' and learners' adaptations to unfamiliar environments including teacher training, the information and communication technologies, and French as the language of instruction in a linguistic minority situation.

Kumari Beck (PhD) is an Associate Professor and Co-Director for the Centre for Research on International Education in the Faculty of Education at Simon Fraser University. Her research focuses on university internationalization, equity in higher education, curriculum and pedagogy in higher education, and the ethic of care in teacher education.

Pam Bishop (PhD) is currently Associate Dean, Graduate Programs and Associate Professor, Educational Leadership in Western University's Faculty of Education. Her research focuses on successful leadership in schools that support students who are disadvantaged by poverties of one sort or another. She has worked as a teacher, principal, curriculum writer, and senior research fellow.

Joanna Black (PhD) is a Professor of Art Education in the Faculty of Education at the University of Manitoba. Her research interests and published works are on the subjects of human rights education, Indigenous art education, new media in education, and digital visual arts pedagogy. For over 35 years, she has worked as an art educator, art director, museum educator, curator, art consultant, and a K-12 teacher.

Jeff Brown (PhD) is a Professor in the Centre for Preparatory and Liberal Studies at George Brown College. His research interests focus on ethics and critical pedagogy. His work has appeared in a number of publications, including

TESL Canada Journal, Language Problems & Language Planning, Symposium, and *Dialogue*.

Alana Butler (PhD) is an Assistant Professor in the Faculty of Education at Queen's University. She completed a PhD in education from Cornell University in Ithaca, New York. She has 15 years of teaching experience in a range of settings that include preschool, ESL, high school, adult literacy, and university.

Wanda Cassidy (PhD) is an Associate Professor, Associate Dean (Graduate Studies), and Director of the Centre for Education, Law and Society in the Faculty of Education at Simon Fraser University. Her research and writing focus on legal literacy, cyberbullying, and the ethic of care. She was co-investigator on an SSHRC-funded study on ethic of care in schools, which led to the award-winning DVD *Dare to Care in Schools: Transforming Schools through the Ethic of Care*.

Doug Checkley is a PhD Candidate at the University of Lethbridge. His research is focused on supporting refugee students, with a focus on the high school science classroom. Previously, he had 12 years of teaching and administration experience in high school teaching science and ELL.

George J. Sefa Dei (PhD) is Professor of Social Justice Education and Director of the Centre for Integrative Anti-Racism Studies at the Ontario Institute for Studies in Education of the University of Toronto (OISE/UT). He is a Fellow of the Royal Society of Canada.

Helal Hossain Dhali is an Assistant Professor at the Department of Women and Gender Studies in Dhaka University, Bangladesh. He is a PhD Student in the Faculty of Education at McGill University in Montreal, where he is studying the role of education in the youth perception of extremism. His areas of interest include education, extremism, environment, and gender.

Douglas Fleming (PhD) is an Associate Professor at the University of Ottawa. His research focuses on ESL methodology, policy development, citizenship, and equity. He taught and held administrative positions with the Toronto District School Board. He has also served on the executive of the Citizenship Education Research Network and conducted curriculum and professional development projects at the local and international levels.

Carole Fleuret (PhD) holds a bachelor's degree in orthopedagogy, a master's degree in French didactics, and a doctorate in French didactics from the Université de Montréal. Her research interests include the acquisition of writing, spelling development, and the study of the socio-cognitive and cultural dimensions of the acquisition of second-language writing through, among other things, approximated spellings and children's literature.

Ratna Ghosh (PhD) is Distinguished James McGill Professor and William C. Macdonald Professor of Education at McGill University in Montreal. Her publications in books, journals, and encyclopedias, as well as her prestigious grants and teaching, reflect her varied research interests. Currently, she is working on several projects on the theme of education and violent extremism.

Kendra Gottschall (PhD) is a Social Worker and Professional Practice Lead (Inter-Professional Practice and Learning) with the Nova Scotia Health Authority, Eastern Zone. Her research interest is in the broad field of (dis)Ability, particularly as it relates to adult education.

Ed Harrison (PhD) is an Assistant Professor of Education at the University of Northern British Columbia (Northwest Campus, Terrace). In addition, he has taught for Simon Fraser University and Coast Mountain College. He also taught in the British Columbia public school system for years. He is currently the Bachelor of Education Coordinator for UNBC-Terrace.

Nancy L. Hutchinson (PhD) is a Professor Emerita in the Faculty of Education at Queen's University. For the past 30 years, her research has focused on the inclusion of at-risk youth and of individuals with disabilities in their classrooms, schools, communities, and workplaces.

Allyson Jule (PhD) is Professor and Dean of Education at Trinity Western University. Her research interests are in gender and education and gender and language use. She is a 3M National Teaching Fellow and an Associate of the International Gender Studies Centre, Lady Margaret Hall, Oxford. She has published many articles, books, and edited collections on various educational topics.

Rowena Linton is a PhD Candidate in Social Justice Education at the Ontario Institute for Studies in Education of the University of Toronto (OISE/UT). Her research interest is in Black students' schooling experiences and academic successes, as well as in developing anti-racist curriculum, teaching, and learning practices and pedagogies. Other research interests include Black women's narratives of resistance.

Christina Luzius-Vanin is an MEd Student in the Faculty of Education at Queen's University. As an emerging professional, she has gained teaching experience working in classrooms within a mental health treatment centre. Her current area of research is in exploring how students living with early psychosis experience secondary school.

Dilmurat Mahmut (Maihemuti Dilimulati) is a PhD Candidate in the Faculty of Education at McGill University. His research interests include Muslim identity in the West, equity and education, education and violent extremism, and immigrant integration in Canada and beyond. Currently, he is studying Uyghur immigrants' identity reconstruction experiences in Canada.

Dawn McBride (PhD in Counselling Psychology) is a Registered Psychologist and Associate Professor in Counsellor Education, University of Lethbridge. Her main areas of research and clinical practice centre on promoting value-based ethics, educating teachers and others about emotional regulation to help reduce activation symptoms, and practicing transactional analysis.

Verna McDonald (PhD) spent 20 years teaching in urban, rural, and suburban K-12 schools in Canada and the United States. She then earned a master's degree in educational psychology and a doctorate in multicultural education. She has researched and implemented cross-cultural, bilingual, and experiential teacher education programs in California and British Columbia.

Sharon Pelech (PhD) is an Associate Professor in the Faculty of Education at the University of Lethbridge. Her research interests are in science education, hermeneutics, curriculum theory, ecopedagogy, and place-conscious pedagogy. She completed her PhD in interpretive studies at the University of Calgary.

Leigh Potvin (PhD) is an Assistant Professor in the Department of Experiential and Community Studies at Cape Breton University. Her research focuses on straight privilege and LGBTQ+ allies. More specifically, she challenges allies to move from anti-homophobic approaches to queering their pedagogies and curriculum.

Brett Reynolds (MEd) has been teaching English since 1992. He currently teaches in the TESL certificate program and the English for Academic Purposes program at Humber College. He edits TESL Ontario's *Contact* magazine and is an assistant editor at *TESL-EJ*.

Kyle Robinson is a Lecturer at the University of Regina and a PhD Candidate in the Faculty of Education at Queen's University. His research focuses on advocacy by parents of students with disabilities. He is also interested in the inclusion of students with exceptionalities in secondary schools.

Marie-Josée Vignola (PhD) is an Associate Professor in the Faculty of Education at the University of Ottawa. Her research interests include French as a Second Language (FSL) teacher training as well as FSL programs in the Canadian context. She is also interested in the writing process of Francophones from minority communities.

Alyson Worrall (PhD in Teacher Education) is a Registered Psychologist in private practice in Lethbridge, Alberta. She has extensive experience working in both secondary and post-secondary education. Her interests in teacher education include how student teachers make the transition from student to professional teacher.

David C. Young (PhD) is a Professor and Chair of the Department of Curriculum and Leadership at St. Francis Xavier University. His research is focused on the broad topic of educational administration and policy. More particularly, his current writing deals with issues surrounding law and education.

INDEX

community: classroom as, 204; importance of
to students, 12–13; school as, 40–41, 43–44,
46–47; and teaching anti-racism, 283–284
compassion: argument for its importance in
classrooms, 2–3; colonial perspectives of,
11–13; components of, 255–256; cross-
cultural definitions, 13–14; cross-cultural
understanding of, 16–17, 24–26; definitions,
11; described, 9–10; and ethic of care, 3–5;
expanded meaning of, 24–25; in high-poverty
schools, 256–263; importance of in fighting
poverty, 253, 266–267; lack of research
on, 168; meaning and use of, 154–156;
and religious responsiveness, 219–224; as
second nature for teachers, 14–15; teacher
assumptions about, 10–11; when it's
warranted as teacher response, 159–160, 168
compassion fatigue, 21–22, 28
compassionate actions, 25, 26–27, 219–224
compassionate assertiveness, 176–177, 190
compassionate communication: assessment of,
189; five tips on, 192–193; seven steps of,
179–188; between teachers and parents of
children with disabilities, 195–197; between
teachers and students with disabilities, 203–206
compassionate listening, 181–182, 183, 190
Conceptual Framework of Self-Advocacy
(CFSA), 199–201
conceptual thinking, 260
conflict resolution, 176–177, 179–188, 190
Constitution, patriation of, 214–215
cooperative sustainability, 18
*Corporation of the Canadian Civil Liberties
Association v. Ontario (Minister of Education)
and Elgin County Board of Education*, 216, 217
counsellors, 39–40, 47, 143, 145, 146
Counter Extremism Project (CEP), 231
countering violent religious extremism (CVE):
in Europe, 246n9; importance of education
in, 233–234; recommendations for in
classroom, 244–245; teachers approach to
in classroom, 240–242; through care in
education, 236–237
critical caring, 4

critical praxis, 160–161
critical thinking, 40, 284–285
cross-cultural, 13–14, 16–17, 24–26, 28
cultural awareness, 149–150
cultural genocide, 69
cultural sensitivity, 140
curriculum: adjusting for refugee students,
148–149; of anti-racism education, 278;
demands of, 40, 41, 46; of high-poverty
schools, 263–264; ideas for queer content in,
85; including Indigenous culture in, 57–58;
queering of health and physical education,
80–82; queering of mathematics, 76–79;
suggestions for Indigenous, 62–65; and
Universal Design for Learning, 164
cyberbullying, 18, 20

Darling-Hammond, L., 255–256
Davin, Nicholas Flood, 214
Davis, William, 215
Day of Pink, 83, 84–85
decolonization, 276, 283
Dei, G. J. S., 275, 279
Deleuze, G., 116
denominational rights, 215–216
depression, 94, 96, 105, 242, 243
digital technologies, 114–116
Dillon, R. S., 171
disciplining students: alternatives to, 45–46, 47;
and ethic of care, 40; family role in, 12; in
high-poverty school, 258, 259; and refugee
children, 146; and sending children out of
class, 37–38; and textual borrowing, 166
disruption, 206
diversity: in Canada, 1–2, 113–114; and
Universal Design for Learning, 163
drug use, 96
Dutch elm disease, 63
dysconsciousness, 23, 28

education online, 231–232
elm trees, 63